Second Edition

THE TWI WORKBOOK

Essential Skills for Supervisors

Second Edition

THE TWI WORKBOOK

Essential Skills for Supervisors

Patrick Graupp
Robert J. Wrona

CRC Press
Taylor & Francis Group
Boca Raton   London   New York

CRC Press is an imprint of the
Taylor & Francis Group, an **informa** business

A PRODUCTIVITY PRESS BOOK

CRC Press
Taylor & Francis Group
6000 Broken Sound Parkway NW, Suite 300
Boca Raton, FL 33487-2742

© 2016 by Taylor & Francis Group, LLC
CRC Press is an imprint of Taylor & Francis Group, an Informa business

No claim to original U.S. Government works

Printed on acid-free paper
Version Date: 20151023

International Standard Book Number-13: 978-1-4987-0396-3 (Paperback)

Visit the Taylor & Francis Web site at
http://www.taylorandfrancis.com

and the CRC Press Web site at
http://www.crcpress.com

To the memory of all the people associated with the creation and administration of the TWI program during World War II, especially the trainers who so diligently delivered these programs to companies across the United States and made such a profound contribution to the war effort.

Contents

SECTION III JOB METHODS

Foreword

It is with great pleasure that I am privileged to write the foreword to the new and updated *TWI Workbook* by Patrick Graupp and Robert Wrona. As you probably know, Robert Wrona has been the primary driving force behind spreading the Training Within Industry (TWI) concepts in North America and around the globe for the past couple of decades, in conjunction with the TWI Institute. In Patrick Graupp you have, without a doubt, the finest TWI master instructor in the English language around the world. The first edition of their workbook was of tremendous value, and the latest version is even better.

Let me step back for a moment and reflect upon why I think this topic of TWI is so fundamental yet so vital. For decades various organizations have been attempting to emulate the Toyota Production System, commonly known as Lean concepts. Unfortunately, very few organizations have been successful in obtaining similar results or sustaining captured results in the long run.

Every year we see new Lean tools or buzzwords that purportedly will fix the situation once and for all. I, for one, am very dubious every time I hear a new Lean tool mentioned. The tool may work and may have roots in the Toyota Production System. However, I have little interest in the fad of the moment or what various Lean organizations might be doing. Let me attempt to explain why I think that way.

In the realm of science, practitioners make a big deal out of first principles and fundamental elements. Success in sports or other areas also starts with the fundamentals. I think the same analogy applies to the success behind Toyota Motor Corporation and many other companies as well. The question is not necessarily, what are they doing today that I can copy (although it might help)? The more interesting question to me is what did Toyota actually start doing differently in the early 1950s when the company started making dramatic improvements on the shop floor that saved the company from going bankrupt and launched them on their improvement journey? In other words, what were the fundamentals, first principles, and basic building blocks of their system?

Of course there was no single magical silver bullet in Toyota's case. The hard work of Taiichi Ohno and many others within the company set the stage for improvement and lasting success. The architects of the Toyota Way or system of improvement absolutely changed processes on the shop floor. However, more xvi ■ *Foreword*

importantly, they changed the mindset of leaders and how those individuals viewed their daily job responsibilities.

In particular, one key building block for Toyota from 1951 to 1953 was the adoption of the three main TWI courses of Job Instruction (JI), Job Relations (JR), and Job Methods (JM). One course per year was introduced and rolled out. All supervisors and eventually all managers were trained in these core concepts. More importantly, the training morphed into an actual way of doing daily work. In other words, from these humble courses sent to Japan from America emerged a systematic new way of both thinking and doing things. For example, it considered how to train people on the job in accordance with the TWI JI principles. It created a way of handling people and resolving problems that was established on the shop floor and embedded into the culture in line with TWI JR. And finally, it included a way of analyzing jobs and eliminating unnecessary details (does elimination of waste sound familiar?), which started with TWI JM concepts.

There is of course more to the Toyota Way or system of production. However, the undeniable fact remains: this was the first structured management and supervisory training program rolled out companywide in the organization. The basic concepts, especially JI-related ones, enjoyed decades of continual refinement and application inside of Toyota. My first day on the engine assembly production line as a trainee consisted of learning the proper major steps, key points, and reasons why for attachment of brackets, a throttle body, a wire harness, and a couple of stud bolts. I still remember the experience to this day, more than 25 years later, and the proper attitude displayed by my team leader and trainer.

There are many other important skills to learn during your career and about Lean in general. However, I am hard-pressed to think of any that are more fundamental or broadly applicable than the concepts outlined in this workbook. The contents have worked in service industries, health care, laboratories, and production environments around the world. Spend time carefully thinking about the first principles and fundamental elements in this material, like Taiichi Ohno and others inside of Toyota did more than 60 years ago. The fundamentals have provided value to American companies before and after World War II. The concepts have provided decades of value to Toyota and other companies around the world as well. I am certain if you study the content and apply it diligently and patiently, you will find success as well.

Good luck on your improvement journey.

Art Smalley
President, Art of Lean, Inc.

Foreword to Original Edition

The Training Within Industry (TWI) programs have a long track record of dramatically boosting productivity and quality and may well be the most successful supervisor training programs ever developed. Over the past four decades, they have supported the *kaizen* efforts of some of the world's most efficient companies. In particular, they have played a central role in the conceptual development of Lean production, instilling its most important principles in the minds of millions.

In my experience, most Lean initiatives in the United States have failed to deliver the results that managers expected from them. The most common reason for this is short-term thinking. Instead of viewing Lean production as a deep cultural transformation, many managers see it only in terms of the tools—such as the 5S, *poka-yoke*, *kanban*, and quick changeover—which are the most visible part of Lean production. While it is these tools that immediately strike the eye on a quick tour of a Lean facility, they are, in fact, only a relatively small part of the picture. If they are used in the absence of any other changes, productivity and quality will improve, but only by a fraction of what is possible. Most companies that try to implement Lean production fail to tap its full potential. They stop short of adopting its underlying philosophy and building the broader infrastructure needed for Lean tools to make a real difference.

Consider Toyota, the company that pioneered Lean production and which remains one of the best in the world at implementing it. At the time of this writing, Toyota's market value surpasses that of the Big Three's (GM, Ford, and Chrysler) combined; so do its profits. In terms of people, Toyota is smaller than each of these three companies. Moreover, while the media offer a constant litany of layoffs and plant closings at the Big Three, Toyota has not laid anyone off worldwide since 1951. Even though its competitors use the same Lean tools, Toyota's Lean initiative is more deeply committed to kaizen, and it is through this that the company has built an overwhelming competitive advantage. The TWI programs both inspired and generated much of Toyota's success. Yet most U.S. companies embarking on the Lean journey—which often means trying to be like Toyota—are not even aware that TWI exists. Given the intense current interest in Lean production and Lean Six Sigma, this is truly surprising, especially in light of TWI's history.

The three TWI programs—Job Relations (JR), Job Methods (JM), and Job Instruction (JI)—were carefully designed by some of the best training and management experts in the United States and were rigorously field-tested before general release. As you will see, their message is unique. In five punchy 2-hour modules, each course inspires profound and lasting change in the way participants think and act. When the TWI programs came to Japan, many Japanese companies wholeheartedly adopted them and their fundamental message. Toyota was only one of these companies.

No two people in the West are better equipped to teach you about TWI than Patrick Graupp and Bob Wrona. I first became aware of Patrick Graupp in the late 1980s as I browsed in a bookstore in Tokyo and came across his book *The Life of John Japanese*. In the book, Patrick told of his experiences living in Japan and working at Sanyo for more than 15 years. I enjoyed the book tremendously and was particularly intrigued to learn that he was a TWI instructor. Several years later, I wrote an article for a Japanese magazine about the TWI programs and their role in Lean production. Patrick happened to read the article and got in touch with me. We met and talked, and I have followed his career and doings with interest ever since. One of the most experienced TWI instructors in the world, Patrick is able to deliver the courses in both Japanese and English. He has taught them in all kinds of industries and to all levels of the workforce.

In the late 1990s, I received a telephone call from Robert Wrona of the Central New York Technology Development Organization (CNYTDO), a not-for-profit organization in New York. When he told me that his organization wanted to offer the TWI programs to companies in New York State and was looking for a good person to teach them, I immediately thought of Patrick Graupp, who by that time had moved back to the United States. Since then, Patrick, Robert, and the CNYTDO have run programs all over the country, with excellent results.

It is my hope that this book gets the attention it deserves from organizations interested in kaizen and Lean production and that TWI once again has the chance to demonstrate its extraordinary power to American businesses.

Alan G. Robinson
Coauthor of *Corporate Creativity (Berrett-Koehler, 1997),
Ideas Are Free (Berrett-Koehler, 2004), and
The Idea-Driven Organization (Berrett-Koehler, 2014)*

Acknowledgments

When we started communicating with each other coast to coast in the late 1990s, we really had no idea if or how we could combine our common interest in TWI to reintroduce these programs into the American mainstream, let alone how they would be received. Then, like others involved in breakthrough events, we were simply swept up in a movement that has been escalating since the initial pilot project was completed in September 2001 and continues until this day, almost 10 years after the initial publication of *The TWI Workbook*. There is no question that the right timing had a lot to do with the success of *The TWI Workbook*. As with the original book, however, this second edition was an opportunity made possible only with the help of a great number of people.

Once again, we owe a great debt of gratitude to Kazuhiko Shibuya, Patrick's mentor from his days working for Sanyo Electric, who told him on his first day of work at Sanyo's training center in Japan, "You have a lot of things to learn, but first, TWI." Mr. Shibuya, who learned TWI in the 1960s from the first Japanese conductors trained by the Americans, visited the United States in 2008 as a guest of the TWI Institute to introduce two TWI programs popular in Japan: Job Safety and Problem Solving. Mr. Shibuya then worked closely with Patrick to develop these programs for the market outside of Japan, and they are included in this new edition.

We are continually grateful to Alan Robinson and Dean Schroeder for writing the research article, referenced in Masaaki Imai's books on *kaizen*, that is responsible for bringing TWI back into the daylight both in the United States and around the world. Alan was the person who introduced Bob to Patrick when he took time from a very busy schedule to return a phone call from Bob, who was simply looking for additional information about the TWI program after reading that article. Alan had met Patrick while researching his article.

We continue to feel deep gratitude to Paul Smith, Barry Weary, and Gayle Spaulding, who were instrumental in implementing TWI at the ESCO–Syracuse plant and for sharing their implementation process as detailed in the appendix in this edition. They were our first major engagement and what they accomplished continues to serve as a benchmark for successful TWI implementation.

We are very much indebted to the work of Jim Huntzinger and Dwayne Butcher for their continuous support and promotion of TWI through their firm Lean Frontiers. From the very beginning of this journey, they have been steady partners in the reintroduction of TWI into American industry and business.

We would not have been able to document the role of TWI at Toyota without the Toyota Way series of books published by Professor Jeffrey K. Liker and his coauthors, who found and documented the TWI connection in each book. More than anything else, these books opened the eyes of the world to the inherent value of TWI. We are also grateful to Art Smalley, who provided us with information about the TWI connection at Toyota that was hidden in the open when Lean was originally discovered. We gleaned much value from Mr. Smalley's interviews with key people who worked with Taiichi Ohno when he embraced the TWI program and made it an integral part of the Toyota Production System (TPS).

We are also grateful to Masaaki Imai, who published the role TWI training plays in supporting continuous improvement in his 1996 book *Gemba Kaizen*,* which first introduced Bob to TWI. Mr. Imai continues to promote TWI with statements like this in the second edition of his book, published in 2012: "One of the most important emerging developments in management since the year 2000 has been the discovery and spread of Training Within Industries (TWI)."

We would like to thank all the people, too numerous to mention, who brought us into their plants and firms across the country and around the world to introduce their people to TWI. You taught us the true and lasting value of this great program called TWI.

Special thanks to Michael Sinocchi at Productivity Press for his unwavering support of TWI and Gary Peurasaari who did an exceptional job as content editor. Along with all the great staff at CRC and Productivity Press, this book would not have made it to its final form without their insight, wisdom, and hard work.

---

* Masaaki Imai, *Kaizen: The Key to Japan's Competitive Success.* (New York: McGraw-Hill, 1986), Chapter 4.

About the Authors

Patrick Graupp began his training career at the Sanyo Electric Corporate Training Center in Japan after graduating with highest honors from Drexel University, Philadelphia, Pennsylvania, in 1980. There he learned to deliver Training Within Industry (TWI) from his mentor Kazuhiko Shibuya. Mr. Shibuya was trained by Kenji Ogawa, who was trained by the four TWI, Inc., trainers sent from the United States to help Japan rebuild industry in 1951. Patrick earned an MBA from Boston University, Boston, Massachusetts, while leading Sanyo's global training effort. He was later promoted to the head of human resources for Sanyo North America Corp. in San Diego, California, where he settled.

Patrick partnered with Bob Wrona in 2001 to conduct TWI pilot projects in Syracuse, New York, that became the foundation for the TWI Institute, which has since trained a rapidly expanding global network of more than 1000 certified trainers who are now delivering TWI training in the manufacturing, health care, construction, energy, and service industries in the United States and around the globe. The first edition of their book *The TWI Workbook: Essential Skills for Supervisors* was a Shingo Research and Professional Publication Prize Recipient for 2007. Patrick's other books include *Implementing TWI: Creating and Managing a Skills-Based Culture* (Productivity Press, 2011), *Getting to Standard Work in Health Care: Using TWI to Create a Foundation for Quality Care* (CRC Press, 2012), and *Building a Global Learning Organization: Using TWI to Succeed with Strategic Workforce Expansion in the LEGO Group* (CRC Press, 2014), which won the Shingo Research and Professional Publication Prize for 2015.

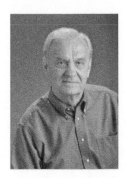

Robert J. Wrona began his manufacturing career at Chevrolet in Buffalo, New York, where he was promoted to shop floor supervisor after earning a BS from Canisius College, Buffalo, New York. He moved on to Kodak in Rochester, New York, where he became interested in organizational development while earning his MBA from the Rochester Institute of Technology, Rochester, New York. Bob joined a high-volume retail drugstore chain in Syracuse, New York, when it was a 12-store operation. He standardized store operating procedures, developed internal training, and reorganized central distribution as the company profitably grew into a regional chain of 140 in 11 years.

Bob returned to his manufacturing roots as an independent consultant to help small- and medium-sized organizations engage people in their work to improve quality and performance. Fifteen years of hands-on implementation confirmed that shop floor supervision lacked the skills to lead people in the new world of Lean production. He discovered Training Within Industry (TWI) when studying kaizen and contacted TWI master trainer Patrick Graupp in 1998, who shared his interest to resurrect TWI from the archives.

The opportunity came in 2001, when Bob became a Lean consultant for CNYTDO, Inc., which provided support for them to reintroduce TWI in Syracuse, as detailed in their 2007 Shingo Prize–winning book *The TWI Workbook: Essential Skills for Supervisors*. Bob and Pat also collaborated to write *Implementing TWI: Creating and Managing a Skills-Based Culture*, which was published by Productivity Press in 2011.

Introduction

U.S. Mass Production Provides a Strategic Advantage during WWII

William (Bill) Knudsen* worked for Ford Motor Company from 1911 to 1921, where as head of production he led the way to the development of the first modern assembly line to mass-produce the Model T automobile at Ford's Highland Park plant. To keep the line moving smoothly and efficiently, his engineers "built the skill into the tool" so that unskilled operators could be trained solely on how to use the tools to quickly make many copies of parts to specifications that fit the other finished parts of an assembly. By creating a continuous linear sequence that allowed every part to be fitted where and when it was needed, Ford and Knudsen had triggered a second industrial revolution based on mass production, one that lowered costs by making more, not fewer, of a product—and one that ruthlessly weeded out the old and obsolete to make way for the new.†

Not content with just producing Model T's, Knudsen pioneered a new manufacturing process labeled "flexible mass production." Unlike Ford's mass production of a single product, Knudsen's process would allow for constant modification and change to assemble mixed-model automobiles on the same line. His determination to see his ideas realized led to his resignation when the concept was rejected by Henry Ford. Shortly thereafter he was recruited by Alfred P. Sloan to join General Motors, where he was put in charge of engineers who had already pioneered the concept of using standardized interchangeable parts for a variety of different models in an effort to turn around the unprofitable Chevrolet division that was a candidate for closure. Knudsen immediately replaced all of the old Chevrolet machines and tools with his newer, heavy multipurpose machines featuring strengthened fixtures that allowed engineers to set lower limits within the precision capabilities built into the tools. This rapid systematic retooling of the assembly line increased Chevy's ability to produce a variety of cars in quantities that met customer

---

* Wikipedia: William Signius Knudsen (March 25, 1879–April 27, 1948) was a leading automotive industry executive. His experience and success as a key senior manager in the operations sides of Ford Motor Company and later General Motors led the Franklin Roosevelt administration to commission him as a lieutenant general in the U.S. Army to help lead U.S. war materiel production efforts for World War II.

† Arthur Herman, *Freedom's Forge* (Published in the United States, an imprint of The Random House Publishing Group, a division of Random House, Inc., New York, 2012), 20–23.

demand, reducing the Chevy–Model T sales ratio from 13:1 to 2:1 in 1926. By 1937, the Sloan–Knudsen formula had made General Motors the largest industrial corporation in the world. In 3 years it would have to save the world.*

With the worsening international situation, President Roosevelt invited Knudsen to meet him in the White House on May 30, 1940, to inform him that although the U.S. government had spent almost $1.3 billion on new armaments, there would soon be a need for much more. The president asked Knudsen—and he accepted—to take a leave of absence from GM to engage key leaders in American business to help the government quickly ramp up production of armaments the Allied armies needed to win what was rapidly becoming a global war. His first major act in this effort was to convince automobile manufacturers to suspend annual model changes to free up people to concentrate on the production of airplanes and other war materiel. "Knudsen coined a phrase to describe the auto industry's commitment to war production: 'the arsenal of democracy' based on Knudsen's flexible manufacturing that changed the entire nature of the military buildup that spilled over into every sector of the American economy as manufacturers converted to wartime production."†

America was soon in full production with 25,000 prime contractors and 120,000 subcontractors making war materiel, with thousands more to come. "A new 'Rule of Three' would take root in the American munitions business. In the first year after a production order, output was bound to triple; in the second, it would jump by a factor of seven, at the end of the third year, the only limits on output were material and labor—whether it was trucks or artillery pieces or bombs or planes."‡ With ample resources in terms of factories and materials, the only limit on output was manpower, in particular how to replace skilled workers who would be called to serve their country in the military. The high level of unemployment that persisted in the United States coming out of the Great Depression provided enough people across the country that were immediately available to replace these skilled people, however, the challenge then was how to quickly train these people who had never worked in a factory before to operate the new machines Bill Knudsen was having installed in factories across the nation to produce the armaments of war.

TWI Plays a Major Role in Improving Productivity

To meet defense demands, emergency government groups were set up to plan production increases and the Training Within Industry (TWI) Service become the first emergency service organized under these auspices. The TWI Service issued the following bulletin on September 24, 1940, calling for a completely new approach

* Arthur Herman, *Freedom's Forge* (Random House, 2012), 67.
† Ibid., 115.
‡ Ibid., 157.

to the training of a new workforce of people that had never before worked in industry: "The underlying purpose of this activity [TWI] is to assist defense industries to meet their manpower needs by training within industry each worker to make the fullest use of his best skill up to the maximum of his individual ability."*

The TWI Service recruited leaders and assembled a staff, drawn largely from industry, to work diligently to answer a very simple question: "What can we do to make more people productively useful?" Industry responded by having its own people collect, develop, and standardize the TWI techniques laid out by the TWI Service. Most notable were the three J programs:

1. *Job Instruction (JI) training.* Trains supervisors how to instruct employees so that they can quickly remember to do a job correctly, safely, and conscientiously.
2. *Job Methods (JM) training.* Trains supervisors how to improve job methods in order to produce greater quantities of quality products in less time by making the best use of the manpower, machines, and materials currently available.
3. *Job Relations (JR) training.* Trains supervisors how to lead people so that problems are prevented and gives them an analytical method to effectively resolve problems that do arise.†

TWI trainers then trained people within industry who would, in turn, train other people in industry, creating a multiplier effect that allowed a minimum of qualified trainers to reach a maximum number of people who could then respond to this challenge in the shortest period of time. To measure the impact of TWI training on the war effort, the TWI Service monitored 600 of its client companies from 1941 until it ceased operation in 1945. The last survey, performed just after TWI had shut down operations, detailed the following percentages of firms reporting *at least 25% improvement in each of the following areas*‡:

Increased production	86%
Reduced training time	100%
Reduced labor-hours	88%
Reduced scrap	55%
Reduced grievances	100%

Interest in TWI as a production method, however, had already started to fade in the United States by 1944 as orders from the military declined. But what the program had helped to accomplish in this relatively short period of time is nothing short of miraculous. As noted by Arthur Herman in the preface

---

* War Production Board, Bureau of Training, Training Within Industry Service, "The Training Within Industry Report: 1940–1945," U.S. Government Printing Office, Washington, DC, September 1945, 3.
† Note: TWI defines a *supervisor* as anyone who is in charge of people or who directs the work of others. This can include managers, superintendents, group leaders, team leaders, working leads, or even operators who have been assigned to train other operators.
‡ Alan G. Robinson and Dean M. Schroeder, "Training, Continuous Improvement, and Human Relations: The U.S. TWI Programs and the Japanese Management Style," *California Management Review* 35 (Winter 1993), 44.

to his book *Freedom's Forge*, the remarkable mobilization of American industry, technology, and material production laid the foundations for a postwar prosperity that would extend across three decades until the 1970s and fuel the economic growth of the rest of the planet.[*]

C. R. Dooley, director of the Training Within Industry Foundation, who viewed the future for TWI from a different perspective, could not have visualized the level of postwar prosperity in the United States when, in 1946, he wrote of his vision for a postwar TWI that is now applicable in today's global economy:

> We have learned a great deal in wartime which we can and must carry over to peacetime in that field of industrial activity, which, for lack of a better name, is called "training." … During wartime, plants needed to use training in order to supply the needs of the armed forces. Now, plants must use training if they are going to survive in competitive situations and if they are going to keep on providing jobs and wage for workers.[†]

Dedicated TWI trainers who had come to respect the TWI program as a national treasure placed their TWI manuals and materials in libraries throughout the United States where they awaited their day of resurrection some 60 years after Mr. Dooley's prophecy. TWI quietly resurfaced, however, in the 1950s in an environment no one could have foreseen, where it was kept alive, helping revitalize a national industry that had been destroyed during WWII.

TWI Thrives in Japan

By the end of the war, Japanese industrial output was running at less than 10% of its 1935–1937 level. The United States needed to help restart Japan's industry quickly to prevent mass starvation, widespread unrest, and, as was greatly feared, the rise of communism. Several staff members of the U.S. occupation of Japan commanded by General Douglas MacArthur had worked on the War Manpower Commission. They were familiar with TWI and the impact it had on ramping up production in the United States and felt that TWI was just the program Japan needed to help rebuild its industry and economy and emulate the strong capitalist roots of the United States. Ideally, they wanted to transform Japan from an archenemy into an economic friend.

As it turned out, Japanese industry enthusiastically embraced TWI. In fact, each of the three J programs had a profound and enduring influence on the Japanese culture. *Job Instruction* introduced a new, sure way of "how to teach" that was just what Japan, having lost much of its skilled labor force to the war, needed.

---

[*] Arthur Herman, *Freedom's Forge* (New York: Random House, 2012), p. x.
[†] Alan G. Robinson and Dean M. Schroeder, "Training, Continuous Improvement, and Human Relations: The U.S. TWI Programs and the Japanese Management Style," *California Management Review* 35 (Winter 1993), 46.

JI trainers appeared in almost every factory to begin training a peacetime work-force. The *Job Relations* program introduced the Japanese to a progressive human relations concept based on humanism in the industrial workplace. According to Japanese leaders at the time, this was one of the most appreciated ideas that TWI brought to Japan because it broke up the Japanese autocratic management tradition just at a time when the people of Japan were questioning "emperor worship" and the infallibility of their leaders. *Job Methods*, the TWI program that stressed continuous improvement, is credited for its key role in the development in Japan of *kaizen* and the *kaizen teian* suggestion system, the very pillars of today's Lean manufacturing principles. Alan G. Robinson and Dean M. Schroeder brought to light these and other contributions TWI made to the rebuilding of Japanese industry and the influence it had on Japanese management in their 1993 article "Training, Continuous Improvement, and Human Relations: The U.S. TWI Programs and the Japanese Management Style."*

The Revival of TWI: Back to Basics

Although global companies like Carrier Corp., GE, Crouse-Hinds, and General Motors no longer have a manufacturing presence in central New York, Syracuse is still home to many small- to medium-size manufacturers of everything from cookies to precision gears, specialty castings, and automated packaging equipment. The people running and working in these plants and others across the nation are in a perpetual "fight for their lives" to stay in business, and those with the will and determination to take on the global competition are working diligently, using Lean concepts to remove waste and add value for their customers. What many of these determined companies have discovered, however, is that there is something missing in all of the Lean lessons they are trying to apply. They understand, for the most part, the concept of Lean and have even had some success in applying Lean tools. But they have not been able to emulate the great accomplishments of the Japanese in productivity and efficiency as exemplified by the Toyota Production System (TPS). To a great extent, this is due to a lack of basic skills; in the absence of these skills, workers are unable to replicate what they learn in classrooms on the workplace floor.

In Syracuse, in 1996, Bob Wrona was working diligently as an independent consultant for small companies struggling to apply the Japanese manufacturing techniques that could no longer be ignored as a passing trend. In his search to understand these techniques, he ran across the article on TWI by Robinson and Schroeder in the *California Management Review*.† With the idea that TWI was a program he could easily deliver on his own, Bob contacted Dr. Robinson, who clarified that his research indicated specialized training was needed to deliver each TWI program, and he referred him to Patrick Graupp, who was

---

* Copies of this article are available from cmr@berkeley.edu.
† Robinson and Schroeder, "Training, Continuous Improvement, and Human Relations."

then the HR manager at the North American headquarters of Sanyo Electric in San Diego, California. Robinson had interviewed Patrick when doing research for this article and referred to Patrick as "the only certified TWI trainer I know of in the Western world" who was trained to deliver TWI in Japan, as it was so successfully delivered in the United States during World War II. A telephone relationship developed by comparing Patrick's TWI training experience with the problems Bob was encountering implementing Lean, which led both of them to conclude that the current need for industry to improve productivity in the United States was similar to the situation in U.S. industry during World War II, and in Japan as well, after the war, when the country rebuilt its industrial base.

The opportunity to test their theory came in 2001, after Bob joined the Central New York Technology Development Organization (CNYTDO)* as a Lean consultant. CNYTDO opened the door for Bob to have Patrick conduct pilot projects for Job Methods in September 2001, and Job Instruction and Job Relations in March 2002. The results of these projects provided a basis for President Robert Trachtenberg to approve TWI as part of CNYTDO's Lean program and to give Bob support for Patrick to recreate the training manuals and materials needed to deliver the programs in central New York. How did two individuals go about even attempting to redeploy the timeless concepts of TWI that had been ignored and forgotten in the West since 1945 while being energetically embraced within the culture of Japan for five decades? As mentioned above, Syracuse, New York, was just the right place at just the right time, and here is how the reintroduction of TWI into the United States got started.

TWI Pilot Projects in Syracuse, New York

With support from CNYTDO, Bob and Pat organized a 2-day Job Methods (JM) program trial run (Table I.1). Ten supervisors from a mix of 10 manufacturers in the Syracuse area participated in learning how JM can help them *to produce greater quantities of quality products in less time by making the best use of the people, machines, and materials now available.* Each company was asked to send a management representative to observe and provide feedback along with the supervisor and team leaders who participated in the training.

Job Methods Pilot Project (September 2001)

With only two vacation days available, Pat modified TWI's original 2 hours per day, 5-day format into a 2-day workshop. Thus, the initial trial run began with a half day of classroom training; the balance was spent reviewing JM

---

* CNYTDO is a private, not-for-profit business located in Syracuse, New York, that is focused on accomplishing economic development through the support of small to midsize manufacturers in central New York State. CNYTDO programs are partially funded by the New York State Office of Science, Technology, and Academic Research (NYSTAR) and the federal Manufacturing Extension Partnership (MEP).

Table I.1 Companies Participating in the Job Methods Program Trial Run

Company	Product	Local Employment (+ or −)
Carrier Corp.[a]	Air conditioning and heating equipment	3000
DHD Healthcare	Plastic injection molding	125
Gray–Syracuse	Investment castings	375
Higbee	Die-cut gaskets and sealing products	60
Kilian Manufacturing	Ball bearings (ungrounded)	300
Nixon Gear	Hardened ground gears and sprockets	60
Rollway Bearing	Precision ground bearings	230
Schneider Packaging Equip.	Automated case packing equipment	180
Solvay Paperboard	Reclaimed paperboard	180
Syracuse Castings Corp.	Highway grating and hatches	90

[a] Union representation.

breakdowns of participant projects, both in the classroom and on the shop floor of two host companies. In spite of the limited time, everyone was surprised with the impact the JM projects generated at the participating companies.

Overall satisfaction with JM was rated at 4.1 out of a possible 5.0 on the closing survey. Most participants and observers said they would recommend this training to other companies and expressed interest in the other J programs. When asked what they disliked about TWI, several people responded that the 2-day format for JM was too compressed. One participant summed up this consensus: "I like the idea of 2 hours a day for 5 days better. I understand this would not have worked for our trial run. It would give more time to think about the ideas that were presented at the training." This was the first of many lessons learned about the wisdom and forethought that went into the original development of the TWI programs. In fact, all subsequent attempted adjustments confirmed the need to adhere to the original parameters of the program, which were established during World War II and codified in a manner to discourage adjustments by individuals:

> No TWI program was brain trusted or just "written." All grew from demands for assistance on definite common needs; all went through many try-outs with groups of supervisors in plants. These programs for industry came from industry—the experience of many people in many plants was pooled, individual approaches were merged. The nation's war plants both provided the materials and the proving ground. No one person was responsible—it was group work, on a large scale.[*]

---

[*] War Production Board, "Training Within Industry Report," 177.

In the end, these valuable lessons saved countless hours of what would have been wasted effort had we tried to change the fundamentals just for the sake of updating TWI from what many people mistakenly viewed to be an antiquated World War II training approach. Since then, our focus to reintroduce TWI in its original form and format has not wavered.

Job Instruction and Job Relations Pilot Project (March 2002)

Enthusiasm from participating companies and from people who attended the JM pilot enabled Bob to quickly fill two classes in the same week to pilot the JI and JR programs. Eight of the 10 companies that had participated in the JM pilot enrolled in the JI and JR programs. Among the participants were representatives from three companies who had sent only observers to the JM pilot. This time, programs were delivered as outlined in the original format (ten hours of content to a class of ten participants over five 2-hour meetings), the truth of which our original JM workshop trial bore out.

Job Instruction Training

Patrick introduced JI as a method that "worked every time" for teaching people to "quickly learn to do jobs correctly, safely, and conscientiously" by breaking down jobs for learners to get just the right amount and kind of information to master jobs fully in a short period of time. The results of this effort, he said, would be "less scrap, rejects and rework, fewer accidents, and less tool and equipment damage."

The participants and the observers were taken aback by such high expectations for a training program. By the end of the week, however, they rated the program 4.4 out of a possible 5.0, commenting that they had enjoyed the interaction between instructor and learners, the diversity of problems presented, and learning concepts applicable to any function (e.g., production or office). In particular, they were impressed at learning a method that was clear and concise and included preparatory steps like breaking down a job for training.

Job Relations Training

The aim of JR is to provide a foundation for developing and maintaining good employee relations between supervisors and their people, and between people throughout an organization. Bob, at first, was of the opinion that there were already too many soft skills programs available on a local and a national level and had to be convinced to include JR as a program component. (Most companies, in fact, feel their employees already have sufficient training in employee relations matters.)

To our surprise, the participants gave JR the highest satisfaction score of all the TWI programs, 4.8 out of a possible 5.0, compared to 4.1 for JM and

4.4 for JI. What they liked most about the program was using the JR four-step method of analyzing problems, as well as the variety of problems covered in the class demonstrations. When queried, many participants stated the concepts learned were easy to apply, helping them become better supervisors.

ESCO Turbine Technologies–Syracuse Leap of Faith (May 2002)

Impressed with the September JM workshop, Paul Smith, director of human resources at ESCO Turbine Technologies–Syracuse, a producer of precision casting parts used in aircraft engines, power generators, and missiles, arranged for two key operators to participate in both the JI and JR training in March, and for Barry Weary, production manager, and Gayle Spaulding, human resources manager, to accompany him to observe and evaluate the training. Following the pilot projects, they commented: "TWI is exactly the kind of program we have been looking for." The team was confident that the JI training could replace their current method of assigning one of their best assemblers to train new employees, the so-called buddy system, which inevitably did not reduce rework. The only question they had for us was how soon Patrick could deliver the JI, JR, and JM programs on site and help them to establish the full TWI program as an in-house project to instruct internal trainers who could then teach the program to the company's approximately 400 employees.

The training was spread over several months to give ESCO time to introduce one module at a time. A few months between deliveries were also needed for Patrick to edit his training delivery manuals, which would be the key tools to develop in-house trainers, who could then deliver the TWI classes on their own following the manuals. His manuals were still in rudimentary form where Sanyo training staff, in the 1980s, before personal computers and desktop publishing software, had literally cut and pasted the manuals together in paper form. Fortunately, Jim Huntzinger, founder of Lean Frontiers, who himself had discovered TWI in the 1990s, had acquired copies of the original JI, JM, and JR trainer delivery manuals from interlibrary loans and shared these with Patrick to use as the standard when remaking the Sanyo trainer delivery manuals. Minor deviations from the original manuals were corrected, and most significantly, numerous additions to the manuals that had been inserted by the Japanese over several decades and translated by the Sanyo training staff were also incorporated into these new versions. These additions did not change the core of the manuals but were additional instructions and dialogue for trainers that made the manuals easier to learn and deliver.

Patrick had participated in and led TWI train-the-trainer sessions going back to his early days at Sanyo, when the company was growing rapidly and opening manufacturing plants around the world where TWI was successfully used to develop local trainers who trained the TWI skills within the new facilities. So he was skilled at putting on these programs. It was not until

Patrick's mentor Kazuhiko Shibuya traveled to the United States in 2008 to introduce us to the TWI Problem Solving program (see Chapter 15), though, that we learned of the direct link Mr. Shibuya and Patrick have with the original WWII American TWI trainers who developed the first group of master trainers in Japan:

1951 Kenji Ogawa was one of the 35 Japanese TWI trainers trained by TWI, Inc. trainers sent by the U.S. government to help Japan rebuild an industrial base destroyed during the war.

1960 Mr. Ogawa trained Kazuhiko Shibuya, who helped develop the TWI programs for Sanyo Electric Corporation.

1980 Mr. Shibuya hired, trained, and mentored Patrick Graupp on how to train new trainers who took TWI to Sanyo plants that were being opened around the globe.

2002 Patrick left Sanyo to partner with Bob Wrona at CNYTDO to resurrect the TWI program in the United States, where it was born.

This time frame for embedding the TWI programs at ESCO also gave Bob time to obtain JI and JM classroom simulation materials from Japan, recreate the laminated pocket cards, and gather all forms and materials the new ESCO–Syracuse TWI trainers would need to deliver 10-hour classes on their own after being trained by Patrick. The impact TWI had on the company was tremendous and was instrumental in helping the plant stay open during the challenging economic period that began on September 11, 2001. The full case study on how ESCO deployed JI training to create and sustain standardized work is detailed in the appendix of this book and serves as a model for Lean companies to understand how JI, when properly implemented, can take a company down a path to standardized work.

2006: The Tipping Point for TWI

The publication of *The Toyota Way Fieldbook* in 2006 revealed that "the training method used by Toyota today is essentially a replica [TWI] program developed in the United States in the 1940s."

> All leaders within Toyota are required to learn the Job Instruction Training method. The course format and structure is also used for many other training courses within Toyota and is based on 5 two-hour sessions, for a total of 10 hours. The course is led by a trainer who received certification from one of Toyota's "master trainers," someone with exceptional skills and many hours of experience…. First the trainer tells and shows the method, then … students are required to identify a practice job to demonstrate in the classroom with guidance

from the instructor and other students. Whenever possible, the training demonstrations can be conducted in the work area.*

Toyota management adopted the TWI program in 1950 to provide supervisory development training in response to the labor union's demand to improve the quality of supervision at a time when the company was near bankruptcy. The timing coincided with Taiichi Ohno's thoughts on kaizen, flow, multi-process handling, visual control, standardized work, and so forth, that were already established and being coached to his disciples. Job Instruction (JI) was introduced in 1951, Job Methods (JM) in 1952, and Job Relations (JR) in 1953. According to Isao "Ike" Kato, who led Toyota's training program throughout this era, JR was well received and remains almost intact to this day. JM did not fit in as well with the notion of improvement Ohno built into TPS; however, he particularly valued JI, which had the most impact by far, and "JI remains in Toyota today in virtually unchanged fashion from the original."†

With the publication of such works as *The Toyota Way* and, most notably, *Toyota Talent*, the manufacturing world was introduced to TWI on a wide scale, and the high reputation held by Toyota in the Lean community gave universal recognition to the enduring value of the TWI programs.

Forward Progress with TWI since 2006

With Toyota leading the way, we anticipated and received an increased interest in TWI from companies in the United States and around the globe that were not getting the full benefit from their Lean efforts and were struggling with workshop issues related to supervision and standardized work. At the same time, Lean consultants and companies who became aware of TWI began modifying the standard TWI delivery method, signaling that the time had arrived for the United States to have a national program guaranteeing quality standards for TWI trainers, as was done by the TWI Service during WWII and by the Japan Industrial Training Association (JITA), which continues to guarantee the quality of the national TWI program in Japan.

> When a programme is operated nationally, quality control is necessary so that there can be a guaranteed quality standard, nation-wide, and so that poor local results will not have an unfavourable reaction on the national programme.‡

---

* Jeffrey K. Liker and David Meier, *The Toyota Way Fieldbook*, (New York: McGraw-Hill, 2006) 249–250.
† Isao Kato, "TWI Influence on TPS & Kaizen," summary notes from Art Smalley's interview with Mr. Isao Kato, February 8, 2006, www.artoflean.com.
‡ C. R. Dooley, "Vocational Training, I.L.O. (Montreal, 1946)," in *Training within Industry in the United States, Third Conference of American States Members of the International Labor Organization*, Mexico City, April 1946, Report III, 177.

To help establish and monitor quality standards for trainers, CNYTDO invited everyone we knew who expressed an interest in TWI becoming a national program to attend a 1-day symposium in Syracuse, New York, on August 21, 2006. Nineteen of the 29 people invited attended and discussed the need for a quality standard to ensure that TWI trainers delivered the training as outlined in each trainer delivery manual in order to ensure that people were properly trained in the usage of each method. That afternoon they toured the ESCO–Syracuse plant to see how a JI auditing process minimized variation by confirming that operators did their job in conformance with standards.

Many of the participants, however, felt strongly that while they greatly admired the fundamentals of the program, TWI should remain an open-source model where practitioners would not be tied down to the 1940s model but be allowed to evolve and develop it. When further attempts by CNYTDO to create a consensus in forming a national organization failed, CNYTDO formed the TWI Institute in 2007 to take on that responsibility. With Patrick Graupp as the most likely candidate to set quality standards in accordance with the original material he was trained on at Sanyo, the TWI Institute established itself to be the authoritative resource for TWI training just as it was conceived, developed, and practiced by the TWI founders during WWII. To provide a venue for TWI users to share experiences and for interested organizations to learn about TWI, the TWI Institute partnered with Jim Huntzinger and Dwayne Butcher to help launch the first TWI Summit in 2007, which has since become an annual event where companies using TWI can benchmark with each other, while companies new to TWI can learn from others.

To date, the TWI Institute has trained more than 1000 company, independent, and consultant trainers in every corner of the world who use TWI Institute manuals and materials to deliver the TWI programs in their native language as they were originally created and promoted.

How to Use This Workbook

We have designed this workbook for supervisors to practice how to apply the four-step method for each J program. Sections II through V of the workbook discuss the four-step method for each J program and provide examples and supervisor team exercises. In these exercises, supervisors participate in a hands-on experience in applying the four-step methods to actual jobs and, in the case of JR, people problems, from their own worksites. TWI forms used in these exercises can be downloaded at the TWI Institute website: www.twi-institute.org. Keep in mind as you go through the team exercises that the only way to really learn TWI is to practice it rigorously on actual jobs and solving problems.

Throughout the workbook we will reproduce, as faithfully as possible, the learning sequence and elements of the original TWI programs.

(These fundamentals are described in Chapter 2.) By following this "learn by doing" approach, you will be able to receive the full benefit of these incredible training programs. To help you get a practical view of how contemporary companies are using the J programs, you should refer to the ESCO TWI implementation process detailed in the appendix to keep on the right path. For a much more detailed review, with multiple case studies, of how companies today are going back to the basics with the J programs and successfully implementing TWI, refer to our follow-up book, *Implementing TWI: Creating and Managing a Skills-Based Culture* (Productivity Press, 2011).

The TWI programs are a great legacy to the ingenuity and commonsense approach of the pioneers of American manufacturing. It is our great honor and pleasure to present them to you in this workbook, and we are confident that you will reap great rewards by learning them and putting them into practice.

Changes to the New Edition

Introduction (New Material)

A new introduction gives a more complete description of how TWI was reintroduced into American industry, including events and information that were not available when the original book was published.

Chapter 1: Role of TWI at Toyota (New Material)

While the original content of this chapter focused on how the TWI methodology supports kaizen, our experience working with companies over the past 10 years has demonstrated a much more prevalent focus on how TWI creates and supports standardized work as the foundation for Lean and ultimately continuous improvement. The TPS model serves as a benchmark for why standardized work is a foundation for continuous improvement and helps put TWI in the proper context of Lean as it should be practiced today.

Chapter 3: Four Steps of Job Instruction (Additions)

We have added two new subheads to the Job Instruction four-step method following the Toyota TWI methodology. While the original JI course always taught that giving the reasons for the key points makes the training more complete, Toyota memorialized this practice in its four-step method. After much discussion and consideration, we have chosen to follow this pattern as well. In addition, many new insights and explanations on how and why Job Instruction is such a powerful training tool have been added throughout the chapter. These insights came from our experience teaching and using the method, experience that was not available when we first wrote the book.

Chapter 4: How to Get Ready to Instruct: Break Down the Job (Additions)

We have added more explanation and tips to determining important steps and finding key points, the most difficult part of the breakdown process. A whole new section on making a balanced breakdown has been added, with new examples of Job Instruction breakdowns to emphasize the need for practice in order to perfect the skill of making breakdowns.

Chapter 11: Problem Prevention Using JR's Foundations for Good Relations (Additions)

The importance of problem prevention was not reflected as strongly as it needed to be in the original edition, so content was added to accomplish this.

Chapter 12: Four Steps of Job Safety: Preventing Accidents before They Happen (New)

Chapters 12 through 14 are brand new to *The TWI Workbook*. Job Safety was a program developed by the Japanese in the early 1960s to fill a need they felt was missing from the original TWI lineup. The JS program follows the same standard conventions of the other three TWI programs, with a focus on how to prevent accidents from happening in the workplace. This chapter introduces the need for safety as well as the JS four-step method.

Chapter 13: Two Key Aspects to Safety: Things and People (New)

This chapter goes into greater detail explaining the JS four-step method using two examples highlighting two important aspects of safety and accident prevention: things and people. It provides a deeper practice of the incident chain, which teaches readers to recognize the underlying causes, direct and indirect, that form a chain reaction of events that eventually lead to an accident or injury. Eliminating these causes and breaking the chain of causation are the ultimate goal of the JS method.

Chapter 14: Practicing the JS Method (New)

In this chapter, readers will be taken through an actual example where they themselves have to foresee causes of danger and come up with countermeasures to prevent an accident from happening. The goal of the JS is to take action *before* an accident occurs, and this is the real nature and practice of the method. The chapter will close by giving instructions on how readers can use the JS method to conduct a workplace inspection to find and eliminate potential causes of accidents and injuries in their own workplaces.

Chapter 15: TWI's Problem Solving Training (New)

This chapter comes from our book *Implementing TWI: Creating and Managing a Skills-Based Culture* (Productivity Press, 2010). We studied and practiced TWI's Problem Solving training after we wrote the original *TWI Workbook* and found it to be an exceptional program that integrates and elevates the three original TWI skills into a problem-solving focus. We reprint it here so readers can take advantage of it when learning and putting the TWI skills to good use.

Conclusion—TWI: Key to Changing the Way People Work in Lean (New)

We created a new conclusion that compares the historical role of TWI with what companies today are experiencing using the TWI methodology in the modern environment. Companies in various industries from manufacturing to service to health care are today leveraging these fundamental skills to form a solid foundation for Lean activities and continuous improvement. Moreover, international companies are finding that TWI provides a "common language" for them to create and sustain standards across multiple cultures.

Appendix: ESCO Turbine Technologies–Syracuse: Using Job Instruction as a Foundation for Standardized Work (Enhanced Case Study)

We were very fortunate to work with this local plant between 2002 and 2007, where, like Toyota, they embraced JI to successfully establish a foundation for standardized work. We have enhanced this case study with new material that became available after the first book was published in order to show the implementation process. Other case studies in the first edition were eliminated, and readers should refer to our follow-up book, *Implementing TWI: Creating and Managing a Skills-Based Culture* (Productivity Press, 2010), for a thorough review of implementation case studies.

TWI FUNDAMENTALS

Chapter 1

Role of TWI at Toyota

One of the most important emerging developments in management since the year 2000 has been the discovery and spread of Training Within Industries (TWI).... The TWI program was the foundation of the structuring and development of the roles, responsibilities, and skills of supervisors at Toyota, and without TWI, it is safe to say that their gemba would not be so excellent as it is with.

Masaaki Imai[*]

When helping Lean companies introduce the Training Within Industries (TWI) Job Instruction (JI) methodology as a starting point to create a foundation for standardized work, we always are asked, "How did we ever miss this?" Actually, the role of JI in standard work is easy to miss when people have not yet had the opportunity to attend the JI training sessions over a 5-day period, the content of which we will introduce in this book. If TWI had been identified early on, along with all the other Lean tools, perhaps Lean standard work would not currently be classified by the Lean Enterprise Institute as "one of the most powerful but least used lean tools" (www.lean.org/workshops).

To this day, when Lean companies learn how to create JI breakdowns and then use them to train people in the current best way using the JI four-step method, they wonder how they ever thought they could reach standard work without a solid training methodology like TWI's Job Instruction. Actually, it is easy for Lean companies to miss. The people who studied Toyota when creating the Lean concepts did not recognize the key role of TWI that included creating and sustaining standardized work at Toyota. It was not until *The Toyota Way Fieldbook* (Liker and Meier) was published in 2006 that TWI Job Instruction was identified as a critical part of Toyota Production System (TPS) shop floor supervisor training to create, teach, and sustain standardized work. Their follow-up book, *Toyota Talent*, in 2007, confirmed that Toyota TWI JI training had not changed since it was introduced to Toyota by

---

[*] Masaaki Imai, Gemba Kaizen, *A commonsense approach to a Continuous Improvement Strategy*, 2nd ed., printed in the United States, 2012, 113.

the American TWI, Inc. trainers in 1951. It was also in 2006 that Art Smalley* began posting what is now a wealth of valuable information about the Toyota–TWI connection on his website www.artoflean.com, which includes interviews with retired executives like Mr. Isao Kato,† who worked with Taiichi Ohno at Toyota when he was experimenting with new concepts in the "Ohno line" that became the model for the TPS.

When Kato was asked by Smalley what he felt was more important, JI or standardized work, Kato replied: "If you do JI properly you can eliminate so many problems that plague operations. You can stabilize operations, improve productivity, enhance quality, and establish the fundamental elements of the job on paper for analysis. Then it is a much smaller step to next balance the line to takt time and to add the other elements of standardized work."‡

Although Lean has dramatically improved the competitiveness of companies and the value they deliver to customers around the globe, it is clear from Toyota history that TWI plays an essential role as a foundation to the most basic elements of what we consider a Lean organization, best characterized by TPS. Lean companies must now learn how the TWI approach filled a huge gap that Ohno encountered when developing and rolling out the Ohno line in the 1950s. Kato explained the tight relationship Ohno made between TWI and standardized work: "Mr. Ohno embraced JI as a way to teach supervisors how to break down their jobs, create job breakdown sheets, and train others. Of course, the standardized work chart is needed on top of this job breakdown to balance the line to takt time and analyze it for improvement. However, Mr. Ohno would scold people if they had not broken down the job properly and written it down on paper for either the sake of JI or standardized work."§

While the role of TWI at Toyota over the last 60 plus years is clearly documented, over the past 10 plus years of our practice, many other successful implementations of TWI have now become known and are available for study. There is much you can learn from ESCO Turbine Technologies–Syracuse on how this low-volume specialty products manufacturer penetrated a niche market by utilizing JI to create and sustain standardized work, as outlined in the case study in the appendix of this book. In addition to those of you that work in manufacturing, those in specialized manufacturing, health care, service industries, distribution, and construction can also learn from the following books, which show how

---

* Art Smalley has more than two decades of experience with the Toyota Production System and leadership development working for Toyota; he is one of the few Americans to ever work for Toyota Motor Corporation in Japan. Smalley learned TPS principles firsthand at the Kamigo engine plant, which was founded under Taiichi Ohno and to this day remains the preeminent model for many aspects of the Toyota Production System.

† Isao "Ike" Kato spent 35 years with Toyota Motor Corporation in a variety of management positions in manufacturing, HR, training and development, and supplier development. Mr. Kato was known internally in Toyota as the primary developer of training courses for standardized work, kaizen, and supervisor development.

‡ Isao Kato, "TWI Influence on TPS & Kaizen," summary notes from Art Smalley's interview with Mr. Isao Kato, February 8, 2006, www.artoflean.com.

§ Ibid.

organizations applied JI to create standardized work, train people in the standard, and then audit people to sustain and continuously improve that standard:

> Patrick Graupp and Robert J. Wrona, *Implementing TWI: Creating and Managing a Skills-Based Culture*, Taylor & Francis Group, Productivity Press, Boca Raton, FL, 2011

> Patrick Graupp and Martha Purrier, *Getting to Standardized Work in Health Care: Using TWI to Create a Foundation for Quality Care*, Taylor & Francis Group, CRC Press, Boca Raton, FL, 2013

> Patrick Graupp, Gitte Jakobsen, and John Vellema, *Building a Global Learning Organization: Using TWI to Succeed with Strategic Workforce in the LEGO® Group*, Taylor & Francis Group, CRC Press, Boca Raton, FL, 2014

> Robert Baird, *The Four Components of a Fast-Paced Organization: Going beyond Lean Sigma Tools*, Taylor & Francis Group, CRC Press, Boca Raton, FL, 2014

Even if you have a very small organization, there is much you can learn and benefit from TWI training. For example, a few companies we have worked with adopted the JI method to train new hires, or to onboard temporary workers to perform entry-level jobs. Companies with only a few people rely even more on cross-training employees so that "everyone can do everything." However, there is a need for both JI and Job Relations (JR) to keep the team, however small, running smoothly. Moreover, without the resources to maintain a Lean office or an operational excellence function, small companies can still have frontline employees learn Job Methods (JM) skills to make countless improvements that benefit the bottom line.

In addition, teachers we know have built the JI method into their teaching curriculum. A multitude of parents, coaches, and scout leaders trained in JI at work informed us of the successes they have had using JI to train children. It is not unusual for a married supervisor trained in JR to report he or she used the JR method to help solve personal problems in a way that improved his or her marriage. This kind of feedback provides critical insight into the culture change characteristic of JI, JR, and JM implementations. The early struggles of Toyota show how TWI helped make that culture change, which is much the same as the struggles organizations are having with Lean today.

Early Struggles of Toyota

Formed in 1933, the Toyota Motor Company (TMC) emerged from World War II in 1945 as a small manufacturer of inferior cars. With about 3000 workers, no working facilities that survived the war, and the Japan economy in chaos, TMC designed a new automobile in 1947 and proceeded to rebuild the firm. Rampant inflation in 1949 led the government to introduce anti-inflationary measures that dried up commercial credit, and TMC's financial situation deteriorated to the point where the company could not meet payroll. Toyota's labor union went on strike over impending layoffs, and this led to bitter negotiations until bankruptcy was imminent. President Kiichiro Toyoda and his executive staff resigned after management and labor agreed on fewer workforce reductions. The strike (the only one in Toyota's history) appears to have had a profound effect on the company's approach to employees that resulted in a paradigm shift about the role of people in operations, and this ended up being more important even than the many process and technical innovations that all became part of TPS and Lean manufacturing.[*]

One agreement sought by the union was for Toyota's management to create some form of supervisor development and training. The HR department investigated existing programs, including TWI, which was evaluated and ultimately adopted by Toyota just when Ohno was "experimenting with multiprocess handling (which require some standards for the job, a notion of takt time, and thus requires a way to teach others takt time changes)." First Job Instruction (JI) was introduced in December 1951, then in succession Job Methods (JM) in June 1952, and finally Job Relations (JR) in March 1953…. JR was well received and remains almost intact to this day as a training course…. JI was a big success and had the most impact of the three training courses by far. JI remains in Toyota today in a virtually unchanged fashion from the original.[†]

Ohno embraced JI as a way to teach supervisors how to break down their jobs and train others. The standardized work chart was needed on top of this job breakdown to balance the line to takt time and analyze it for improvement. In a historical sense, JI came at a critical juncture for Toyota, as Ohno was now in a position between 1950 and 1955 to begin to roll out the learning points from the Ohno line to other areas in the company. "The JI thinking is really critical and somewhat under-appreciated in the TPS formulation."[‡]

During this time, Ohno developed the core elements of Lean manufacturing at Toyota, experimenting with machine-intensive production and developing the key concepts of takt time, process flow, standardized work, single-minute exchange of die, and basic pull systems. Although very little was written down by Ohno, Art Smalley obtained a good perspective about how difficult it was to establish the basic tenants of Lean from interviews and conversations with retired Toyota executives who understood the challenges Ohno had to overcome when rolling out TPS.[§]

[*] Q. Lee, "Toyota Survives War and Aftermath: Surviving & Thriving during Crisis," *Strategos* Lean Manufacturing Strategy Newsletter, www.strategosinc.com/toyota_crises.htm.
[†] Isao Kato, "TWI Influence on TPS & Kaizen," summary notes from Art Smalley's interview with Mr. Isao Kato, February 8, 2006, www.artoflean.com.
[‡] Ibid.
[§] Art Smalley, "Basic Stability Is Basic to Lean Manufacturing Success," www.artoflean.com, 1.

Rolling Out the Toyota Production System: 1950–1973

The TPS evolved in the early 1950s as Toyota struggled to produce small quantities of many varieties of cars under the low-demand conditions the Japanese automobile industry faced in this postwar period. This situation tested the ability of Japanese manufacturers to compete with the mass production efficiencies of established industries in Europe and the United States. The objective of the Toyota system then, as it is today, was "to increase production efficiency by consistently and thoroughly eliminating waste. This concept and the equally important respect for humanity … are the foundations of the Toyota production system."[*]

Ohno felt that Japanese business had lost sight of cutting costs when Japan entered into a high-growth period toward the end of 1955 when the Japanese automobile industry began to invest in the high-performance machines of American mass production to significantly increase income by feeding "the growing public tendency to consider consumption a virtue."[†] Japanese manufacturers experienced unusually rapid growth in 1959–1960, with a focus on mass production being used extensively in many areas, while Toyota stayed its course by adopting *kanban* in 1962 as the company-wide operating system for TPS.

Impact of the 1973 Oil Crisis

It was only after the oil crisis in 1973 that people started paying attention to TPS's unsurpassed flexibility in adapting to changing conditions even during low-growth periods.[‡] Zero growth and production cutbacks due to the dramatic increase in the cost of gasoline caused profits to plummet in Japan and around the globe. Even at Toyota, where production increases had been achieved since the 1930s, production was reduced for 1974. But it took a global oil crisis for Japanese manufacturing to recognize the genius of Toyota's production system, when Toyota was much better able than its competitors to weather the adverse effects of the oil crisis in Japan.[§]

Although TPS is now seen as an example of excellence, it was not until the 1990's that *lean* took on a whole new meaning with the publication of *The Machine That Changed the World: The Story of Lean Production*.

> We have now spent five years exploring the differences between mass production and lean production in one enormous industry (automotive) …. In this process we've become convinced that the principles of lean production will have a profound effect on human society—it could change the world.[¶]

---

[*] Taiichi Ohno, *Toyota Production System: Beyond Large-Scale Production* (Portland, OR: Productivity Press, 1988), xiii.

[†] Ibid., 111.

[‡] Ibid., 38.

[§] Ibid., 113.

[¶] James P. Womack, Daniel T. Jones, Daniel Roos, *The Machine That Change the World* (New York: Harper Collins, 1990), 7–8.

Today's Lean production system that evolved from TPS has in fact changed the world. However, the negative impact Lean is having on people in the workplace does not exist at Toyota's worldwide plants. The reason for this can be traced back to the 1949 strike that resulted in a paradigm shift at Toyota on the role of people in operations. That shift ended up being even more important than the many process and technical innovations that became part of TPS. Obviously, Ohno fully supported the role of people in operations, so much so that he ended his book *Toyota Production System* with this statement: "Of course, what is important is not the system but the creativity of human beings who select and interpret the information."[*]

Role of TWI in the Toyota Production System

On February 8, 2006, Art Smalley, who learned TWI while working for Toyota in Japan, interviewed Isao "Ike" Kato on the topic of the influence of TWI on TPS and kaizen.[†] Kato spent 35 years with Toyota in a variety of management positions, including training and development, where he became known as the father of standardized work and kaizen courses. This interview with Mr. Kato, who is also a TWI JI master trainer, provides firsthand information about why Taachi Ohno embraced TWI in the early 1950s, the critical role TWI then had and continues to have within the Toyota Production System, and the impact TWI has had on the TPS formulation.

Smalley: Some have called TWI the roots of Lean—do you agree?

Kato: TWI had significant influence on the development of our thinking and the way we structured supervisor training. It is underappreciated from that point of view. However, it is not the overall roots of Lean or TPS. TWI simply did not contain most of what makes up the unique and important aspects of TPS; seven wastes, takt time, flow production, pull systems, kanban, leveling, Jidoka, 5S, etc. It did give us a vehicle to embrace supervisor skill sets and it influenced the development of the Kaizen training course, however, that is certain.

Smalley: What is more important: JI or Standardized Work?

Kato: It is not really a question of importance; it is a question of sequence. I don't think you can do a good job of implementing standardized work or several other elements of TPS without the JI skill set in place. I have observed quite a few companies struggle with implementing standardized work, kaizen, and other items. Often the short term gains

---

[*] Taiichi Ohno, *Toyota Production System: Beyond Large-Scale Production* (Portland, OR: Productivity Press, 1988), 116.

[†] Isao Kato, "TWI Influence on TPS & Kaizen," summary notes from Art Smalley's interview with Mr. Isao Kato, February 8, 2006, www.artoflean.com.

companies obtain fall away over time. One direct reason why is that no proper plan was ever put in place to train people to the new method and the JI technique provides the exact skill set required to do this work. I can't see how standardized work can function without JI in place underneath to support it in the long run.

Smalley: Which of the TWI courses had the biggest impact and why?

Kato: The JI thinking is really critical and somewhat underappreciated in TPS formulation. The capability to break down a job is fundamental in terms of helping create a standard for teaching and training others. It is a much easier and smaller step then to create the three elements of Standardized Work (takt time, work sequence, and standard amounts of work-in-process) after JI is in place. Plus when you change takt time and move work around, JI is the perfect vehicle to train people. For this reason I believe and think Mr. Ohno would agree that JI had by far the biggest impact on TPS formulation.

Smalley: Why in your opinion is TWI critical?

Kato: It helps build capability into the organization at the supervisor level which is critical for TPS to succeed. TPS won't flourish if just staff and engineers are driving it from the side. The first line supervision is critical in making small daily improvements, leading the work teams, and making the whole system stick together. In Toyota we had a saying, "mono zukuri wa hito zukuri" which means "making things is about making people." If people want to succeed with lean or TPS they have to emphasize people development and making leaders capable of delivering improvements. TWI is a great starting point even today and a hidden strength of Toyota's production system.

Advice from Mr. Kato on How to Use TWI in Lean

While Mr. Kato spoke about the historical significance and impact of TWI in early Toyota, we have taken the liberty to sum up his insights and what they mean for readers of this book embarking on the study of TWI:

1. Develop a proper a plan to train people in the JI method to attain standardized work.
2. Break down jobs in basic terms to create a standard for teaching and training others.
3. Put JI skills in place before implementing standardized work in the workplace.
4. Introduce JR and JM as a vehicle to improve supervisor skill sets to develop and lead work teams to make small daily improvements to make the whole system stick together.
5. For long-term success with TWI in Lean today you must emphasize people development.

TWI: The Missing Link to Lean

While we learned from the Kato interview that TPS includes "unique and important aspects" that are not found in TWI, we also learned that TWI had significant influence on the development of Toyota thinking going back to the early 1950s when TWI was first introduced into Toyota. The most timely lesson from Kato for struggling Lean companies today is that "standardized work cannot function without JI in place underneath to support it in the long run." When companies try to apply Lean concepts without mastering these original TWI skills, they find that something is missing. That something is the most fundamental aspect of Lean—engaging workers to apply the tools of Lean to learn and improve their jobs consistently and continuously in a positive work environment. TWI, because it was there at the beginning and is today missing when companies try to emulate Toyota's success, is the *missing link* to Lean that ultimately makes the implementation of Lean successful.

Although the basics of Lean and TPS began with the teachings of Henry Ford and Taiichi Ohno, it was Toyota that truly empowered people by providing them with the skills they lacked to apply the tools of TPS to learn and improve their jobs. Jeffrey K. Liker explains this connection in *The Toyota Way*:

> Even more influential than Henry Ford was the methodology and philosophy of the American military's Training Within Industry (TWI) service…. It was based on the belief that the way to learn about industrial engineering methods was through application on the shopfloor and that standardized work should be a cooperative effort between the foreman and the worker (Huntzinger, 2002)…. The Toyota Way of going to the source, observing in detail, and learning by doing were all very much influenced by TWI (Dietz and Bevens, 1970) and became the backbone of Toyota's standardization philosophy.[*]

Chapter 2 introduces the basic concepts of TWI and the commonalities of the J programs that teach companies to develop in their people the necessary skills to make Lean production work and transform Lean production into a philosophy of action performed by everyone on a continuous basis.

---

[*] Jeffrey K. Liker, *The Toyota Way* (New York: McGraw Hill, 2004), 141.

Chapter 2

Fundamentals of the TWI Program

When the Training Within Industry (TWI) courses were created during WWII, the developers ran hundreds of trials to find just the right formula for accomplishing successful training that had the widest impact in a short amount of time. What is more, they had to be able to scale the delivery so that its use could spread quickly throughout industry. After all, the war was on and the rapid ramp-up of industrial output in all sectors was imperative for victory. What we have found to be unequivocally true today, after more than 10 years of delivering TWI in manufacturing as well as in the health care, administrative, and service industries, is that this same formula that performed so well in wartime still works in a contemporary work environment. As we saw in Chapter 1, Japanese industry proved the effectiveness of this formula by embracing the TWI methods and utilizing them fully in the revitalization of their economy. Fortunately for us, the Japanese maintained the TWI practice in its original form so that we could rediscover it decades later and actually see it and know how it works. This would not have been possible just by studying the historical record.

This chapter introduces TWI's foundational principle, the five needs model for supervisors, and the four-step methodology for each J program, which creates commonality among the programs. It also describes the key elements of the standardized training format that successfully teach the methods each and every time the training is delivered. It is these concepts that make TWI timeless and powerful.

Five Needs Model

TWI's three distinct programs, Job Instruction, Job Methods, and Job Relations (Job Safety was developed by the Japanese after WWII; this has been discussed in Section V), derive directly from the five needs model for good supervisors that TWI developed during World War II. Table 2.1 describes the five

Table 2.1   Five Needs Model for Good Supervisors

Knowledge of the work	This refers to the kind of information that makes one business different from all other businesses: materials, products, services, processes, equipment, operations, etc. Even in a routine job, people are required to regularly increase their knowledge of the work and, if a new product or a new process is introduced, learn a new type of knowledge. Many people spend their entire lives working at one job and continue learning new things about it. If they move to another industry, they have to learn a new knowledge of that work. Since the knowledge of the work is unique to each business, people need to acquire it independently, so the TWI program does not cover this type of knowledge.
Knowledge of responsibilities	This refers to the particular company situation regarding policies, regulations, rules, agreements, schedules, organizational structure, etc. These are different for each company, even companies that operate in the same business or industry. Hence, this knowledge must be supplied locally and, as with knowledge of the work, is not covered by the TWI program. Nevertheless, to succeed at their jobs, supervisors must have a clear understanding of their authority and responsibilities as a member of management. These are the "ground rules" under which every supervisor works, and if they are not understood and used correctly, it will be difficult, if not impossible, for a supervisor to direct the work of other people and coordinate with other areas of the company.
Skill in instructing	This is concerned with helping supervisors develop a well-trained workforce. When this skill is acquired, supervisors can reduce the number of defects, rejects, and rework; have fewer accidents; and have less tool and equipment damage. No matter how much knowledge or skill a person has about the work itself, if he or she does not have skill in instructing, it will not be possible to pass on that knowledge and skill to others. Supervisors will acquire this skill in the Job Instruction section of the TWI program.
Skill in improving methods	This deals with utilizing materials, machines, and manpower more effectively by having supervisors study each operation in order to eliminate, combine, rearrange, and simplify details of the job. With this skill, we can use the resources that are currently available more effectively to achieve greater production of good quality products and services. Supervisors will acquire this skill in the Job Methods improvement section of the TWI program.
Skill in leading	This helps the supervisor to improve his or her ability to work with people. The results of a supervisor's work depend on the output of other people, and without their cooperation, work will not be carried out effectively. Using this skill, a supervisor can get that necessary cooperation, and fewer problems will arise. Even if problems do come up, utilizing this skill will help to solve them. Supervisors will acquire this skill in the Job Relations section of the TWI program.

essential needs that must be satisfied before any supervisor can fulfill his or her responsibilities on the job successfully. The TWI developers defined a *supervisor* as "anybody in charge of people or who directs the work of others," which applies to each of the three programs. As you will see, the contents of each need, in particular the three skills, clearly define the objectives of each J program and show, as well, how they fit together as an overall program for supervisor development.

The first two needs focus on *types of knowledge*, while the last three focus on *types of skill. Knowledge* is something you acquire by reading a book or attending a class. *Skills* are learned through practice and repetition. This important distinction can be illustrated by analogy: If you read a book on how to swim, will you be able to swim? It is only by getting in the water and practicing repetitively that you actually learn the skill and perform it well. Likewise, acquiring knowledge about TWI must be accompanied by acquiring skill, which is only attained through practice.

Once the TWI developers established the five needs model, they structured the TWI programs around a common set of parameters or traits that were tested extensively in actual industry during wartime production, pared down to essentials, and perfected on the job. These parameters have made teaching the three skills in the J programs consistent and, more importantly, effective.

Common Trait: J Program's Four-Step Methods

Using Charles Allen's four-step methodology developed prior to World War I, TWI developers incorporated the scientific method when creating the four-step method approach for each J program. Table 2.2 compares the four steps to the steps in the scientific method.

Giving each program a common four-step pattern created common traits among all three programs that made it easy for supervisors to pick up and practice each method quickly and to "carry it with them" on pocket-size cards developed for each course.

According to James R. Huntzinger, Charles Allen's four-step methodology was also the basis for the development of standard work and *kaizen*. Mr. Huntzinger, who did considerable research on TWI and its connection with Toyota as part of his master's thesis for the Milwaukee School of Engineering in 2004, graciously shared with us a section of his thesis, which includes the following comparison of the TWI steps and the kaizen process (Table 2.3).

As Huntzinger notes, "Toyota's methods for Standard Operations are exactly what TWI developed during WWII: Job Instruction, Job Methods, and Job Relations." Figure 2.1, by comparing the TWI "pocket card" used by Toyota to the original TWI card from the 1940s, shows direct similarities between Toyota's four-step method and the original TWI four-step method. The third card shown is the one currently used to teach the TWI programs.

Table 2.2 J Program's Four-Step Methods Are Based on the Scientific Method

Steps	Job Instruction	Job Methods	Job Relations	Scientific Method
1	Prepare the worker	Break down the job	Get the facts	Observation: Define the problem and its parameters.
2	Present the operation	Question every detail	Weigh and decide	Hypothesize: Suggest a possible explanation or solution.
3	Try out performance	Develop the new method	Take action	Testing: Collect information (data) and test hypothesis.
4	Follow up	Apply the new method	Check results	Results: Interpret the results of the test to determine if hypothesis is correct.
				Conclusion: State a conclusion that others can independently evaluate. (Start process over.)

Source: Amended from Dinero, D. A., *Training Within Industry: The Foundation of Lean*, Productivity Press, New York, NY, 2005.

Table 2.3 Comparison of the TWI Steps and the Kaizen Process

Steps	TWI			Kaizen
	Job Instruction	Job Methods	Job Relations	
1	Prepare the worker	Break down the job	Get the facts	Observe and time current process
2	Present the operation	Question every detail	Weigh and decide	Analyze current process
3	Try out performance	Develop the new method	Take action	Implement and test new process
4	Follow up	Apply the new method	Check results	Document new standard

Figure 2.1 Similarities between Toyota, TWI, and TWI Institute pocket cards. (The original Job Instruction card is from the 1944 Job Instruction training manual. The Toyota Job Instruction card is courtesy of the Toyota Motor Corporation, Toyota Motors Manufacturing, Kentucky [TMM-K], and James R. Huntzinger. The TWI 2015 card is courtesy of the TWI Institute.)

Common Trait: Learn by Doing

The next important common trait to the TWI programs is the "learn by doing" approach. The training must include hands-on practice if it is to work effectively. In each TWI training program, participants are required to demonstrate TWI methodology on an actual job or problem from their respective worksites. Thus, each participant gets practical experience using the method firsthand on current job issues.

For example, in the Job Instruction training course, participants must bring in a job they are familiar with that is performed in their area so they can practice teaching that job in the training room. Though technology has improved since these programs were designed, people are still people and need to practice to learn a skill. While training tools like videos and simulations can certainly assist in learning, nothing replaces getting your hands on the actual tools and materials and role-playing the training scenario until it is perfected. Moreover, when the trainees apply the method to real jobs they do on a day-to-day basis, they immediately recognize the application of the method to their work and can begin using it from day 1.

Common Trait: Training Session Format

The TWI method also specifies the format of the training classes so that each course is structured in the same way: five 2-hour sessions (10 hours) over 1 week, with a maximum of 10 trainees in each session. TWI established this 10-hour program format because the developers determined that getting a supervisor away from the floor for more than 2 hours on any given day was nearly impossible. They also determined that 2 hours was the maximum length of time a person could effectively concentrate in one sitting. The number of participants was limited to 10 because of the limited time available to view the required demonstrations.

In the first session of each course, the instructor presents a demonstration problem that everyone can easily relate to and shows poor or incorrect ways in which people attempt to handle these problems. Then the instructor introduces the TWI four-step method for that particular J program to show how supervisors can handle such problems more effectively. After trainees spend the first session or two on learning methods, most of the remaining course time is used for demonstrating actual and current jobs or problems brought in by each supervisor. It is here, in the practice of doing, that the real learning of the methods takes place.

Over the course of the 5 days, participants have time to think over and digest what they are learning and practicing even as they go about their daily work. Some may even have the opportunity during the week of putting the skills right into practice on the shop floor, and this is always encouraged. When the total training period is cut short or spread out over several weeks, the results of the training do not take full effect. The same is true when fewer than 8 to 10 people participate in a group because not enough demonstrations are seen to review and learn the methods.

Think of it this way: If I were preparing for a piano recital this coming Sunday and today is Monday, which would be better, for me to practice a fixed amount each day or to procrastinate all week but then practice all day on Saturday? Of course we know the answer here because a skill is perfected a little bit at a time and cannot be crammed into a single day. In the TWI classes, the small group of 8–10 people are practicing and learning together, and they get better and better at performing the skill each day until, by the final session, they have mastered it. We have seen organizations attempt to be more efficient with this training plan and do it in, for example, two full days, but the results are never satisfactory.

Training Manuals: A Standardized Methodology for Delivering Training

The TWI developers wrote precise training manuals, providing standardized methodology for delivering each J program. These manuals document everything that the trainer needs to practice, say, and do during the 10-hour training session. Using a standardized methodology ensures the quality of each delivery, even by people who are not necessarily training experts, and creates a multiplier effect by allowing those who learn to teach the manuals to train others to teach them as well.

The training manuals enabled this train-the-trainer process that created the enduring value of the programs. Today, new TWI trainers oftentimes resist the rigidity of the manuals that quite literally dictate what to say and when, what to write on the board and where and when to write it, what to discuss with the group and the answers you are trying to draw out of them, as well as the pacing at which you must keep all of this moving forward. However, with practice and experience, the quality of the outcomes convinces most as to the wisdom and brilliance of what the TWI founders left behind for us to follow.

The manuals lay out several other standard tools as well, the most important of which is the *job breakdown sheet* germane to the JI and JM programs. The breakdown sheet for JI identifies important steps and key points of the job being taught, while the breakdown sheet for JM guides the user through finding and questioning the details of the job being improved and then helps the user develop the new improved method. You cannot train a person in a job or improve the job until you break it down into its component parts. TWI provides an approach that does this effectively and succinctly.

> **TWI note:** Most likely because of legal concerns on taking notes about employee issues, the original TWI manual instructions emphasize no note taking in the Job Relations program. Consequently, there was no breakdown sheet for JR. We also encourage this practice and most organizations follow it.

Identifying Roles and Responsibilities in the TWI Programs

People from all kinds of industries and varying skill levels participate in the J programs. Although the TWI developers designed these programs primarily for

Table 2.4   Defining Roles in the J Program Training

	Role	*Responsibility*
1	TWI trainer or trainer	Conducts TWI programs to teach participants, supervisors,[a] or employees the TWI method. The trainer teaches TWI.
2	Participant, supervisor, trainees	The person being trained in the TWI method by the TWI trainer.
3	Instructor	For the JI program, this is the trained participant or supervisor that instructs (trains) employees in a job at his or her workplace. The instructor teaches the specific job, not the TWI JI method.
4	Learner, workers, employees, operators	People at the workplace that the instructor is training.

Source: Amended from Dinero, D. A., *Training Within Industry: The Foundation of Lean*, Productivity Press, New York, NY, 2005.

[a] Supervisor can also mean manager, director, superintendent, group leader, team leader, working lead, VP, etc.

Table 2.5   Defining Participants Taking the J Programs

J Program	*Participants Taking Program*
Job Instruction (JI)	Anyone who instructs another person in how to do a job; usually this is a supervisor[a] or experienced employee.
Job Methods (JM)	Supervisors or any designated employee.
Job Relations (JR)	Anyone whose job responsibility includes reaching objectives that are dependent on the efforts of other people, especially any level of supervisor and union officers.

Source: Amended from Dinero, D. A., *Training Within Industry: The Foundation of Lean*, Productivity Press, New York, NY, 2005.

[a] TWI defines a *supervisor* as anyone who is in charge of people or directs the work of others. This can include managers, superintendents, group leaders, team leaders, working leads, VPs, etc.

the manufacturing sector, they based them on fundamental principles of supervision that apply to any industry. For the purposes of this workbook, the reader can use Tables 2.4 and 2.5 to assist in identifying who is training, instructing, or learning and who is the trainer, supervisor, or worker for any particular J program.

JOB INSTRUCTION

II

Chapter 3

Four Steps of Job Instruction

Frontline supervisors are responsible for three key areas that ensure work in a company flows smoothly: *production*, *quality*, and *cost*. Their job is to produce a quality product, in time for delivery, and within the budgeted costs. (Note that *production* means any kind of output, not just manufactured products, that the company produces and sells to make a profit. If the company produces a service, that service is included in the definition of *production*.)

With the demands of just-in-time, zero inventory, quality, and low prices driving the hotly competitive marketplace, falling behind on production schedules can mean the difference between survival and failure. It is the supervisor's daunting task to handle myriad small but vital details each minute of the working day to deliver on these "metrics." Indeed, supervisors in all lines of work face an endless stream of challenges in managing staff and getting their jobs done. When things go wrong, it does not necessarily mean a supervisor is negligent or irresponsible. Sometimes important things simply fall between the cracks. Good supervisors, however, have the skills to apply all the tools available to them to counter or even anticipate problems.

Most supervisors, when asked what kinds of problems they face delivering on the responsibilities of production, quality, and cost, usually say the following:

- Production deadlines are not met.
- Too much scrap and rework.
- Too much damage to tools and equipment.
- Employees do not follow the work specifications.
- The quality of the product is not up to standard.
- Machinery breaks down.
- Accidents take place on the factory floor.
- Work is delayed or stopped.
- Employees are not interested in their work.
- People are careless.
- Too much time is needed for people to become experienced.

Supervisors routinely face these (or similar) challenges. As a result, they often find themselves in a firefighting mode. These problems are never scheduled, but they can never be ignored. Supervisors are the ones responsible for managing them and finding effective solutions. The irony is that the daily management of such routine problems keeps supervisors from attending to important tasks that can prevent these very problems from occurring in the first place.

Supervisor Team Exercise: Use the list above and compile a list of common problems and challenges that your company team firefights. Rank them from major to minor. A major problem might also be one that occurs constantly. Be specific and list actual incidents. How are these problems holding you back from fulfilling your responsibilities? How do they affect production, quality, and cost?

Workforce Instruction: Two Ineffective Methods

The one thing that all supervisors can do to prevent these problems from occurring is to have a *well-trained workforce*. Training employees to do their jobs is one of the key responsibilities of all supervisors, no matter what industry you work in. (Note: Recall that Training Within Industry [TWI] defines a *supervisor* as not only a person in charge of others, but also anyone who directs the work of others.) The need to train employees on job procedures (whether to accommodate changing work demands, changes and improvements in procedures or standards, workforce turnover, the increasing need for cross-functional training, the continual progress of technology, or the pervasive use of short-term temporary workers) is a regular and vital task in every working environment. Moreover, worker performance, regardless of whether people are new or experienced at the tasks, is not always at an optimal level. With innovations in production and service methodologies, such as cellular manufacturing or computer-automated service stations, operators in production plants (as well as those in service outlets and offices) are being asked to understand and perform a much wider variety of jobs than ever before. Something must bridge the gap between what they already know and what they now need to know.

Most supervisors understand the need for good training, and they do not neglect to instruct employees on how to do jobs. What is at issue here is the method of instructing. Is it viable, effective, or complete? Poor instruction will lead to the many problems pointed out above. Let's look at two common, but incorrect, methods of instruction: *showing alone* and *telling alone.**

---

* In *Training Within Industry: The Foundation of Lean* by Donald Dinero (Productivity Press, New York, NY, 2005), you can find course outlines of the 10-hour TWI classes that show the format of a live training course. In this workbook, we do not follow exactly to this format but cover all the material presented in the class.

Showing Alone

One method supervisors commonly use to instruct employees is *showing* them how to do a job. Showing a person how to do a job is a very important element of instructing, but when used alone, it can lead to very serious problems, as the following story demonstrates.

The failure to do the job correctly was not this person's fault. No matter how simple it may seem, no job can be mastered by observation alone. Seeing a job done does not always translate into being able to do it. Many motions are difficult to copy, and most learners usually miss the tricky points. Even if they can do the job, it is usually no more than a copy of the motions and does not mean they understand the job. Yet, surprisingly, countless people today are simply being shown how to do their jobs with little more explanation than "Do it like this." The showing alone type of instruction is one of the major causes of the problems noted above.

Pat's CD Plant Story

Back in the fall of 1990, I was working at a Richmond, Indiana, plant that produced compact discs, and I was primarily in charge of processing customer orders and organizing the plant load scheduling. Early on, I was put in charge of running the final packaging and shipping areas of the plant. The most important elements of the manufacturing process for the record companies themselves were at the back end of the line, where their many efforts to enhance product marketing through novel packaging and distribution took place. Because I was the direct communication link between the customer and the factory floor, the company found it extremely effective for me to take charge of these back-end functions and implement customer instructions directly to the line.

One morning, I arrived at work to learn that an altercation had occurred with one of the employees the previous evening and that person had not shown up for work. By the time I got there, the supervisor in charge had remedied the situation by bringing in a temporary employee to fill the position, and he had the new person already on the floor working. I was immediately concerned with the work being done by this new person and quickly slipped out to a corner of the packaging floor to observe this temporary worker doing the simple but important job of inspecting the CD title numbers.

The most serious error that can occur in the CD manufacturing process is to have the CD labeled incorrectly. For example, you purchase a Ray Charles CD and all of the packaging that comes with the CD indicates that it is Ray Charles, but when you actually play the CD, it is, say, Beethoven. Today the label inspection process is automated and mislabeling is a rare and unusual occurrence. However, in the early days of CD manufacturing, such automation was not yet available and the inspection had to be done by hand.

With this manual process, the inspector begins with a stack of unpackaged CDs, which are stacked on poles of about 100 CDs per lot. Using both hands, the operator lifts a bunch of CDs, still on the pole, from the upper one-fourth of the stack, again from the middle of the stack, and then again from the lower one-fourth of the stack. Without taking the CDs off the pole, the inspector leans over and reads the number on the center of the CD at each of these points to confirm that the title is correct, the theory being that if two lots were to have been mistakenly mixed together, the error would be detected within the lot of 100 CDs by spot-checking these three points on each stack.

I watched the temporary worker perform this exact procedure. From a distance, she appeared to be doing everything right. Even her body motion told me that she was doing a good job by the way she kept her fingers straight, to prevent fingerprints, and leaned over to see into the center of the stack of CDs. Something still bothered me, though, and I decided to have a word with her.

She told me the supervisor in charge told her he was very busy and to just do what the person next to her was doing. He said he would be back to help out when he had a chance. And so, with no further instructions, the new temporary operator observed the work of the person next to her and began performing the operation exactly the same way. The supervisor hadn't returned, and I asked her if she had asked other people working around her about doing the job. She said she had not wanted to bother them.

I then asked her what she was looking for when she inspected the CDs, and to my dismay, she told me *she did not know*! She did not know about the codes stamped onto the CDs nor that she was supposed to be confirming the correct title number with the print on the CDs. She had been going through all of the correct motions, lifting up the piles of CDs in order to observe the one CD underneath, but had not one clue as to what she was supposed to be looking for. She had been working very diligently for 1–2 hours with no purpose.

Telling Alone

Telling a person how to do a job is another common method of instruction. Again, this is a very important element of instructing, but when used alone, it can lead to serious problems. One example that demonstrates the shortcomings of only showing or only telling how to do a job comes from the original TWI training program. Although it focuses on a job from a bygone era, it applies to similar jobs people are being asked to do today. It is also an ideal example for introducing an approach for breaking down a job and using the Job Instruction (JI) four-step method.

Imagine you are a new employee about to learn a job you have never done before. Your supervisor stands in front of you and says you are about to learn the fire underwriter's knot. Without showing you a thing or making any gestures or motions, your supervisor gives you the following explanation of the job:

Telling Alone

Take an ordinary piece of twisted lamp cord. Hold it vertically with your left hand, between the thumb and the first finger, 6 inches from the end. Untwist the loose ends, forming a V. Straighten the loose ends between the thumb and first finger of the right hand. Hold the wire at the beginning of the V. Take the right-hand loose end with the right hand and make a clockwise loop, bringing the loose end across *in front of* the main strand. See that this loop is about 1 inch in diameter and that the stub protrudes to the left of the main strand about 1½ inches. Hold the wire at the junction of the loop and the main strand. Take the other loose end with your right hand. Make a counterclockwise loop. To make this loop, pull the loose end *toward you* and pass it *underneath* the stub, *behind* the main strand. Pass the loose end through the right-hand loop, from back to front. Hold the ends evenly between the thumb and the first finger of the right hand. Pull the knot taut. Shape the knot between the thumb and first finger of the left hand as it is pulled taut.

Would you be able to perform the job? In training classes throughout the world over the past 35 years, we have given course participants this explanation of the fire underwriter's knot. A supervisor is then handed a piece of twisted lamp cord and asked to perform the job. The reaction is always the same—an incredulous smile while the rest of the class breaks into laughter. The task, of course, is impossible to accomplish. Yet, in workplaces everywhere, employees are given similar verbal-only instructions on how to do their jobs. Most people do not learn through verbal explanation alone. More often than not, many people are also too intimidated to say they do not understand or are too afraid to ask questions. In combination, these two things make instruction by telling alone virtually impossible.

Many operations are difficult to describe in words, and few of us can use the exact words or the right number of words to explain a procedure correctly and completely. Often, the person hearing the words cannot put the pieces together in the same logical order. The brain can only absorb so much information at one time, so we mix things up and focus on certain points while neglecting others.

Over time, with enough telling and enough showing, a capable person will be able to do the job. Eventually, through trial and error, he or she will even learn the nuances or tricks of the job. But this approach is not cost-effective or efficient, and many mistakes and accidents will occur before the job is mastered.

Supervisor Team Exercise: Have team members share an incident when a person just told them how to do something. A good example to use is instructions on using software, such as PowerPoint or Excel. Did you get it the first time? How soon did you lose your way? Have team members discuss the last time they showed someone how to do something with no explanation and were disappointed or surprised at the results. Was the person able to do the job? Did something else happen? Jot down a few of these instances. What did the learner or employee do wrong? Why?

Using the JI Four-Step Method

So how is JI different from other training methods supervisors now use? When applied properly, the four steps of Job Instruction (JI four-step method) can ensure a successful training experience every time. More importantly, this method works quickly and efficiently while ensuring that the learner remembers how to do a job *correctly*, *safely*, and *conscientiously*. The effectiveness of the JI method was fully validated by the time the TWI programs were instituted in the 1940s. Furthermore, JI is based on fundamental principles of human learning that are timeless and always true, a fact confirmed by supervisors who were formerly K-12 teachers and have noted that JI incorporates the fundamentals they were taught in teacher training courses. To illustrate the effectiveness of JI, let's revisit the fire underwriter's knot.

Fire Underwriter's Knot Demonstration

In the actual worksite, the employee being trained with JI hears and sees the instructor's words and actions. So as we go through the demonstration, refer to the diagrams and photographs of the job. Now imagine that you are a brand new employee with very little experience, and this is one of the first jobs you are to learn. Pay attention to what the instructor *says and does and the order in which things are performed*. Tying the knot is not what matters here. It is just an example to help you understand the TWI instruction process. Let's begin.

The Fire Underwriter's Knot Demonstration

Instructor: Hello, Mary. How are you?

Operator: Fine, thank you.

Instructor: My name is Bill Jones and I'm the supervisor in this production area. It's nice to meet you. Have you been working here long?

Operator: No, this is my second day.

Instructor: Well, are you getting along OK?

Operator: All right, I guess.

Instructor: It takes some time to get used to a new place. But if you need anything at all, please let me know. Today, I'd like to get you started on this job. [*Instructor shows completed set—Figure 3.1.*] It's called the fire underwriter's knot. Have you ever done this job before?

Operator: No.

Instructor: Do you like to do things like camping or sailing where you have to tie knots and things?

Operator: No, not really. But I do a lot of knitting and when you knit you have to tie all kinds of different knots.

Instructor: Great! This is going to be really easy for you then. It's just like that. But it is a very important job. [*Instructor shows inside of socket—Figure 3.2.*] As you can see, the knot goes right inside the socket here. When the cord is pulled on,

Figure 3.1   Completed knot.

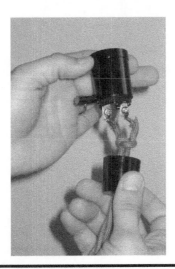

Figure 3.2   Inside view of lamp socket.

the pressure goes to the knot being pulled against the inside of the plastic case. If it isn't tied correctly, these bare ends could be pulled from their fittings and that could cause a short circuit or even start a fire if there is a spark. So it's an easy job, but a very important one.

Operator: I see.

Instructor: OK, Mary, why don't you come around and stand right behind me, to my left, and watch what I'm doing over my left shoulder. Can you see all right?

Operator: Yes.

Instructor: First, I'm going to do the job while explaining the important steps of the job. Are you ready?

Operator: Yes.

Instructor: [*Instructor **performs the job** as he explains and points out the important steps—Figure 3.3.*] This job has five important steps:

- The first important step is *untwist and straighten.*
- The second important step is *make right loop.*
- The third important step is *make left loop.*
- The fourth important step is *put end through loop.*
- The fifth important step is *pull taut.* Did you get that all right?

Operator: Yes.

Instructor: Let me do it for you again. This time, I'll tell you the key points for each step. [*Instructor **performs the job** again as he explains and points out the key points.*]

- The first important step, *untwist and straighten,* has one key point. That key point is *6 inches.*
- The second important step, *make right loop,* also has one key point. That key point is *in front of main strand.*

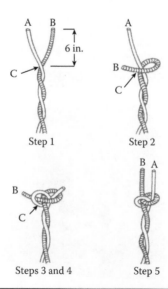

Figure 3.3   Steps 1–5.

■ The third important step, *make left loop*, has three key points. The first key point is *pulling toward you*. The second key point is *under stub*. The third key point is *behind main strand*.

■ The fourth important step, *put end through loop*, doesn't have any key points.

■ Finally, the fifth important step, *pull taut*, has three key points. The first key point is *ends even*. The second key point is *sliding loops down*. And the third key point is *firmly*.

Did you get all that?

Operator: Yes. But why did you have to pull the strand toward you?

Instructor: Good question. Let me do the job one more time, telling you the reasons for all of the key points. Then that will answer your question. [*Instructor **performs the job once again** while explaining the reasons for the key points.*]

■ The first important step, *untwist and straighten*, has one key point, *6 inches*. The reason for that is that it leaves just enough length on these loose ends for the next operator to screw down the ends to the socket fasteners. Any more than that will be cut off and thrown away.

■ The second important step, *make right loop*, has one key point, *in front of main strand*. If this end does not go in front of the main strand, the knot will not tie correctly.

■ The third important step, *make left loop*, has three key points. The first key point is *pulling toward you* [*see Figure 3.4*], and the reason is because it puts a crease in the wire and that makes it easier to do the next motion. The second key point is *under stub* [*see Figure 3.5*]. If this loop doesn't go under this stub, the knot will not tie correctly. The third key point, *behind main strand*, has the same reason—if you don't do it behind the main strand, the knot will not tie correctly.

■ The fourth important step is *put end through the loop*, and there are no key points.

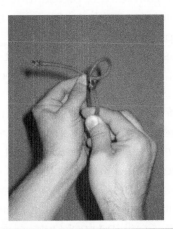

Figure 3.4   Key point: pulling toward you.

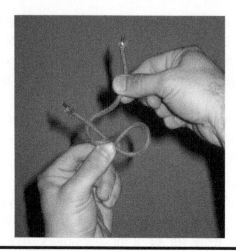

Figure 3.5   Key point: under the stub.

■ The fifth important step, *pull taut*, has three key points. The first key point is *ends even*. If you don't keep the ends even, the knot will be unbalanced and will not tie snugly. The second key point is *sliding loops down*, and we do this so that the knot will close and be formed all the way down in the proper place, 6 inches from the end and not higher. The third key point, *firmly*, is so that the knot will not come loose later on.

Do you have any questions?

Operator: No. I think I get it.

Instructor: All right, then. Why don't you try it for yourself? You take a seat here at the workbench and just do it once for me without saying anything. [*Instructor has the operator sit in his place and goes and stands where she was standing, behind her left shoulder. He immediately jumps in and corrects any errors that she may make as she does the job.*]

That's very good. [*Instructor picks up the finished piece and observes it carefully.*] You're a quick learner.

Do the job again for me, please. But this time, tell me each of the important steps of the job as you do them. How many important steps were there?

Operator: I think it was five—yes, five important steps.

Instructor: That's right. Tell me what the five important steps are as you do the job.

Operator: [*Operator* **does the job again** *while saying the important steps. Instructor helps her to remember any important steps she can't remember.*] The first important step is untwist and straighten. The second important step is make a right loop. The third important step is make a left loop. The fourth important step is put the loose end through the loop. The fifth important step is pull the knot taut.

Instructor: Excellent! That's very good. [*Instructor picks up the finished piece and observes the work carefully.*] Let me ask you to do the job again, Mary. This time tell me both the important steps and the key points for each of those steps.

Operator: [*Operator **does the job again** while saying the key points for each important step. Instructor helps her to remember any key points she can't remember.*] The first step, untwist and straighten, has a key point: 6 inches. Is that right?

Instructor: Yes, that's it.

Operator: OK. The second important step is make a right loop. The key point is in front of the main strand. That's the only key point for step 2.

Instructor: That's right.

Operator: The third important step has three key points. The first key point is....

Instructor: What is the step again?

Operator: The step is to make a left loop.

Instructor: Right. And the three key points are?

Operator: The first key point is pulling the wire toward you. The second key point is ... I can't remember it.

Instructor: Where does the loose end go in relation to this stub?

Operator: Right! The second key point is under this stub. And the third key point is behind the main strand. The fourth important step is to put the loose end through the loop, and there are no key points.

Instructor: Correct.

Operator: And then the fifth important step is to pull the knot taut. There are three key points. The first key point is to hold the ends even. The second key point is sliding the loops down. And the third key point is firmly.

Instructor: [*Instructor picks up the finished piece and observes the work carefully.*] You're really getting it. It sounds like you have a good understanding of the job. But just to be sure, let me ask you to do it again, and this time, tell me the reasons for each of those key points.

Operator: All right. [*Operator **does the job again** while saying the reasons for each of the key points. Instructor helps her to remember any reasons she can't remember.*] The first step, untwist and straighten, has a key point: 6 inches. And the reason is because that is just the right amount of length for the next process to screw the ends down to the socket. Any more will be cut off and thrown away. [*Operator continues giving the reasons for all of the key points until the job is completely finished.*]

Instructor: Well, it looks like you're ready to get going on your own now. Please continue doing this job for the rest of the morning.

If you have any problems, just ask me. I'm usually over there
at my desk or in the area. If you don't see me, ask Jane. That's
Jane over there and she is the assistant line leader. I've already
told her about you and she is ready to help at any time. I'll
come back and check on you every 5 minutes or so for the
next half hour, just to make sure you're getting started OK.
By that time you should be getting the hang of it, and after
that, I'll just come by every half hour. But never be afraid to
ask a question if there is anything at all that is bothering you.
I really believe that the best employees here are the ones who
ask lots of questions. If things are going smoothly by noon,
I'll leave you on your own. Does that sound good?

Operator: Great. I think I should be fine.

Instructor: All right. Why don't you get started then?

In the countless demonstrations of this job that we have performed over the
last 35 years, the operator is always able to perform the fire underwriter's knot
job well in less than 20 minutes. Yet, not one person in any of these training
groups was able to tie the knot after just being told how to do it or just being
shown how to do the job. The JI method does both, in a methodical and effective fashion.

The JI four-step method is defined as *the way to get a person to quickly
remember to do a job correctly, safely, and conscientiously*. It is quite simple, and
it works every time if performed properly. To ensure this, TWI developers created the JI four-step method pocket card that each supervisor (instructor) should
have on hand at all times when training. Figure 3.6 shows the back side of the
pocket card (we will look at the front side in Chapters 4 and 5).

Supervisor Team Exercise: Team members should reread the fire
underwriter's knot exercise using Figure 3.6. If possible, have one team
member play the instructor and the other the operator. Using the pocket
card, identify the points in the exercise where the instructor is following
each step and detail of the JI four-step method. Note how the exercise
exactly conforms to the training card. The instructor should memorize
the training card and always have it handy, particularly when instructing
someone how to do a job.

Now that the team has gone through an actual example of how to use the
JI four-step method to instruct people, it is time to understand how to use each
step, strictly following the order of the steps. These steps apply to any job in
any industry. Follow along with the pocket card as we review each item of
each step.

HOW TO INSTRUCT

Step 1: Prepare the worker

- Put the person at ease
- State the job
- Find out what the person already knows
- Get the person interested in learning the job
- Place the person in the correct position

Step 2: Present the operation

- Tell, show, and illustrate one **Important Step** at a time
- Do it again stressing **Key Points**
- Do it again stating **reasons for Key Points**
  - *Instruct clearly, completely, and patiently, but don't give them more information than they can master at one time*

Step 3: Try out performance

- Have the person do the job—correct errors
- Have the person explain each **Important Step** to you as they does the job again
- Have the person explain each **Key Point** to you as they does the job again
- Have the person explain **reasons for Key Points** to you as they does the job again
  - *Make sure the person understands*
  - *Continue until you know they know*

Step 4: Follow up

- Put the person on their own
- Designate who the person goes to for help
- Check on the person frequently
- Encourage questions
- Taper off extra coaching and close follow-up

**IF THE WORKER HASN'T LEARNED,
THE INSTRUCTOR HASN'T TAUGHT**

Figure 3.6   Back side of the JI four-step pocket card.

Step 1: Prepare the Worker

In the initial step, the instructor must do several things to put learners into the correct frame of mind. These may appear simplistic at first glance. But because every person is unique, instructors must take into account attitude and demeanor at the time of training to ensure that the trainee is receptive to learning the job. Otherwise, you will have wasted your time or, even worse, created conditions that lead to problems.

Detail 1: Put the Person at Ease

People are, by nature, nervous and uncertain when they learn a new job. They may be afraid that they are not capable of doing the job or will have difficulty getting accustomed to the new work. They may have had a bad training experience in the past. Anxiety and uncertainty create "noise" in the minds of learners. They are a barrier to communication and cause learners to miss important points.

In the fire underwriter's knot example, the instructor tried to put the new person at ease by asking her how long she had been with the company and by assuring her that he was there to help out if needed while she got accustomed to her new surroundings. You could also begin by talking about local events or even the weather. Your task is to get a trainee to relax and focus on learning the job. While you do not want the training session to devolve into idle chatter, a little time spent building a relationship helps to ensure training success.

Detail 2: State the Job

Amazingly, many supervisors rush their employees into a training situation without informing them exactly what they are asking them to learn. Make sure learners fully understand, up front, the job they are being asked to do. Otherwise, they will be puzzling over where your instruction is going and will miss important points. It is like building a jigsaw puzzle: without the picture on the box, we are simply fumbling with the pieces not knowing which piece should go where.

For example, tell the learner the name of the job he or she is going to be learning and then show a completed sample. This lets the learner see what the finished work should look like. Because you have removed the mystery of the work and the fear of the unknown, you have already made the learner less anxious.

Detail 3: Find Out What the Person Already Knows

The instructor should find out as soon as possible whether the learner has done the job (or something similar) before or has a hobby requiring the same types of skills. A quick review of the process should provide this information. If the learner has never done this particular job before, finding out whether he or she has similar or related knowledge and skills can help the instructor evaluate and adjust the amount of instruction needed to teach the job properly. Accelerate or slow down instruction depending on the learner's background and experience.

In the fire underwriter's knot example, the instructor asked the operator if she did things like camping or boating, activities requiring knot tying. She replied that she did neither, but subsequently revealed that she enjoyed knitting, a hobby that also requires skill in tying knots. Knowing this, the instructor could guess with some certainty that this particular person would not have any trouble learning to tie the knot and should be able to master it quite quickly. If the learner had none of these related interests, the instructor might have slowed down the instruction, anticipating that the learner would need a little more time to learn this job.

By comparing the job at hand with something the learner already knows, even if only marginally related, you build confidence and reduce anxiety. In teaching the knot, for example, the instructor can try something as simple as telling the learner that this job is similar to tying a shoe, something everyone can do.

Detail 4: Get the Person Interested in Learning the Job

JI teaches people to learn to do their work *conscientiously*. That means that they have to take an interest in what they are doing and pay attention to details. The most effective way of getting people interested in learning a job is to make them realize the importance of doing the job right. For that, they need to know how their effort, no matter how small, fits into the bigger picture—the finished product or service. No one is ever enthusiastic about doing a mindless, meaningless task. The following fable illustrates this point.

Fable of the Two Stonecutters

Two stonecutters working side by side at a job site are doing exactly the same work. When asked what he is doing, the first stonecutter, sweating and very bored and frustrated with his life, complains bitterly that he is "cutting stones." When asked the same question, the second stonecutter, doing exactly the same work and beaming widely, exclaims that he is "building a cathedral." The moral: when people know the purpose of their work, they will have a positive attitude.

In the demonstration of the fire underwriter's knot, the instructor actually took apart a finished lamp socket to show the learner where the knot goes and how it is used in the finished product. The instructor pointed out that if done incorrectly, the bare wire ends could be pulled loose from their mounts, causing a short circuit or, worse, a fire. This explanation was not meant to scare the learner but to show just how important the job would be to the finished product. Knowing the importance of the job honors the person doing it and motivates that person to learn to do it well.

Detail 5: Place the Person in the Correct Position

The final part of preparing learners is to make sure you place them in a position where they can best see and hear the instruction. This may seem obvious, but sometimes the obvious is the very thing supervisors neglect to do. For instance, an untrained supervisor unwittingly trains an employee how to do a job backwards—because the employee is facing the instructor.

The proper place for the learner to stand to watch the job demonstration is behind the instructor, looking over his or her left shoulder, the view the learner will have when performing the job. Since most people are right-handed, this gives them the clearest view of what the right hand is doing. If you are a left-handed instructor, you may want to have the learner stand behind you looking over your right shoulder. However, be aware that the learner will do the job exactly as shown. Your procedure may be awkward for right-handed learners.

The best place to teach a job is at the actual spot where the work will be performed on a regular basis. If there is anything dangerous at the worksite, this is the time to be sure the learner is in a safe position. Be aware that it may be difficult for the learner to see or hear what you are doing or saying because of noise or inadequate space. Always ask if you can be heard and seen clearly. If not, you may decide to go to a training room or other suitable area, taking all necessary tools and materials to teach the job with you. (This situation is discussed in more detail at the end of Chapter 4.)

Supervisor Team Exercise: Each person on the team should choose a simple job that is actually done in his or her department, one that you are responsible for training. Give the job a name. (**Note:** You will be using this job as a practice instruction demonstration throughout this part of the workbook.) If there are job sheets or other documentation relating to the job, gather them together. Team members should go over how they normally instruct or do jobs in their departments. Take note of the different approaches. Now go back over your own practice job applying step 1. What gaps can you see between your approach and JI? Do you use step 1 at all? If you skip any of the details in step 1, does this explain some of the problems you typically have? The kinds of problems we discussed at the beginning of this chapter?

Step 2: Present the Operation

In step 2, the instructor moves from the preparation phase to an actual presentation of the job. Here, the instructor gives a careful and detailed demonstration of the job to the learner. Again, it is imperative that you tell the learner what it is you are demonstrating.

In the knot-tying example, the job was broken down into important steps and key points to facilitate the instruction. Following a job breakdown is the way to make sure that the learner understands all of the vital information in the right order and avoid confusing the learner with information overload. Learning how to do job breakdowns using important steps and key points is a vital skill for supervisors proficient in JI. Chapter 4 provides a detailed discussion of the job breakdown sheet, but for now, it is enough to know that an important step is a logical segment of the operation when something happens to *advance the work*. Key points represent whatever is key to doing a step properly, such as things that *make or break* the job, anything that would *injure the worker* (i.e., safety), or things that make the work *easier to do*.

Detail 1: Tell, Show, and Illustrate One Important Step at a Time

Begin by *showing* the job one important step at a time, *telling* the learner what each step is as you do it. You can use sketches or diagrams of the job to illustrate any fine points that may be difficult to conceptualize. It is a good idea to start out by telling the learner how many steps there are in the entire job: "This job has five important steps; the first important step is ...." By doing this, you give the worker a clear idea of what to expect, and you focus attention on the five important things to be learned.

Since important steps are the logical segments of the operation, do not make these steps hairsplitting, micromotion details of the job. They should be simple, commonsense reminders of what is really important in getting the job done. When demonstrating the job, be sure to do the following:

- Speak clearly and deliberately.
- Make eye contact with the learners to ensure they are following you.
- As you move along, ask learners if they understand what you are demonstrating.

In Chapter 4, you will learn to use your breakdown sheet, which lists important steps and key points, to ensure you explain the important steps in the right order without missing anything. Never show the breakdown sheet to learners because they must focus their full and undivided attention on the specific job you are demonstrating.

Detail 2: Do It Again, Stressing Key Points

Most people do not learn to do a job by seeing it demonstrated just once. With a second demonstration, people know what to expect the next time around, and this helps them understand what they saw the first time. Once people have an overall picture of what is going on from start to finish, they can begin to absorb the intricacies of the job. Here, you introduce them to the key points of the job—any relevant special trick or a knack that is not readily apparent but which constitutes the real skill of the job learned over time.

Key points are the skills and insights that make people experienced. JI speeds up this maturing process and transfers this experience quickly and smoothly so that learners do not spend weeks, months, or even years figuring things out.

As with the important steps, be sure to articulate each key point clearly as you demonstrate the job. The learner needs to see and hear your demonstration at the same time. Use your breakdown sheet to make sure you present all key points in their correct sequence.

Detail 3: Do It Again, Stating Reasons for Key Points

Repeat the job again one more time, explaining the reasons for each key point. If a person knows the reason for a key point, he or she will better remember and execute that key point, and this is one of the most powerful aspects of the Job Instruction method. It is very common for even experienced workers to not know why they do jobs in the way they are supposed to perform them.

However, without knowing the reasons, it is easy to stray from the standard procedure, which has "no meaning" to us. Having a sense of purpose allows us to do the job conscientiously, thinking about what we are doing, and also enables us to understand and recognize when things change in the process so we can have them corrected.

This presentation process may seem cumbersome and repetitive, but what may seem redundant to you is, for the learner, a natural part of the learning process. Each time you demonstrate the job, you give a little more information even as you repeat what was stated in the previous round. In doing this, you reinforce information presented before while adding depth of detail to the learner's understanding. In addition, you create a logical structure for the learner by drawing connections between each key point and its corresponding important step.

Caution Point: Instruct Clearly, Completely, and Patiently, but Don't Give Them More Information than They Can Master at One Time

This caution point on the card is in italics to alert the instructor that this applies to all of the other items in this step. By teaching "clearly, completely, and patiently," you can be sure the learner has understood your instruction. And by not giving them more than they can handle at one time, you avoid confusing the learner with too much information. Learning is like eating. You can only chew and swallow small amounts at one time. By regulating the amount and content of information in each demonstration of the job, the learners can absorb it more quickly and completely than if they tried to swallow it whole.

> **TWI note:** Never give learners more information than they can master at one time. There is only so much information the brain can absorb and process at any given time. That is why in step 2 you need to present the operation several times, starting with the overall guideline and then drilling down into greater detail each time you go through the presentation. The more times the learner sees the demonstration, the more familiar he or she will become with the process. Gradually, the learner will become more capable of grasping and connecting information that is needed for doing a job.

Three quick run-throughs of the job to teach the important steps, key points, and reasons for key points may be enough for someone already experienced. For learners who are completely unfamiliar with even the basic motions of a job, you may need to repeat and demonstrate instructions several times. Do this as many times as necessary.

Supervisor Team Exercise: Choose an instructor and a learner from the team. Have the instructor read the "telling alone" explanation (page 25) of the fire underwriter's knot to the learner. Ask the learner to try doing the job. Then have the instructor repeat the dialogue for step 2 explaining the important steps, key points, and reasons for key points (pages 28–30) while actually showing how to tie the knot. You can use two pieces of light rope or insulated wire twisted together to simulate the lamp cord. Bear in mind that it is very difficult *not* to say everything we know about something in one continuous flow. It takes practice to learn how to hold back information. Switch roles with others in the group until everyone gets a turn to practice.

Step 3: Try Out Performance

In most cases, by the time you are satisfied that you have completed step 2 successfully, the learner is already anxious to try doing the job. Do not feel that you have to rush into step 3 until you are sure the learner has fully understood all of the important steps and key points, as well as the reasons for the key points. Recognize, however, that if a learner is anxious to try the job out, it is likely that your efforts to motivate have succeeded.

Never assume the learner can do the job without verification. Stay and observe until you are confident the learner can continue doing the work without your assistance.

Detail 1: Have the Person Do the Job—Correct Errors

First, have the learner perform the job silently, without either of you saying anything. This is the time for the learner to show you what he or she can do. At this point in the training, the learner merely needs to do the job and not worry about explaining how or why. (Exception: If the job entails judgment calls, like an inspection, the learner can confirm the call aloud.)

Observe the work carefully and stop the learner immediately if he or she is doing anything incorrectly. Do not let the learner proceed, because it is extremely difficult to unlearn something done incorrectly even once. If a learner is unable to do any part of the job, show and tell again, as you did in step 2, the correct way of doing the step. Then have the learner continue demonstrating the job using the correct procedure. Recognize that you may have to go back and repeat step 2 at a slower pace.

Many supervisors get confused on this detail because they think they should not let the learner do the job silently, which is like showing alone. While the instructor should never show alone, it is essential for the learner to demonstrate that the job has been fully understood without instructions or explanations. TWI always starts at the simplest level and moves toward complexity. Having the learner perform the job silently the first time is the simplest level. It allows the learner to focus on just doing the job.

On the other hand, some learners have a tendency to mumble to themselves as they try to do something for the first time. This is just a regular habit, so go ahead and let them do that. If you tried to stop them from talking, it would make them more uncomfortable and nervous. But this talk is not an explanation of the job they are doing, nor does it mean they understand the job in its totality. Make sure to you continue with each detail of step 3.

Detail 2: Have the Person Explain Each Important Step to You as He or She Does the Job Again

Now that you know the learner can do the job physically, you want to make sure that he or she understands the job mentally and is not just imitating the motions. Ask the learner to do the job again and tell you all of the important steps. The learner does not need to repeat the important steps verbatim, but listen carefully for accurate content. If the learner is having trouble remembering the steps, provide one or two key words as a hint. This will usually stimulate a recall of the whole step. Use the same breakdown sheet used in step 2 (in this case as a check sheet) to make sure the learner has stated all important steps in the correct order.

Learners also typically state some of the key points here, and this means they have not clearly articulated each of the important steps to the job. Point out that we are not looking for the details yet but want to confirm the major parts of the job that move it forward. It is essential that they learn the important steps in this round so that they can identify, in the next round, the key points one step at a time. We can quickly learn a large number of details (key points) if we remember them a few at a time, step by step. But we can only accomplish this when we have fully retained the important steps ahead of time.

If the learner cannot state any of the steps, stop the job and have the learner begin again. Interrupt when the learner gets to the end of an important step. Ask the learner to describe what he or she just did and sum up the learner's explanation by saying the important step. Continue this process with the next important step.

When the learner has completed doing the whole job, take a moment to pick up the completed work and examine it carefully. Even if you are sure the job was done correctly, this careful review of the finished work shows the learner how much you care about the quality of the work. An encouraging "Well done!" after the inspection inspires confidence.

Detail 3: Have the Person Explain Each Key Point to You as He or She Does the Job Again

Have the learner do the job once again, this time telling you the key points for each important step. This will confirm the learner understands the vital elements to doing the job well. Use the breakdown sheet to make sure *all* key points were stated with the right step and in the correct order.

Because the job is still new, some learners may confuse important steps and key points. This is normal. Your job is to help the learner distinguish important steps from key points and one important step from another while mastering the key points for each of those steps. This may take some time and work, so have patience. Your breakdown sheet will show you how to do this. Asking questions reinforces the process: "What was the first important step again?" "How many key points were there in that first important step?" "So what is the first key point in this step?" and so on. Above all, make sure it is the learner, not you, who is restating the important steps and key points.

Detail 4: Have the Person Explain Reasons for Key Points to You as He or She Does the Job Again

Finally, have the learner do the job yet again while telling you the reasons for the key points. In this way, you can be sure that he or she understands why the job must be done following each key point. This in-depth understanding will enable the learner to fully master the job because it can now be done conscientiously and consistently. People are not machines mindlessly repeating tasks without question. They need a good reason to do what they do, and this motivates them to do it well.

Caution Point: Make Sure the Person Understands

This caution point is italicized on the JI pocket card and applies to all of the other items in this step. In each part of step 3, the instructor's job is to make sure the learner physically and mentally understands the job while demonstrating it. The instructor's role is to be attentive to everything the learner says and does, jumping in whenever necessary. Never assume the person understands the job, or you may run into problems down the road. If the learner is having trouble repeating the important steps, key points, and reasons for key points, continue to review them until the problem is resolved.

Caution Point: Continue until You Know They Know

This caution point is also italicized on the JI pocket card. There is no set number of times the learner should repeat the job while the instructor observes and gives instruction. *The correct number of times is the number of times it takes for the learner to fully learn and be able to perform the job.* Although the TWI model shows that you should repeat step 3 four times, you should continue this process until you are satisfied that all important steps and key points have been mastered. Do not leave the scene until you are confident that the learner knows how to do the job. Be patient. Reassure the learner that you are not going to bail out until the job is completely mastered. No matter how busy you are, you will avoid or minimize future problems if you take the time to instruct correctly and completely.

No. 123

JOB BREAKDOWN SHEET

Operation: Tying the fire underwriter's knot

Parts: Twisted lamp cord

Tools & Materials: None

IMPORTANT STEPS	KEY POINTS	REASONS
A logical segment of the operation when something happens to advance the work.	Anything in a step that might 1. Make or break the job 2. Injure the worker 3. Make the work easier to do, i.e., "knack", "trick", special timing, bit of special information	Reasons for the key points
1. Untwist and straighten	6 inches	Leave enough length for the next operation.
2. Make right loop	In front of main strand	The knot will not tie correctly.
3. Make left loop	1. Pulling toward you 2. Under stub 3. Behind main strand	1. It's easier to do the next motion. 2. The knot will not tie correctly. 3. The knot will not tie correctly.
4. Put end through loop		
5. Pull taut	1. Ends even 2. Sliding loops down 3. Firmly	1. The knot will tie evenly. 2. So the knot ties in the correct position. 3. So it won't come apart.

Figure 3.7   Job breakdown sheet for fire underwriter's knot.

Supervisor Team Exercise: Return to the fire underwriter's knot example. Using the same instructor–learner teams from the previous exercise, go through step 3 and have the learners try out performing the job using the step 3 sequence. Remember that learners are not to look at the breakdown sheet or notes as they perform this step. Instructors should use the breakdown sheet (see Figure 3.7) as a check sheet to be sure the learners have learned the job completely.

Step 4: Follow Up

The final step of the JI four-step method is follow up. No matter how diligently you have performed the initial three steps—prepare the worker, present the operation, and try-out performance—you must never assume that you have achieved perfect instruction or covered every detail. Things are seldom done perfectly. Moreover, remember that people and processes can and do change. It is impossible to predict what effects changes will have on the work being done, which is why you must follow up on the instruction to make sure you are not blindsided by the unexpected.

Detail 1: Put the Person on His or Her Own

From the moment the instructor transfers the job, it is the worker's responsibility to do the job correctly each time, showing that he or she knows the job is important. The instructor needs to make it clear to the learner that he or she has taken on this responsibility.

At this point, the instructor should advise the learner how much work is expected over a given time period (e.g., the next hour or the next full day) or how often the work is to be performed if it is not an ongoing task. Knowing how much work must be finished and by when will give the learner a sense of pacing, which is always a big concern when doing something for the first time. Without this knowledge, some learners might feel compelled to rush needlessly to prove themselves. This can lead to mistakes or accidents.

Detail 2: Designate Who the Person Goes to for Help

In the early stages of doing a new job, a learner will have questions or need help. Unless otherwise instructed, most learners have a tendency to ask people nearby. This can be disruptive and counterproductive, especially when the people nearby, regardless of their willingness to help, are not familiar with the job in question or do not know how to give correct instruction. The most appropriate person to get help from is you, the person who taught the job. Make this clear to the learner immediately. Obviously, you will not always be available, so you must designate someone else who can fill in (e.g., another leader in the area or an experienced worker). Be sure to let these individuals know that you have appointed them to help and that they have the appropriate knowledge to provide instruction.

Detail 3: Check on the Person Frequently

Most errors occur soon after the learner starts doing a job alone for the first time. During this critical period, check back frequently, even every few minutes if necessary. How often you check back depends on the nature of the job. In situations where accidents or serious failures can occur, checking frequently may even mean staying at the site and keeping an eye on the worker's performance for a period of time. Remember that it takes time to become experienced. Be available to help and give additional instruction when needed. As the worker becomes familiar with the job, check less frequently.

Detail 4: Encourage Questions

Most employees are hesitant to ask questions. Some fear that questions will show a lack of ability or experience and might jeopardize wages or promotions. They may even fear being fired. Even experienced workers hesitate to ask questions because they unrealistically (and usually mistakenly) believe they are supposed to know everything about the job. As a supervisor, you want all workers to be asking questions, especially if answers to those questions can help prevent problems. Encourage *all* questions and answer them.

The key to encouraging questions is to create a stable, secure, and open work environment where people are not afraid to ask questions. You must work hard at this by letting your people know that it is OK to ask questions and by taking the time to listen and respond. Furthermore, by creating strong and steady Job Relations with your people (discussed in Section III of this workbook), you will create a mutual trust that will encourage people to ask any question without hesitation or fear of consequences.

Detail 5: Taper Off Extra Coaching and Close Follow-Up

As the learner becomes more experienced, gradually taper off extra attention and bring the follow-up phase to a close. This period will change with the nature of the job and the skill of the person doing it. For some jobs it may be a few hours and for others a few days or even weeks. If you have instructed well, you can rest assured that the work will be carried out properly and with few problems.

> **Supervisor Team Exercise:** Return to your practice job. Review with your team the follow-up parameters for each team member's job. Determine how much work each new worker will be expected to do, how often you will need to check up on the worker, who will serve as your backup person, and how you will encourage the worker to ask questions. Consider potential changes or problems that might occur.

If the Worker Hasn't Learned, the Instructor Hasn't Taught

The JI four-step method, when used properly, is a sure and reliable way of getting people to learn jobs. The key tenet to the JI method is *if the worker hasn't learned, the instructor hasn't taught*. In other words, the supervisor has the responsibility of ensuring that employees perform their jobs well.

When things go wrong in a working environment, it is very easy and very common for supervisors to blame problems on the low skills or lack of proper attention on the part of the people who perform the work. The supervisor may even replace a person who cannot perform up to speed (at times, this may indeed be the needed action). The truth of the matter is that most employees are actually capable of doing much more than what they are being asked to do. Moreover, most people go to work each day with the intention of doing a good job and are proud of the work they do. With proper training, most people not only do the jobs that are required of them, but also try to show their supervisors the full breadth of their ability and ambition.

Many supervisors feel it is an unfair burden for them to be held totally responsible for an employee's performance. After all, they protest, no matter how hard you try, some people simply refuse to listen or follow good instruction. This is not an instruction problem; it is a leadership problem. Poor performers generally do not have a good relationship with their supervisor and resist the supervisor's guidance. TWI addresses this issue with its Job Relations program, covered in Section III of this workbook, which develops leadership skill that helps supervisors build and maintain strong relationships with the people they supervise and encourages their cooperation. In an environment that provides good leadership, employees depend on their supervisors to train them properly so they can succeed at their jobs.

Teaching new employees is an obvious supervisory responsibility, but even veteran employees need to learn new skills to keep up with new jobs and earn promotions or to adjust to transfers, changes in work duties, changes in procedures, or changes in work standards. New products and services, as well as new technologies, come at workers with increasing speed and must be addressed. Above all, no company should ever be satisfied with the current level of performance; improving ways of doing things should be a continual process.

How to keep up in a changing environment is covered in Job Methods improvement in Section II of this workbook. If supervisors are trained to instruct their employees (old and new) properly and continually, the problems discussed earlier in this chapter can be alleviated or eliminated, and changes can be addressed appropriately. The ability to train is, in fact, one of the most important qualities a supervisor must possess. Using the method described in this chapter will hone this training ability.

It is important to reemphasize that training ability is perfected through practice, and for this reason, putting the JI four-step method into practice immediately is essential. Before doing that, however, you will be learning a few essential preparatory items, the most important of which is the job breakdown. In Chapters 4 and 5, you will examine the "get ready" points of JI and learn how to use them to enhance your use of the JI four-step method.

Supervisor Team Discussion: Have members of the team discuss how they feel about the statement "If the worker hasn't learned, the instructor hasn't taught." Channel the discussion by asking about prejudice against people perceived as slow learners, insubordinate workers, or workers who do not want to take responsibility. Under what circumstances would it be uncompromisingly true that the supervisor is fully responsible for the performance of employees through proper training? How is the skill of the supervisor, in both job instruction and leadership, a critical component of this?

Chapter 4

How to Get Ready to Instruct: Break Down the Job

In Chapter 3, the fire underwriter's knot example and related exercises showed effective (and ineffective) ways to teach someone a job. But although the description of Job Instruction (JI) using the four-step Training Within Industry (TWI) methodology was fairly detailed, other elements must be in place before you are ready to take these ideas to the shop floor. If you go with what you know now, you may still run into a variety of problems. Because the concepts covered in Chapter 3 follow a specific pattern, you might, for example, unwittingly give too much information or fail to present the job as clearly as you should. You might jump too soon from one point to another or backtrack because you missed a point earlier. In step 2, you might introduce new ideas in the wrong place or miss critical points because you have not clearly organized information about the job. In step 3, you might fail to confirm that the learner has in fact grasped all of the important steps and key points or confuse the learner by adding new information in step 3 that was not presented in step 2.

These training shortcomings are common throughout all industries and job types. They show that instructors, although they may know how to do a particular job without even thinking, need to be fully prepared to deliver the training. Carefully considering the steps and critical points of a job before trying to teach it is the best way to begin.

There is usually more to a job, even a simple job, than you realize, especially if it is something you do not do on a regular basis. For this reason, even if you fully understand the JI four-step method, you need a solid foundation that will prepare you to teach it properly.

> *JOB INSTRUCTION*
>
> **HOW TO GET READY TO INSTRUCT**
>
> **Before instructing people how to do a job:**
>
> 1. **Make a timetable for training**
>   - Who to train
>   - For which work
>   - By what date
> 2. **Break down the job**
>   - List **Important Steps**
>   - Select **Key Points**
>   - *Safety factors are always Key Points*
> 3. **Get everything ready**
>   - The proper equipment, tools, materials and whatever needed to aid instruction
> 4. **Arrange the worksite**
>   - Neatly, as in actual working conditions

Figure 4.1   Front side of the JI four-step pocket card.

There are four important things that you need to do *before* you instruct a job. These four "get ready" points are printed on the front side of the JI pocket card introduced in Chapter 3. Titled "How to Get Ready to Instruct" (Figure 4.1), this side of the card lists things you need to do before you give instruction using the four steps listed on the other side. Let's examine these four get ready points.

1. *Make a timetable for training.* Do the training by plan, not by accident. You usually make plans for any part of your work, and training should be no different. When you make a timetable for training, you are planning whom to train, on which job, and by what date.
2. *Break down the job.* List the *important steps* of the job and identify the *key points* for each of those steps along with the reasons for those key points; clearly organize the operation in your mind so that you can be sure you are correctly teaching the *one best way* of doing the job.
3. *Get everything ready.* Have all of the proper equipment, tools, materials, and supplies needed to aid the instruction. If you use makeshift tools or use the wrong equipment or forget something or don't have the necessary materials, you set a poor work standard for the person who has to do the job and undermine your authority as a supervisor.
4. *Arrange the worksite.* Arrange things neatly, just as you would in the actual working conditions. A cluttered tool chest, a poorly arranged workbench, a cluttered desk, or any single thing that is out of place sets a poor example for employees.

Because the second get ready point, break down the job, is the most important and the most difficult point to learn, it merits special attention.

Thus, Chapter 4 will focus only on this subject. Chapter 5 will cover get ready items 1, 3, and 4. Although break down the job is the most critical of the four preparatory steps, the instructor needs to follow all four get ready points to ensure a successful JI session.

Get Ready Point 2: Break Down the Job

If someone asked you to give a short speech at an event or to talk at a business meeting about the progress of a project you are leading, you would probably make some notes beforehand, perhaps in outline form, so that you present your thoughts in an understandable, logical order. Doing this would help you to remember important information as well as keep you from digressing from the subject at hand. At the same time, you want your outline to be flexible so that you can adjust your comments in response to audience reaction to what you are saying. In preparing for JI, you also need to make notes regarding the jobs you want to teach to workers.

Specifically, you need to break down jobs into their *important steps* and then find the *key points* for each of those steps. You will also be finding the reasons for each of these key points, which you will use during instruction. When you break down a job, you document the *one best way* for doing that job and thus create a job standard for the work. However, the purpose of these job breakdowns is *not* to try to describe every conceivable step, motion, point, or precaution that may relate to the job. Nor are they instruction sheets that document in detail how to do the job. In fact, you don't even show the breakdown sheet to learners. The breakdown sheet is merely a tool for collecting notes from yourself to yourself to help you organize your thoughts and the operation's procedures as you train the employee. Figure 4.2 shows the breakdown of the fire underwriter's knot example we used in Chapter 3.

The breakdown sheet has two columns: one for important steps and one for key points. You can add a third column for the reasons for the key points, but for now let's focus on understanding and finding the important steps and the key points.

> **Supervisor Team Exercise:** Print a blank JI breakdown sheet from the TWI Institute website (www.twi-institute.org) and familiarize yourself with the format. The workbook demonstrates how to use the JI breakdown sheet to identify the important steps and key points in the fire underwriter's knot example; the team will use this as a template for filling out important steps and key points for their practice jobs. Use the sheet from the TWI Institute website for this exercise.

No. 123

JOB BREAKDOWN SHEET

Operation: Tying the fire underwriter's knot

Parts: Twisted lamp cord

Tools and materials: None

IMPORTANT STEPS	KEY POINTS
A logical segment of the operation when something happens to advance the work.	Anything in a step that might 1. Make or break the job 2. Injure the worker 3. Make the work easier to do, i.e., "knack", "trick", special timing, bit of special information
1. Untwist and straighten	6 inches
2. Make right loop	In front of main strand
3. Make left loop	1. Pulling toward you 2. Under stub 3. Behind main strand
4. Put end through loop	
5. Pull taut	1. Ends even 2. Sliding loops down 3. Firmly

Figure 4.2   Job breakdown sheet for fire underwriter's knot (without "Reasons" column).

What Is an Important Step?

An important step is a logical segment of an operation when something happens to *advance the work*. Let's say you need to change the blade of a hacksaw and you keep the spare blades in a drawer. "Grasp the handle of the drawer" is not a step worth noting on the breakdown sheet because the operator will know to do this motion intuitively. What about "Pull open the drawer"? This is a step, but it is not an important step, because simply opening the drawer does not advance the goal of changing the hacksaw blade. "Take out the proper blade," however, is an important step and should be noted. For this step, it is not necessary to go into any greater detail.

It is important to keep in mind that these breakdowns are not hairsplitting, micromotion studies that people commonly use when documenting or analyzing a job procedure. They are simple, commonsense reminders of what is essential when teaching a job. Remember that your purpose is to teach people to *quickly remember to do a job correctly, safely, and conscientiously,* so don't overload them with any more information than they absolutely need to have.

For example, if you were to write down every detail of the procedure in the fire underwriter's knot example, it would look like this:

1. Take an ordinary piece of twisted lamp cord.
2. Hold it vertically with your left hand, between the thumb and first finger, 6 inches from the end.
3. Untwist the loose ends, forming a V.
4. Straighten the loose ends between the thumb and first finger of the right hand.
5. Hold the wire at the beginning of the V.
6. Take the right-hand loose end with the right hand and make a clockwise loop, bringing the loose end across in front of the main strand.
7. See that this loop is about 1 inch in diameter and the stub protrudes to the left of the main strand about 1½ inches. Hold the wire at the junction of the loop and the main strand.
8. Take the other loose end with your right hand.
9. Make a counterclockwise loop. To make this loop, pull the loose end toward you, pass it underneath the stub, behind the main strand.
10. Pass the loose end through the right-hand loop, from back to front.
11. Hold the ends evenly between the thumb and first finger of the right hand.
12. Pull the knot taut.
13. Shape the knot between the thumb and first finger of the left hand as it is pulled taut.

In this detailed description, there are 13 steps and 193 words, as compared with 5 steps and 36 words in the brief, but better, job breakdown of the fire underwriter's knot shown in Figure 4.2. Keep in mind that the instructor might need to use all 211 words in the course of explaining the operation. However, for the purposes of organizing the procedure in your mind, 36 words is all you need.

A simple procedure for choosing important steps is presented below. Using this checklist will help you create a concise but complete list of important steps for tying the fire underwriter's knot.

Four Steps to Finding Important Steps

1. Start doing the job, slowly and meticulously.
2. Ask yourself at each stage, "Has the job advanced?"
3. If so, question what you have just done.
4. If you think it can be an important step, write it down in the column for important steps on the breakdown sheet with a succinct phrase to convey the meaning.

With the fire underwriter's knot example (refer to Figure 4.2), you began doing the job holding the wire and untwisting it into a V shape. Now ask yourself whether the job has advanced because of this action. Even though the shape of the wire has changed, the answer is no. The first logical step in the advancement is when these loose ends are straight and ready to be tied. Therefore, the motion of straightening the untwisted ends is the first important step: *untwist and straighten.*

Continue tying the knot, taking the right-hand loose end and making a clockwise loop. This motion definitely advanced the job because you have to have this loop in place to tie the knot properly. So the second important step is *make right loop.* Here you might be tempted to add the word *clockwise*, which is an excellent word describing the direction of a motion, but because the act of making the loop is easy to see and understand, the extra word becomes unnecessary. Moreover, adding *clockwise* to step 2 would then make you want to add the word *counterclockwise* to step 3, *make left loop*, just for balance. Both words are just extra words because the procedures are already well balanced and easy to remember without them.

To finish this example, continue doing the job by putting the loose end of the stub through the right-hand loop. Because this advances the job, you make it the fourth important step, *put end through loop.* Finally, you pull the knot taut and this completes the job, making for a fifth and final important step, *pull taut.* These five steps capture the essence of what it takes to understand this job quickly and completely. Because they are simple and direct, they are easy to remember and repeat. Notice that each step involves something that moves the job forward. It is not until you get to key points for each step that you go into details.

Both body movement and mental activity can be regarded as important steps. In many jobs, the operator may have to think about something in order make a calculation or a decision before moving on to the next step. Whether using the body or the brain in order to advance the work, these can all be regarded as important steps. For example, it may seem, on the surface, that inspection or measurement tasks do not serve to advance the work because nothing has physically changed with the job. But because we know something we didn't know before, this gets us closer to our goal of completing the job and can be considered an important step.

> **TWI note:** The important steps in a breakdown should correlate with learners' abilities. Each step can be compared to the amount of food you can keep in your mouth at any given time. If the experience or ability of the learner is low, each step must be small enough to chew and swallow easily. If it is high, larger amounts can be chewed and swallowed. This means that you can have different breakdowns for the same job.

Supervisor Team Exercise: Have team members perform their practice jobs and identify the important steps. Remember, important steps are what you do. First, perform the job until you reach a segment that moves something forward. Confirm by asking yourself, "Has the job advanced?" Then ask yourself whether what has just been done is an important step. If so, use a succinct phrase to convey the meaning and write it in the "Important Steps" column on your breakdown sheet. Once the team determines it has the needed steps for each job, perform the practice jobs one last time to review the important steps.

What Is a Key Point?

Five to ten percent of every job entails hard or tricky parts that take time to learn and that embody the real skill of doing the work. People gain these know-how skills through years of experience, which give companies a competitive advantage that is difficult for imitators to replicate and repeat quickly. Because these skills are developed over time, businesses value long-term, experienced employees. TWI calls these know-how skills key points because they are the key to doing steps of a job properly. In fact, *knowing the key points of a job and how to pick them out quickly and easily is perhaps the most important task for the instructor.*

A good instructor finds these key points and passes them on so learners can gain needed skills as quickly as possible. Knowing a job's key points helps to reduce the number of accidents and defects that occur while people are becoming experienced. Supervisors can also use breakdowns to capture the knowledge of experienced employees and pass it down to a new generation of workers.

Key points represent the difficult things in performing a job. They can be points that new workers fail to do or misunderstand. They can also be things that all learners find hard to remember or take time to master. We can classify key points into three types. Understanding them will help you recognize the key points in any given job.

Three Kinds of Key Points

1. *Make or break the job.* These are things that make for success or failure in job performance.
2. *Injure the worker.* Safety factors, no matter how small, are always key points.
3. *Easier to do.* This includes any special knack or "trick of the trade," the special bits of information or timing that make a job easy to do.

As with important steps, there is no need to identify everything, but if the activity meets one of these three conditions, you can consider it a key point. Some good examples of key points are listed below:

■ Using a micrometer to get an accurate measure of the thickness of a piece of material. If you don't turn down tightly enough, the measurement is not accurate. If you turn down too tightly, you compress the material and, again, the measurement is not accurate. The key point, *how tight you turn down on the barrel*, is a matter of feel.
■ Assembling plastic parts. You will know the parts are attached properly when you hear the pins snap into their holders. *Hearing this sound* is the key point.
■ Changing the grindstone of a grinder. By tapping the stone with a hammer, you can judge when there is a crack. If the stone rings like a bell, there is no crack; if the sound is dull and short, it is cracked. The key point is the *quality of that sound.*
■ Attaching certain kinds of electrical wiring. The key point is *attaching the negative wire to the steel screw and the positive wire to the brass screw.*
■ Diluting sulfuring acid, you have to pour acid into water gradually. If a worker pours water into the acid, the acid and water will react and splash. This may injure the worker. *The order of combining the ingredients* is the key point.
■ Using a knife. *Always cut away from and not toward yourself to avoid injury* is the key point.

When giving key points, as much as possible avoid using negative expressions. Telling learners what to do is preferable to telling them what not to do. If you teach them, for example, not to touch the surface of a part because it puts oil and dirt on the clean side, they will still not know how to properly hold the part so that their fingers can avoid touching the surface. An exception to this rule may be when there are only two possible courses of action, in which case not doing one option leaves only the other option available. Some safety factors may also require a negative expression (e.g., "Do not touch bare wires"). In general, though, always look for positive expressions.

Identifying the Key Points in the Fire Underwriter's Knot Example

Below are the six steps to identifying key points. We will use these six steps to go through the fire underwriter's knot example to identify the key points for each important step. Once this is covered, we will discuss the reasons for the key points and the importance of observing and involving experienced workers. Then we will provide some sample breakdowns that will prepare the team to apply the six steps to their practice job.

Six Steps to Identifying Key Points

1. Do the important step.
2. While performing the step, recite the three conditions that define a key point: *make or break, injure the worker, easier to do.*
3. If you find something you think might meet one of these three conditions, ask yourself why you do it that way or what if you didn't do it that way. (The answer here is the reason for the key point.)
4. Confirm that this is a key point by asking yourself which of the three conditions this meets. For example, does this *make or break* the job because you could not do the next operation?
5. If you conclude that it does meet one of the conditions, write the key point down on the breakdown sheet.
6. Repeat steps 2–5 for the same step until you can't find any more key points in this important step. Then repeat the entire process for any remaining important steps.

Now let's use these six steps to find the key points in the fire underwriter's knot example.

Important Step 1: Untwist and Straighten

1. Do the first important step: *untwist and straighten.*
2. While performing the step, recite the three conditions that define a key point: *make or break, injure the worker, easier to do.*
3. Is there anything you are doing here that might meet one of these three conditions? Yes, we need to make sure we leave *6 inches.* Ask yourself why you do it that way or what if you didn't do it that way. The answer is because *if you do not leave 6 inches, there won't be enough wire length to complete the next operation.* (Note: This is the reason for the key point.)
4. To confirm that this is in fact a key point, ask which of the three conditions it meets. In this case, not leaving 6 inches would *make or break* the job because you cannot do the next operation. Therefore, you can conclude that 6 inches can be a key point.
5. Write the key point down on the breakdown sheet. All you need to write is *6 inches.*

6. Repeat steps 2–5 for the first important step until you can't find any more key points in this step. (In this case, there are no other key points for the first important step.)

Important Step 2: Make Right Loop

1. Do the second important step: *make right loop*.
2. While performing the step, recite the three conditions that define a key point: *make or break, injure the worker, easier to do*.
3. Is there anything here that might meet one of the three conditions? When you make the loop, you have to pass the stub *in front of the main strand*. Why do you do it that way or what if you didn't do it that way? If you don't, or if you passed the stub *behind* the main strand, *the knot will not tie correctly*. (Note: This is the reason for the key point.)
4. To confirm that *in front of main strand* is a key point, ask which of the three conditions it meets. In this case, it clearly *makes or breaks* the job.
5. Write the key point on the breakdown sheet: *in front of main strand*.
6. Repeat steps 2–5 for this step. Here, you might consider whether the size of the loop and the length by which the stub protrudes to the left of the main strand might be key points. Because there could be variability in either of these and the knot would still tie correctly, these things do not make or break the job and are not key points. You could leave these details to the worker, and he or she would still do the job correctly. There are no other key points in this step.

Important Step 3: Make Left Loop

When you *make the left loop*, continue reciting the three conditions for a key point—make or break, injure the worker, easier to do—so that you stay focused on what you are looking for. Key points are usually hidden, almost invisible at first glance, so you have to be diligent about knowing what they are in order to flush them out. For example, when you make a left loop, you first pull the loose end toward your chest to put a kink or bend in the wire. When you ask yourself why you do this, the answer is to get the wire coming from a better direction to *make it easier to do the next motion*, which is to pass it under the stub. If you don't put a 90° bend in the wire, it will be parallel to the stub and the stub will tend to pop out of the loop after it is made. This meets the condition easier to do, and the key point is *pulling toward you*.

Continue questioning the same step to see if there are any more key points. In step 3, there are two other key points, *under stub* and *behind main strand*, and both of these are make or break conditions. If they are not in place, *the knot will not tie correctly*.

Important Step 4: Put End through Loop

Step 4 is quite different from the other steps because it has no key points. Many instructors mistakenly think that they have to have a key point for every step, but if the process is straightforward and clear, as in this step, no key point is necessary.

Important Step 5: Pull Taut

In step 5, *pull taut*, several important things meet one of the three conditions that define a key point. First, you need to line up the two loose ends of the wire before you pull the knot taut. With the *ends even*, the knot is square or forms evenly. The knot is nice and tight, and *it will not come loose later*. This meets the make or break condition for a key point. Further observation reveals that if you didn't form the knot while pulling it taut (i.e., by sliding the loops down so that the knot is closed in the right position), the knot could close and tie higher up on the wire. If this occurs, you *will not have the 6 inches you need for the next operation*. This, too, is a make or break condition, and the key point is *sliding loops down*. Finally, after the knot is pulled taut, you tug on it *firmly* to make sure it is good and tight. This is a make or break condition because it ensures that *the knot will not come loose later*.

Listing the Reasons for the Key Points

When you identify how each key point meets one of the three required conditions, you will always be able to see the reason for that key point because it confirms why you have to do the step a certain way and shows what will happen if you do not do it that way. Writing these reasons on your breakdown sheet will help you during the instruction process. As noted in the previous chapter, if the learner knows why the key point is necessary, he or she will be more likely to remember and follow it.

Be sure to give the specific reason for each key point and not a generality like "safety," "quality," or "it's a rule." For example, if the key point is "holding by edges," simply saying "safety" does not help the learner to fully understand the reason why he or she must do it this way. Explaining "to avoid burning fingers" will better teach the learner the safe way of holding the part while convincing him or her to do it that way every time. The purpose for giving the reasons for the key points is to help the learner understand the job fully and deeply, so get into the details of why this job must be done this specific way. If you don't know the reason yourself, go and find someone who does.

When teaching the job, emphasize that these are the reasons for the key points and not the important steps, as this is often a point of confusion. The ultimate reason for any important step is that it advances the job.

In other words, if you don't do it, the job will never get done. The reason for any key point, on the other hand, explains why we do it this way. There may be various ways to accomplish any one step, but by giving a specific reason to do it following the key point, we make sure to get it done correctly, safely, and conscientiously.

Making a Balanced Breakdown

Once you have identified the important steps and the key points, along with their reasons, you can look at your breakdown to see if it has a good balance between these two components. For example, if your breakdown has a long list of important steps with just a few scattered key points here and there, consider consolidating the steps or moving some of them over to the "Key Points" column. It is very common for new trainers to put too much detail into the important steps when many of these steps are really key points to doing larger elements of the whole job. While there is no definitive number of important steps a job may contain, a good breakdown will have from five to seven steps; more than that will be difficult for the learner to remember. (See the "Long Operations" section at the end of this chapter.)

On the other hand, if there are too many key points in one single important step, consider breaking the step into two or more steps. Even though this new step may not necessarily advance the work, there is a limit to how much a person can remember in any one step. Generally speaking, three to five key points is the maximum you can expect a person to remember for any one important step. Be careful not to let any one step carry the weight of the entire job.

Creating this balance does not change the procedure for doing the job. It just makes it easier for the learner to capture and hold the critical elements of doing the job. Figure 4.3 shows a poorly balanced breakdown for the job of attaching a pipe, and Figure 4.4 shows a better breakdown for this same job. Notice how it is possible to rearrange important steps and key points to create a better balance.

In addition, each important step of the operation should contain roughly the same volume of work. When learners do new jobs, it is easier for them to remember the whole process when there is a regular rhythm or beat to each step. Also, don't feel the need to break long expressions artificially. Though we pointed out that important steps and key points should be expressed accurately and simply, learners will find it more difficult to remember a simple action when it is broken into two parts. For example, for "line up the ruler on the baseline," technically speaking, the important step would be "line up the ruler" and the key point would be "on the baseline." But when the learner observes you putting the ruler on the baseline, it is more intuitive for the activity to be summed up in one expression.

No. _____

JOB BREAKDOWN SHEET

Operation: Attach pipe

Parts: Pipe, ring, fixture

Tools and materials: Deburr tool, Scotch-Brite, Windex, cloth

IMPORTANT STEPS	KEY POINTS
A logical segment of the operation when something happens to advance the work.	Anything in a step that might 1. Make or break the job 2. Injure the worker 3. Make the work easier to do, i.e., knack, trick, special timing, bit of special information
1. Pick up the pipe	
2. Inspect for burrs	
3. Debur the inside end	1. No touch before 2. Away from you 3. Feel for smoothness
4. Debur the outside end	Same as #3
5. Shine edge with Scotch-Brite	1. 2–3 inches 2. Rolling back and forth
6. Wipe clean	1. 2 squirts Windex
7. Install ring	1. Down at an angle 2. Light pressure 3. Back and forth into position 4. Snapping in with "click" 5. Check full circumference 6. No bends or breaks
8. Apply flux	
9. Line up with hole	
10. Attach pipe to fitting	1. Check with gage
11. Push in all the way	

Figure 4.3 Job breakdown sheet for poorly balanced breakdown.

TWI note: Job Instruction is designed specifically for teaching skills on the job. However, in any operation there is always a certain degree of knowledge that a worker must have to learn and perform the task. These two elements, knowledge and skill, are best learned in different ways. When we try to teach knowledge about the job while we are performing Job Instruction, we waste precious time during this intensive, one-on-one training setting. We can learn knowledge much more efficiently in a classroom and by reading texts and other educational materials. On the other hand, trying to teach skills in a classroom full of people is rarely effective.

No. _____

JOB BREAKDOWN SHEET

Operation: Attach pipe (revised)

Parts: Pipe, ring, fixture

Tools and materials: Deburr tool, Scotch-Brite, Windex, cloth

IMPORTANT STEPS	KEY POINTS
A logical segment of the operation when something happens to advance the work.	Anything in a step that might 1. Make or break the job 2. Injure the worker 3. Make the work easier to do, i.e., knack, trick, special timing, bit of special information
1. Inspect and debur	1. Inside and outside edge 2. No touch before 3. Away from you 4. Feel for smoothness
2. Shine edge with Scotch-Brite	1. 2–3 inches 2. Rolling back and forth 3. Clean with 2 squirts Windex
3. Position ring	1. Down at an angle 2. Light pressure 3. Back and forth into position
4. Snap ring in place	1. With "click" 2. Check full circumference 3. No bends or breaks
5. Apply flux and attach	1. Lining up with hole 2. Check with gage 3. All the way in

Figure 4.4   Job breakdown sheet for better balanced breakdown.

Observing and Involving Experienced Workers in the Breakdown Process

If supervisors know a job well, they can find these key points on their own. However, with the help of an experienced person, you will be able to find even more key points. Getting experienced people involved in the breakdown process will provide invaluable information on how to do a job, as well as many insights into the best way of doing it. We know, for example, that Toyota likes to have its workers involved in the work standardization process and add their experience and knowledge to the "one best way" of doing the work. By emulating this model of "tribal knowledge," you can perpetuate the real value of your company's work by passing on important skills to future generations of employees.

Interestingly, workers do not always realize they are performing their jobs by using key points. For example, a job instruction might say "look and do," but the worker is really using "feel" rather than sight to perform a particular aspect of a job. This suggests that key points are obvious or commonsense items that anyone can identify. However, key points often point out what the process should feel or sound or look like, and these concepts are not always easy to describe in words. What makes a difference here is the supervisor's point of view and attitude in actively looking for, documenting, and then teaching these critical items. For this reason, it is important to observe the worker doing the job and to note any experienced wisdom that surfaces.

In the appendix to this workbook, we review the ESCO Corporation, where they made a plastic jig that operators actually touch and feel to learn whether a wax part is defective or not. Using their JI training to look for and identify key points, they created a process in which workers learning the job can drag their fingers across the jig and actually feel and recognize, in gradual stages, a bad surface, a marginally passable surface, and a good surface.

Pat's Story: Finding Key Points by Observing Experienced Operators

Pat was once helping a JI class break down a job at a high-end foundry. The final finished product included fuel injection lines for jet fighter planes, and the job in question was to insert quartz rods into corresponding holes in a steel block. These would later be made into an alloy die-cast; the quartz rods melted out, leaving behind the fuel lines. The trick was to get the rods, which were long, narrow, and brittle, into the holes without breaking them. As Pat observed the operator doing the job, he noticed that each time she performed the operation, she first held the rod at a steep angle to the steel block and then slid the tip of the rod gently down the face of the block until it "caught" the hole. She then straightened out the rod and slid it into the hole.

Using the procedure for finding key points, Pat asked the operator why she performed the job that way. The operator looked up incredulously and said she didn't know what he was talking about. He pointed out what he had observed, and only then did she consciously realize just what it was she had been doing to get the tip of the rod positioned properly at the hole. She said that she used to do the job by stabbing the rods at the holes, like throwing darts at the bull's-eye, but she broke a lot of rods that way because the holes were so tiny and hard to hit. By seating the tip of the rod into the hole at an angle, she was able to line up the rods more by feel than by sight. This was an action she had learned through experience, unconsciously, over a long period. By capturing this key point, the company did not have to wait, or waste a lot of broken rods, before the next person doing the job could become experienced in doing it well.

It is not unusual for some employees to resist sharing their special techniques or tricks with others. They may do this for job security (if they are the only ones who know how to do it, they can't be laid off) or simply because they put in the time it took to become experienced and believe others should do the same. But for companies that want to improve, it is imperative to create a culture where employees act as team members and not like "lone wolves" fighting for their survival within the organization. If you honor the experience of your veteran employees, you can make them mentors for others. If this occurs in a way that does not threaten their job security, they will become useful partners in creating and improving company standards while passing on their know-how to a new generation.

Summary and Sample Breakdowns

As you have seen, the breakdown for Job Instruction consists of two major parts: important steps and key points. One easy way to remember the difference between these two items is that *important steps are the "what you do" and the key points are the "how you do it"*. Therefore, important steps usually consist of action phrases beginning with verbs: "insert fastener," "input data," "swab injection area with alcohol," or "turn up heat to 375°." Key points, on the other hand, usually consist of descriptive words using adjectives and adverbs: "with rough side up," "feeding evenly and slowly," "to two decimal places," or "squarely, no chips or nicks." When you put the two together, they make a complete and descriptive sentence, as in "chuck the bit squarely, with no chips or nicks," where "chuck the bit" is the important step and "squarely, no chips or nicks" is the key point. Then, when you add in the reason for the key point, you complete the full explanation: the what and the how and the why we do it that way.

It takes much practice and experience to perfect making good breakdowns for training. While there is no right or wrong breakdown, we can hone our skill at making better breakdowns by seeing what works when we train the job and adjusting accordingly. Keep in mind that instruction is a communication process, and what we are working with here are words and expressions that try to convey meaning from one person to another. This is more an art, like poetry, than a science because there is no one formula that makes a good breakdown.

Because breakdowns are simply notes to yourself, few words are required, and the fewer the words, the better. If you make your breakdowns too precise or use technical jargon, you will only confuse the learner and the important parts of the instruction will be left unclear or misunderstood. With a good breakdown in hand, when you demonstrate the job in step 2 of the JI four-step method, you will be able to explain each of the important steps precisely and emphasize all of the key points to each step, along with their reasons, in the correct order without missing any. In step 3, the trial phase, you can use this breakdown as a check sheet for making sure the learner has understood all of the important steps and key points, with nothing omitted. And when they are able to state the reasons for the key points, you can be sure they will do it that way each and every time.

> **TWI note:** Supervisors may know a job so well that they seldom think about how to put it across to others, so when they teach it, they carelessly miss important parts. On the other hand, sometimes supervisors incorrectly think that they fully understand a job that they really don't and only notice their ignorance when they try to teach it to someone. The TWI developers created the breakdown sheets so that you can think through jobs before instructing.

The following four sample breakdowns are from four different industries (Figures 4.5 through 4.8). You will notice in Figure 4.5 that there are two levels of detail, depending on whether the learner is experienced or new. Example 1A is used for operators who have had other bench lathe experience and are already skilled at each of the operations listed. New people, however, have to learn each operation. Example 1B is the breakdown for just the first step, chuck. There will be breakdowns for each of the other operations; once the operator has learned them all, it will not be necessary to provide that level of detailed instruction. Your breakdowns can be as precise or as general as needed depending on a learner's skill level. Below is a summary of how to do a breakdown.

Summary of the Way to Do a Breakdown

1. Do the job on your own. You may want to refer to any available written materials, such as work standard forms or instruction sheets, and you should talk with experienced operators to be sure you have determined the one best way of doing the job.
2. Write up the important steps of the job, making sure that each step is a logical segment of the operation that advances the job.
3. Do the job again, step by step, and find the key points for each important step. When finding the key points, keep in mind the three conditions that define a key point: What makes or breaks the job? What might injure the worker? What makes the work easier to do? As you find the key points, record the reasons for each of those key points to enhance your instruction.
4. Number or label your breakdown sheet. Doing this will make it easy to find in your files, and you'll be able to use it again and again whenever you have to teach that particular job.

Example 1A **JOB BREAKDOWN SHEET** (Experienced Operator)		Example 1B **JOB BREAKDOWN SHEET** (New Operator)	
Operation: Bore, ream, and face **Parts**: Governor brake disc		**Operation**: Chucking **Parts**: Governor brake disc	
IMPORTANT STEPS	**KEY POINTS**	**IMPORTANT STEPS**	**KEY POINTS**
1. Chuck	Chuck squarely—no chips, no nicks	1. Open jaws	Wrench full into sprockets
2. Indicate	Low speed	2. Clean out chips	Use brush—not hands; get all out
3. Center drill	Angle—give drill double hearing	3. Set piece in jaws	
4. Drill	Lips even; feed even; high for chip clearance; clean drill	4. Adjust jaws to piece	Even pressure all round—not too tight
5. Reverse piece		5. Try for balance	Must center
6. Bore	Feed even and slow	6. Final tighten—jaws	Must hold against pull of cutting tools
7. Plug gauge	Enough stock for reaming	In Example 1A, a job setter in a machine shop did this breakdown in 9 minutes. He uses this breakdown as is for operators who have had other bench lathe experience. For newcomers, he uses one or two of the above steps as a separate instructing unit and makes a separate detailed breakdown for each of these smaller units. Example 1B shows his detailed breakdown for just step 1, chucking.	
8. Ream	Feed evenly; if bell-shaped, check tool		
9. Set cross-slide	No backlash		
10. Turn	Feed evenly; keep "drag" for good finish		
11. Face	Keep "drag" for finish		
12. Gauge hole—plug gauge	Never remove piece—feel		
13. Check			
14. Remove and place in tray	Don't drop		

Figure 4.5   JBS Example 1: two levels of detail for a new or experienced learner.

Supervisor Team Exercise: Using the six steps to determining key points, have each team member fill in the key points for each important step as they perform the practice job. Ask what will make or break the job, what hazards may injure the worker, and what knack, trick, or special information can make the work easier to do. In step 3, where you confirm that an activity is a key point, find the reason why that key point is necessary and list it in the "Reasons" column. Do the practice job and go over the important steps and key points one last time.

JOB BREAKDOWN SHEET

Operation: Printed circuit board (PCB) insertion

Parts: PCB, housing

Tools and material: None

IMPORTANT STEPS	KEY POINTS	REASONS
A logical segment of the operation when something happens to advance the work.	Anything in a step that might 1. Make or break the job 2. Injure the worker 3. Make the work easier to do, i.e., knack, trick, special timing, bit of special information	Reasons for the key points
1. Pick up housing with left hand	Notch to the left	Easy to insert PCB from this position
2. Pick up PCB with right hand	1. With two fingers 2. Holding by edges	1. Easy to grasp 2. Keep oil and dirt off surface of PCB
3. Insert PCB into housing	1. Align notches 2. Top edge first, at an angle 3. Sliding along rails	1. Correct orientation 2. Get in correct position 3. Make sure it is all the way in
4. Push in tight	Until pins come out	So it doesn't come off

Figure 4.6 JBS Example 2 with reasons.

JOB BREAKDOWN SHEET

Operation: Data input

Parts: Monthly sales data sheet

Tools and materials: Computer/Excel

IMPORTANT STEPS	KEY POINTS	REASONS
A logical segment of the operation when something happens to advance the work.	Anything in a step that might 1. Make or break the job 2. Injure the worker 3. Make the work easier to do, i.e., knack, trick, special timing, bit of special information	Reasons for the key points
1. Open sales file	1. Correct product line 2. Entering your password at prompt	1. Each product line has a separate file 2. To ensure security
2. Select current month	Double-clicking on month tab	Easier than using menus
3. Input sales volumes by customer	1. One customer per column 2. Rounding up cents to nearest dollar 3. Numbers only, no "$" signs	1. Makes it easy to read 2. Do not need exact total; used for sales forecasting 3. Cells are already formatted
4. Double-check totals on spread sheet with data sheet	If totals are different, check for entry errors	Easy to find missed entries
5. Save and close file		

Figure 4.7 JBS Example 3.

JOB BREAKDOWN SHEET

Operation: Install IV catheter and inject contrast material for CT examination

Parts: Needle, syringe, IV connecting tube

Tools and materials: Rubber gloves, tape, tourniquet, alcohol, cotton pad, clear band-aid, sodium chloride, contrast material

JI No._____

Date: October 9, 2004

IMPORTANT STEPS	KEY POINTS	REASONS
A logical segment of the operation when something happens to advance the work	Anything in a step that might 1. Make or break the job 2. Injure the worker 3. Make the work easier to do, i.e., knack, trick, special timing, bit of special information	Reasons for the key points
1. Apply tourniquet	Adequate pressure to increase the size of veins	To make the best vein available stand out from the rest
2. Select vein	Straight and large enough to accommodate a standard size catheter	So contrast can enter vein at the rate desired; otherwise a smaller catheter must be used
3. Cleanse area with alcohol pad	Letting the alcohol air dry	Arm sting when a needle is put in the skin when wet with alcohol
4. Insert needle into vein	1. At the same angle the vein is running 2. Pushing the needle in to the length of the catheter	1. To prevent going through the vein 2. To assure stability while in the vein
5. Attach syringe to the catheter	Drawing back on syringe until you see blood flow	Needle is not properly in vein if blood does not flow
6. Inject 2 mL of sodium chloride	Use the full amount of sodium chloride	Clear blood from catheter
7. Secure catheter to arm	Applying clear band-aid at the site of entry	1. To prevent catheter from coming loose when attaching IV line 2. Ability to see entry site
8. Attach IV line	Firm connection	So line will not come off when contrast is going into vein
9. Inject contrast	Feeling vein as contrast is entering vein	To make sure contrast is going into the vein.
10. Remove catheter after the injection; apply gauze and tape to arm	Firmly over the point of entry for gauze to maintain pressure	To prevent continued bleeding

Figure 4.8 JBS Example 4.

Breakdown Sheets and Standardized Work

Learning to make breakdowns of jobs and putting this skill into use is a big step toward the greater goal of work standardization. Breakdown sheets, however, should not be confused with work standards. Strictly speaking, the breakdown sheet for Job Instruction is a training tool for the supervisor to use during the instruction process and should not be used for any other purpose. If your company already has detailed instruction sheets or standard work forms, you can use these as reference materials as you create your breakdown sheets for training. Usually, these forms are very detailed and describe everything about a job. TWI breakdown sheets for Job Instruction give only the amount of information needed to "put across the job to the learner" because it is what the learner both sees and hears during Job Instruction that makes up the full extent of the instruction.

Even if you have instruction sheets or standard work forms, you should still perform the jobs when making the breakdown sheets, because doing so ensures that you are capturing just the right descriptive and simple words for the operations. There is absolutely no substitute for actually going to the worksite and doing the job yourself to make sure you have the procedure down correctly.

> **TWI note:** In Japan, the TWI concept of doing the job the one best way was an important step toward the development of standardized work, which Taiichi Ohno of Toyota claimed was the bedrock foundation of continuous improvement.

Once companies go through the JI training, they usually realize that their instruction sheets for employees are too complicated. These documents typically have the steps and key points intermixed in long narrative descriptions. In many cases, they are not used or even read by the employees. As a result, some companies have found it useful to modify their instruction sheets using the JI important steps and key points format. But these are still reference materials and are not to be used for training.

Small- or medium-size companies that do not have formal written documents outlining how jobs are done often look to the JI breakdown sheet as a vital tool for documenting work standards even though the breakdown sheet for Job Instruction is not designed to be a comprehensive work standardization document. Company managers note that once their supervisors develop and use the breakdown sheet, they are more effective in determining and maintaining the one best way of doing the work. It is important to remember, however, that the breakdown sheet is a training tool used by the instructor. It does not document every single thing that is done in a job. It is not a comprehensive record of the job, and you should not use it as such. Supervisors who know the breakdown sheets they are developing are to become the official version of the job may be tempted to include more information than is necessary. They should resist that temptation.

We cannot emphasize enough that the JI breakdown sheets do not replace detailed instruction documents, which are the proper references for both operators and supervisors to use to confirm details of the work. Just because the names of the tools are similar doesn't mean they perform the same function.

Extra Notes on Key Points

Knowing how to pick out key points quickly and easily is perhaps the most important part of Job Instruction. Four additional points that will help you complete this critical part of the JI method are (1) understanding common key points, (2) teaching feel, (3) dealing with long operations, and (4) instructing in noisy areas.

Common Key Points

In many jobs, there are key points that apply to all of the steps in a given job, and it is cumbersome and confusing to repeat the same key point for every important step. Often these are key points concerning safety (e.g., wearing protective glasses or cutting away from you). Some key points refer to the way a tool is held or a part is used throughout the entire process (e.g., with large opening facing up or squeezing trigger all the way). You should teach common key points as an integral part of the job procedure, listing them on the breakdown sheet as the "zero step" or "0. Common key points" (Figure 4.9).

The first things to point out when instructing a job are the common key points that apply to *all* the steps. You should mention these each time you explain the job in step 2. In step 3, make sure that the learner can repeat them.

Teaching Feel

Many jobs, especially in manufacturing and health care, require some kind of a feel or knack. Some supervisors tend to think that these skills are somehow mysterious or difficult to teach because they are generally the result of years of experience. But if you teach the learner what and where the feel or knack is, he or she will be able to pick it up much faster. And if you teach the correct feel for the job right from the start, the learner will master it with little difficulty and few problems.

IMPORTANT STEPS	KEY POINTS	REASONS
A logical segment of the operation when something happens to advance the work	Anything in a step that might 1. Make or break the job 2. Injure the worker 3. Make the work easier to do, i.e., "knack", "trick", special timing, bit of special information	Reasons for the key points
0. Common key point	1. Wearing protective gloves 2. Squeezing trigger all the way	1. To keep solvent off hands 2. Put just the right amount of solvent onto parts

Figure 4.9   Common key points: the zero step on the breakdown sheet.

Feel and knack key points are very difficult to describe in words, so you have to think of creative ways to teach them. Using expressions like "finger tight," "wrist tight," "arm tight," or "body tight" when referring to how tight to turn down on a tool may help, but demonstrating feel by getting the learner's hands on the tool in connection with these verbal cues is better. Have the learner try it out and keep checking performance until it feels just right.

For example, when measuring the diameter of a piece of stock with calipers, making the setting takes a kind of feel for the job. To put over this feel, the instructor does the following:

1. Adjusts the calipers until they are set correctly.
2. Hands them to the learner and explains to him or her, "This is the correct adjustment. Remember this adjustment." Lets the learner get the feel of it.
3. Tells the learner to adjust the calipers from the beginning, recalling the feeling.
4. If the instructor sees the learner is able to adjust the calipers correctly, takes them back and examines them.
5. Praises the learner if it is done correctly. If not, asks the learner to try again to make the adjustment.

By passing the calipers back and forth several times, the learner can master the feel more quickly.

The example of how the ESCO Corporation made a jig out of plastic to teach operators making wax parts just the right feel for how the surface of the parts should be finished (presented earlier in this chapter in the "Observing and Involving Experienced Workers in the Breakdown Process" section) is another creative way of teaching key points concerning feel. Use your imagination and ingenuity to come up with similar ways of teaching key points about feel and knack.

Long Operations

One of the concerns expressed by supervisors about JI is that it is just fine for production line jobs that take only a few minutes or less to complete, but not suitable for jobs that can take several hours (or even days) to complete. Some of these jobs consist of so many elements that they simply cannot be taught all at once. But it is for such complex and multilayered jobs that correct instruction is most important because both learners and instructors tend to get confused and "lost" when a job has an overwhelming amount of detail. The best approach is to break up the long operation into smaller units and, using the JI four-step method, teach them one segment at a time within the limits of the learners' ability to understand.

One of the caution points in the four-step method is *don't give a person more information than he or she can master at one time*, and this also applies to the total amount of work you can teach at one time. Consider the example of using a micrometer, a delicate measuring instrument that looks like a clamp. Many things go into using this instrument, but they can be divided into four units:

■ Unit 1: Care of the micrometer and its parts
■ Unit 2: The scales and their relation to each other
■ Unit 3: Simple measurements
■ Unit 4: Difficult measurements (requiring readings in fractions of 100)

With this division, steps 1 and 4 (prepare the worker and follow up) will cover the same ground for all four units and should be performed only once. Steps 2 and 3 (present the operation and try out performance) should be performed independently for each of the units. This means that there will be a different breakdown sheet for each unit, and the learner will not proceed to the next unit until he or she masters the unit before. By mastering one skill at a time, instead of everything at once, the learner will learn more quickly and avoid mistakes and accidents.

For a long operation that cannot be stopped in midstream, the instructor can still break the work up into smaller units, but this is a bit more complicated. The instructor will have to do most of the operation or get another experienced person to help out while the learner is taught about each unit. It is a good idea to teach the learner the easiest parts of the job first, and then teach the more difficult units, one by one. Until the learner can do the entire job without assistance, you (or another person) will be completing the untaught units. At first glance, this may seem time-consuming, but consider the alternative: how much time it would take the same person to learn the entire job all at once and how many problems would occur while this person struggled to learn the job.

For extremely large and long operations, you may have no choice but to walk the learner through all of the steps in step 2 (present the operation), carefully explaining the job as you do the whole thing yourself. Although you cannot stop or repeat the job, once the process gets started, you will have plenty of time to reiterate the important steps, fully explain them, and point out all of the key points and then their reasons. You could also record the entire job on video and use it to identify the important steps and key points *before* demonstrating the job, so the learner knows what is coming when he or she sees the actual job being performed. Video can be a very useful aid to speed through a long operation, but it should never replace an actual demonstration of the job.

Then, moving directly to step 3 (try out performance), you can check verbally whether the learner can remember all of the important steps, key points, and reasons for key points. Have the learner recite them to you even though he or she cannot actually do a try-out performance. You may also want to use video here to confirm if the learner can identify the important steps and key points at the correct time and location in the job. This is not ideal, but it gives the learner a rough idea of the job, and he or she will be better prepared to do it the next time the procedure is run. Be sure you are there to follow up (step 4 of the JI method) with the learner once he or she is doing the job independently. Use this time to reconfirm that the learner can do the job and knows all of the important steps, key points, and reasons for key points.

Noisy Areas

A common problem in many factories or other industrial sites is noise, which can make it difficult (and sometimes impossible) for the learner to hear the instructor. The basic JI principle is to teach jobs at the actual worksites. However, in instances where people will not be able to hear the explanation, it is best to go to a quiet place where you can first tell the details of the job and then go to the actual worksite and show the job. This showing must reflect everything that was taught in the telling phase. In step 3, after the learner demonstrates at the actual worksite that he or she can do the job, you will need to go back to the quiet area again and have the learner point out to you all of the important steps and key points to be mastered. In all cases, the learner should always perform the job at the actual worksite.

Now that you have learned how to break down a job, it is time to explore the three other get ready points on the "How to Get Ready to Instruct" side of the JI pocket card. By learning how to plan for training, you can be sure that your training will not be haphazard and will support the overall goals of the company. You can also be sure that all of your efforts will pay off with a well-trained person working to meet high standards.

Supervisor Team Exercise: Review your practice job breakdown sheet to make sure it is complete. Choose an instructor and a learner from the team and practice instructing the practice job using the full JI four-step method and the breakdown you made for that job. Preferably, pick a learner who does not know how to do the job. Observers in the group should take notes on the demonstration and comment on the demonstration after the instructor is finished. Then have others on the team take the roles of learner and instructor until everyone gets a chance to instruct. If necessary, review the sample dialogue or the explanations for each item on the pocket card in Chapter 3.

Chapter 5

How to Get Ready to Instruct: Make a Timetable for Training, Get Everything Ready, and Arrange the Worksite

---

Chapter 4 covered the most difficult part of the "how to get ready to instruct" items: *break down the job.* This chapter examines the other three "get ready" points listed on the Job Instruction (JI) pocket card: *make a timetable for training, get everything ready,* and *arrange the worksite.* As with break down the job, Training Within Industry (TWI) developers road-tested these three JI get ready points in actual industry settings and with groups of supervisors until they achieved the most effective program content and format, and nothing in this chapter deviates from their findings. Supervisors often ignore or forget to apply these three points. Don't. Although they are easier to learn than break down the job, they are just as important. Their proper use can mean the success or failure of your training effort.

As you saw at the beginning of Chapter 3, supervisors encounter a multitude of problems when they fail to train their people and train them well. This is especially true when the pressure is on for production and people have to learn new skills. Under these conditions, many busy supervisors tend to see training as a problem or as something that will just happen naturally. When these attitudes are expressed in words, you hear:

- It takes too much time to train people.
- A lot of mistakes always happen while training new jobs.
- Let them do it on their own. That's the only way they will learn.

Such attitudes and statements are counterproductive. Most thriving businesses know that it is well worth the trouble and effort, in the long run, to arrange schedules to accommodate training in the same way they make plans for any other part of the business. That begins with making a training timetable so that training is well planned and executed.

Get Ready Point 1: Make a Timetable for Training

When you get ready to instruct, the very first thing to do is to plan your training. *Make a timetable for training* means that you will do the training according to a plan and not by accident. More specifically, it means that you need to determine:

■ Who should be trained?
■ For which job?
■ By what date?

Making plans on a regular basis helps to ensure that work proceeds smoothly, meeting demands and important deadlines. The same concept applies to training. Many plants use a simple tool called the skills grid as a loose planning guide. The skills grid, however, is a static document that shows only who can do which job, whereas the training timetable is a dynamic document that guides and organizes your training effort. It is easy to make.

Table 5.1 presents a partially finished training timetable. In the left-hand column of the grid is a list of operations done in a department. The operations, listed one by one, are assembling parts, wiring, combining, knot tying (the fire underwriter's knot), clamping, and adjustment. Similar lists can be created for other working environments or departments. You can modify your headings by listing classification, position, level of skill, type of machine, or any other logical way of differentiating the skills required for the people doing the work. The critical question to ask is, what makes one person's work different from the work of others? In an office, for example, even though all of the people may be processing credit forms, some may work exclusively on large accounts and others may specialize in overdue accounts. In a job shop, different people may work with different machinery. Some of the machinery may be old or new, large or small, or made by different manufacturers with different attachments or features.

After listing the operations, put all of the workers' names across the top of the grid in each column. The names can be listed alphabetically or organized to reflect workers' experience or seniority. Then check off all the jobs each worker can do, as shown in Table 5.1. You will notice that all of the checkmarks are the same except for the star mark for Taylor's clamping. Jones, the supervisor making this timetable, used this mark to show that Taylor, although already trained on the clamping operation, was not yet working at the optimal skill level. The grid also shows that Smith, Lark, and Morse are the most experienced people

Table 5.1   Job Instruction Training Timetable (Partial)

Name: Bill Jones Dept.: 2nd Electrical Department Date: 1/05/xxxx	Breakdown No.	Smith	Lark	Morse	Taylor	Massy	Peters	Baker				Changes in Production
Assembling parts		✓	✓	✓	✓		✓	✓				
Wiring		✓	✓	✓	✓							
Combining		✓	✓	✓		✓	✓					
Knot tying		✓	✓	✓	✓	✓						
Clamping		✓	✓	✓	★	✓	✓					
Adjustment		✓		✓								
Turnover Work Performance												

in the department because they can do almost all of the jobs. Baker, the newest person on the team, can only assemble parts, the easiest job in the area.

The completed training timetable (see Table 5.2) illustrates that Jones then reviewed the timetable to see if there were any urgent training needs in his department. First, he looked for possible *turnover* due to retirement, promotions, transfers, and so forth. He knew that Morse was scheduled to retire at the end of February and made a note, "Scheduled to retire on 2/28," at the bottom of the timetable in the column under Morse's name. He then reviewed the list of names from the perspective of *poor performance* (e.g., excessive rejects or mistakes, injuries, and damage to equipment). As the table shows, Jones felt that the performance of all his people was satisfactory except for Taylor's clamping skill. At the bottom of the grid, under Taylor's name, he wrote, "Needs more training."

Finally, Jones reviewed the job headings from the perspective of *changes in production*, considering how he was meeting the present production quotas in all of the jobs and whether there might be any upcoming increases in production. He learned that a special model was being scheduled to run for 1 week at the beginning of March. This was a two-bulb version of a lamp that would require one more person for the knot-tying operation. In the timetable row for knot tying, Jones noted, "Need 1 more worker at beginning of March." The three notations highlighted for Jones the three issues that would require urgent training: Morse's retirement, Taylor's clamping, and the anticipated need for an additional person to do the knot-tying operation.

Table 5.2   Completed Job Instruction Training Timetable

Name: Bill Jones Dept.: 2nd Electrical Department Date: 1/05/xxxx	Breakdown No.	Smith	Lark	Morse	Taylor	Massy	Peters	Baker					Changes in Production
Assembling parts		✓	✓	✓	✓		✓	✓					
Wiring		✓	✓	✓	✓								
Combining		✓	✓	✓		✓	✓						
Knot tying	123	✓	✓	✓	✓	✓		2/21					Need 1 more worker at beginning of March
Clamping		✓	✓	✓	★ 1/12	✓	✓						
Adjustment		✓	2/7	✓									
Turnover Work Performance			Scheduled to retire on 2/28	Needs more training									

Jones was now ready to make plans to meet these training needs. Specifically, he needed to consider *who* was to be trained on *which job* and by *what date.* He decided that Baker was the most suitable person to learn the knot-tying operation. This would help her to expand her skills in the department at a time when it was needed, at the beginning of March. Jones did not want to do the training too early, knowing that people trained too soon will forget what they have learned before they have a chance to perform the work. On the other hand, he did not want to wait until the last minute, in case Baker needed more time to learn the job. After weighing these issues, he set February 21 as the date to complete the training, as shown in Table 5.2. Baker's training was to be completed on or before this date.

Next, Jones addressed the problem of Taylor's clamping. Since Taylor was already skilled enough to do the job partially, Jones determined that the training would not require much time and that it could be done right away. He scheduled Taylor's training for January 12.

Jones knew that Morse's retirement would leave the department with only one other person, Smith, who could do the adjustment process, the most difficult job in the department. If Smith were absent or quit, Jones would have no one in the department who could do this work. He decided that Lark was the most suitable person to replace Morse in this operation because he was the most experienced of all those remaining in the group. Because adjustment work was difficult to learn, he set February 7 as the date for training, which would give Lark plenty of time to practice and ask questions before Morse left the company. In this way, the transfer of Morse's responsibilities could go smoothly and easily.

Using this kind of training timetable grid may seem simplistic, but it is amazing how simple practices like this can create real order and discipline in a department. It can also help you flush out hidden problems and avoid them down the line. At this point, the timetable is basically complete. All that remains is to put in the breakdown numbers for each breakdown. Since the fire underwriter's knot has already been broken down, the breakdown number is entered on the grid and can easily be retrieved when it is time to train Baker on that job. The next step is to break down the clamping job, as that training schedule is coming up soon. The same is true for the adjustment process.

The model presented above is invaluable and can be replicated for any department. The procedures for making a training timetable are presented below.

Procedure for Making Training Timetable

1. Fill in the supervisor's name, department, and date.
2. Put in the job headings in the left-side column.
3. Put in the people's names across the top.
4. Check off the jobs that can be done by each person.
5. Look for urgent training needs.
   - By operator: Turnover, poor performance.
   - By job heading: Meeting present production quotas, anticipated increases in production.
6. Plan to meet these needs
   - Who to train
   - On which job
   - By what date

The training timetable is a simple tool, but many companies that have implemented TWI Job Instruction have improved on its usage and application to fit their needs. Instead of using just a checkmark in the grid for each job a person is able to do, for example, companies like Toyota use different symbols to represent the different levels of knowledge and experience a person has in a particular job. The simplest level, represented by a circle that has only one quarter of its center filled in, means that the person can just perform the job. The highest level, a completely filled in black circle, means that the person not only has great skill and experience in the job, but also has enough ability to teach that job to others.

> **Supervisor Team Exercise:** Using the training timetable form from the TWI Institute website, have each member of the group plan the needs of his or her department for the next 6 months. If you have a large department, choose one area, keeping the number of employees under a dozen. Begin by using the procedure for making the training timetable, taking special note of who to train, on which job, and by what date.

Get Ready Points 3 and 4: Get Everything Ready and Arrange the Worksite

The final two points on the "How to Get Ready to Instruct" side of the card are get everything ready and arrange the worksite. Because these two points are self-explanatory, supervisors often overlook them. You may feel that you cannot take the time to attend to these points of the JI process, but not doing so can jeopardize successful teaching of the JI four-step method. Once you understand their importance, you will always remember to do them and do them well.

Getting everything ready to instruct means that you assemble all the proper things that aid the instruction and have them on hand. At the top of the breakdown sheet is a space to list all of the parts, tools, and materials needed to complete the job. Use this as your guide to make sure you have not forgotten anything before you instruct. You don't want to end up halfway through teaching a job and then realize that you do not have the proper screwdriver to complete the job correctly. Telling the learner, "Oh, just pretend this pencil is the screwdriver and I'll bring you the right one later" shows poor preparedness and sets a poor standard. The learner will not see the actual work being done with the proper equipment and can get the impression that you don't think that the job is important enough to take the time to prepare properly for the training. Furthermore, the learner may feel that if it was not important enough for the supervisor to bring the right tool, then it must not be that important to use that exact tool in any exact way.

Arranging the worksite means arranging the work area neatly, just as you would expect to find it during actual working conditions. First impressions last, and a positive first impression of the workplace will set a good example for the worker to maintain. Neatness will also promote a high standard of work because there will be no extraneous materials that might distract from or interrupt the work. It does not take long for a tool chest to become cluttered and disorganized or for a desk to become piled with papers. Set a high standard right from the start by arranging the worksite and cleaning up this clutter before the new person comes to learn the job.

Supervisors should never be too busy to set a good example for people in their departments. Setting a good example is what supervisors and instructors should be doing as a regular part of their daily responsibilities. As members of the company's management, you are models of the company's standards, ideals, and culture. Teaching a person a new job is the ideal time to begin setting that good example.

The Ultimate Test for Job Instruction: Teaching Young Children

We mentioned in Chapter 3 that many of our Job Instruction trainers were trained teachers who told us the principles of the JI four-step method were exactly the same ones they used to use to teach children. Therefore, it follows that "operators" ranging in age from 8 to 13 who are properly trained in the JI method and are placed in a world-class manufacturing cell should be able to succeed in assembling complex machines with zero defects in a one-time-only run. What follows is a true story.

In the spring of 2003, the Eastwood Knolls School in El Paso, Texas, decided to create a project (and a challenge) for the students in its GT program (a program for gifted children) by having each child learn to assemble a toy robot in 40 minutes. The initial goal of the project was to teach an appreciation for robotics and the project was to run for 3 months in classes that met once per week. Each robot set contained 103 discrete parts. One of the rules of the project was that all of the children in the GT program had to be equally included in the project, not just a single grade level. The work could not be too simple for the eighth grader or too complex for the second grader. Four teachers were assigned to groups of 25 students of all ages for a total of 100 students, and each student got a robot kit to assemble. One teacher, Ms. Dana Gray, after assembling one of the robots herself, realized it would be a challenge even for an eighth grader. She consulted Conrad Soltero, a field engineer with the local National Institute of Standards and Technology Manufacturing Extension Partnership (NIST-MEP) affiliate, who had just completed the TWI Institute Job Instruction train-the-trainer program, and decided that the only chance her students would have of assembling the robots in 40 minutes would be to use Lean manufacturing techniques. While the other teachers used this time to discuss solely the points of robotics and not the issues around assembly of the kits, Ms. Gray promptly began learning production fundamentals, beginning with the JI technique, from Mr. Soltero.

Ms. Gray reassembled and timed each of the logical assembly steps presented in the robot assembly instructions. To provide point of use storage (POUS) for each station within the cell, she needed to kit individual parts for each of the 25 robot sets. After she collected all data, she recombined some assembly steps to accommodate different skill levels and the takt time needed to assemble the robot in 40 minutes. The cells were all loaded before the children began; this included building up the work-in-process so all of the kanbans would be queued before the clock started. A multimode production process was designed because you could assemble the robot in two configurations. Ms. Gray staffed each station according to its complexity: the older children assigned to the elaborate assembly operations and the younger to the less complex. To ensure production was performed competently and on time, Ms. Gray applied the JI four-step method. Weeks in advance, she prepared, with Mr. Soltero's help, a job breakdown sheet for each station and made sure each child was properly trained for the 40-minute production session.

On the big day, Ms. Gray asked each of her students which of the two robot configurations they preferred and then scheduled the robots built in that sequence to simulate a pull system. Finally, the hour was at hand. Ms. Gray gave the word to begin. The operation came off superbly. Every single robot that came out of the cell passed the required functional test on the first try. Of the three other classes, only one student was able to complete the project on his own by the end of the project period.

Supervisor Team Exercise: First, have a team discussion on training workers. Have there been any instances of not having the proper tools during training? Have there been any consequences, minor or serious, resulting from not using the proper equipment? Second, have each team member report on the cleanliness and orderliness of his or her respective work areas. Grade the areas on a scale of 1–5, with 5 being spotless and organized. Do you organize or clean the area once a day, three times a week, once a week, and so forth? Have each team member state at what point he or she begins to feel disorganized to the point that it affects job performance. If you are always disorganized, you may want to use a Lean tool like 5S (a series of activities to *sort, set in order, shine, standardize,* and *sustain* work areas) to get a handle on things.

JOB METHODS

Chapter 6

Applying Job Methods to a Sample Job to Show before and after Improvements

Section III (Chapters 6 through 8) of this workbook covers the second Training Within Industry (TWI) program, Job Methods (JM) improvement. The best way to understand JM is to see how it is applied to an actual job. This chapter presents a detailed example of the methodology (both before and after improvements) of a particular job—the assembly and packing of the microwave shield. Chapter 7 shows how the supervisor used the JM four-step method to improve this sample job while explaining each of the steps in detail. Team members will apply these steps to improve their practice jobs. Chapter 8 provides a detailed discussion of how to apply the improved method using a written proposal. The TWI note below provides an overview of JM and explains how it differs from JI and JR. The first section of this chapter considers what kinds of work JM can improve.

> **TWI note:** In TWI, we refer to the whole JM four-step method process as the *Job Methods improvement plan*, which is a bit different from Job Instruction and Job Relations. Unlike JI, where you use "get ready" points before you instruct, and JR, where you focus on problem prevention with the "foundations for good relations," the four steps of JM cover all of the activities you perform in the program. Of course, it has the JM breakdown sheet and proposal sheet, but these tools are embedded in the JM four-step method and are not separate activities.

Three Fundamental Classifications of Work

In almost all workplaces, *material handling*, *machine work*, and *hand work* are involved in most of the jobs done every day. This is the simplest way of classifying work. Other work, such as inspection, planning, discussion, brainstorming, and so on, adds value to products and services, but depends on these three fundamental types of work, which provide the understanding and knowledge required to do a job correctly. *When a work process or procedure uses one or more of these three types of work, supervisors can use the JM four-step method to find a better way of getting it done.* But to do this effectively, supervisors need to have a clear idea of what these activities are. Understanding these three fundamental classifications of work is a prerequisite for improvement.

1. *Material handling.* If you ask people the kinds of things they do in the work place every day, most will reply by listing routine tasks, such as going to the stock bins to get screws and fasteners, picking up the copies and bringing them back from the copy room, taking the washed and folded sheets back to the linen closet, or sorting and putting the finished pieces into their respective cartons. All of these activities entail taking something, whether it is a part, a piece of raw material, or a finished product, and moving it to a different location. TWI calls this material handling, and it is a common component of most people's jobs no matter where they work.

2. *Machine work.* When people say that they assemble the wire harnesses, prepare the special-order coffees, process the payroll, or check the temperature trends in the lacquer curing oven, they will seldom mention that these jobs entail machine work. But if you ask them to tell you exactly how they do these things, you will usually hear that there is some kind of equipment involved. In order to make the wire harness, for example, they need to use a crimping tool to tie the wires together; in order to make the special-order coffee, they need to use an espresso machine and milk steamer. In fact, almost all work, whether in an office or in a plant, involves machines. No one would think of processing the payroll without some kind of specialty accounting software. Likewise, a mini-computer (microchip) embedded in the machine processes the graph showing the internal temperature of the curing oven over several hours. TWI classifies each of these and similar activities as machine work.

3. *Hand work.* Despite the advances in technology—machines, mechanical devices, and so forth—there are still things that only human hands can do. Examples of hand work include shaving the rough edges off the wax molds, making up the hotel or hospital room beds, inserting the large and oddly shaped components into the printed circuit boards, and changing the ink cartridges in the printer—all operations that are done with human hands.

The next part of this chapter looks at a sample job that uses all three of these job classifications and examines the current method (CM) of doing this work, as well as a new proposed method, using TWI JM.

Microwave Shield Sample Job: Current Method

Part I of this workbook used the fire underwriter's knot example from the original TWI training program to explain Job Instruction (JI). The microwave shield sample job, also from the original TWI training program, teaches JM. It is important to remember that the job itself is not what matters here; the example simply illustrates the JM improvement method and serves as a guide for improving other jobs in the same way.

This sample demonstration analyzes the making and packing of the microwave shield, a component that is used in electronics equipment to block unsafe electromagnetic waves (Figure 6.1). You make the shield by assembling two metal sheets together and riveting them in four spots. Then the word *TOP* is stamped in the lower right corner.

The materials used are copper and brass sheets, and each one measures 5 inches in height, 8 inches in length, and 1/64 inch in thickness. The sheets are very thin and easily scratched or dented if not handled carefully. The operations involved in this process are inspection, assembly, riveting, stamping, and packing, activities performed by four operators who sit with their backs to each other at four separate workbenches. A material supply box is located at the center of the four workbenches, just 6 feet from each operator. Because each operator performs the same operation, this example will focus only on Bob Burns, the operator in the right-hand corner of Figure 6.2.

On his workbench, Bob Burns has a riveter, a rubber stamp with the word *TOP*, and a stamp pad. Six feet from him (at the center of the workbenches) is a supply box for the copper sheets; just next to this supply box is another box containing the brass sheets. The punching and stamping department supplies and replenishes all of these materials. On the right side of the workbench are two scrap bins, one for the copper sheets and the other for the brass sheets. To the left of the workbench is a carrying box for the completed shields. Fifty feet away from the workbench is a scale used to measure the weight of the finished product. One hundred feet away from this scale is the packing area, with boxes for packing up and shipping the finished product.

Now that you have a general idea of the sample job and the layout of the worksite, let's look in detail at how Bob Burns does the work.

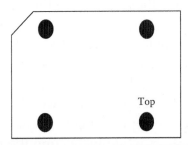

Figure 6.1 Microwave shield sample job.

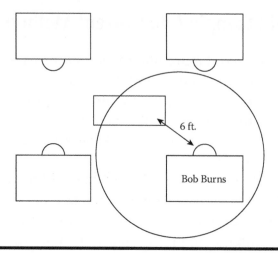

Figure 6.2 Workplace layout.

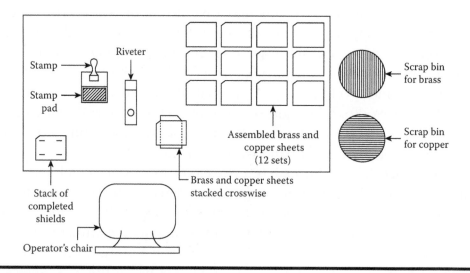

Figure 6.3 Workbench layout.

From his workbench, Bob walks to the supply box for copper sheets and picks up 15–20 copper sheets. Returning to his workbench, he begins to arrange 12 sheets on the bench, one by one, in three rows of 4 sheets. During this process, he inspects both sides of each sheet. If he sees a scratch or a dent, he takes a step to the right side of the bench and throws the defective sheet into the scrap bin for copper sheets. He then returns to the front of the workbench and continues laying out 12 copper sheets on the bench (Figure 6.3).

After Bob has finished arranging 12 undented and unscratched sheets on the workbench, he goes back to the copper sheet supply box to return the leftover sheets. Then he takes a step to the left, to the supply box for brass sheets, and picks up 15–20 brass sheets. He returns to the workbench to inspect and lay out 12 brass sheets *on top of* the copper sheets already on the bench. If he finds any scratches or dents on a sheet while inspecting the brass sheets, he takes a step to the right of the bench and throws the defective piece into the scrap bin for brass sheets. After laying out the 12 brass sheets, he takes the leftover sheets back to the supply box for brass sheets and returns to the workbench, this time empty handed.

Bob then takes each of the sets of sheets, one brass sheet on top of one copper sheet, and stacks them crosswise in a pile just to the right of the riveter. Because the sheets are very delicate, they can bend and scratch easily. Bob has to be careful when handling them, so he picks them up and stacks them very gently. Once this is done, he sits down and begins the riveting process.

Bob picks up the first set and aligns the two sheets carefully. The lineup tolerance for this job is 5/1000 inch (or 0.1 millimeter). Aligning these sheets to such a tight tolerance level is difficult and takes a lot of experience and skill. It also takes a physical toll on the body. The eyes continually strain to see the edges of the two sheets where they line up, get tired, and soon begin to hurt; the operator beings to squint to keep focus, sometimes hunching over the sheets in a way that causes shoulder and back fatigue. This kind of physical stress can lead to long-term problems. In the short term, it can cause quality errors. However, for the sake of moving this example along, let's just say that Bob Burns is keeping up with the quality of the production.

Once Bob has aligned the two sheets, he proceeds to rivet the shield in each of its four corners. He rivets the top left hole first, slides the shield to the left, rivets the top right hole next, turns the shield around 180°, rivets the bottom right hole, slides the shield to the left, and finally rivets the bottom left hole. After finishing riveting all four spots, he turns the shield around to its original position and stamps the word *TOP* onto the bottom right-hand corner. He then places this completed shield on top of the other finished shields just to the left of the riveter and begins to rivet the next shield.

Once he has completed all 12 sets, Bob gets out of his seat and places the 12 completed sets into the carrying box located to the left of the workbench. He then begins the process all over again by going to the supply box for 15–20 copper sheets, and so forth. He continues doing this entire process repeatedly until the carrying box is filled with completed sets. When it is full, this box weighs approximately 75 pounds. Bob Burns has to carry this heavy box of shields to the scale, which is 50 feet away from his workbench.

At the scale, Bob weighs the box of shields and writes the weight on a ticket that he puts into the box. He then takes the box off the scale and puts it on the floor beside the scale. Then Bob goes back to his workbench and continues what he was doing. When three or four carrying boxes have been stacked up next to the scale, a material handler comes along with a pushcart, places the boxes on the cart, and takes them to the packing section, which is located approximately 100 feet away from the scale.

At the packing section, a packer removes the shields from the boxes and inspects them. She counts out exactly 200 shields and packs them into a packing box, tapes the box shut, fills out a packing slip, and prepares the box so it can be picked up and sent to the shipping area. Each box remains in the packing area until the material handler takes it to the shipping area. Finally, the material handler brings all the empty carrying boxes back to their original positions next to the workbenches.

Supervisor Team Exercise: Have each team member identify what kinds of material handling, machine work, and hand work are being done in the microwave shield sample job. Then examine Figure 6.4, paying particular attention to the flow of material (shown by black arrows). Consider all the different movements and activities Bob Burns, the material handler, and the packer do. What do you notice about how they get the work done? Write down your observations and any improvement opportunities you can see off hand. Discuss these. Below the figure are typical answers to this question.

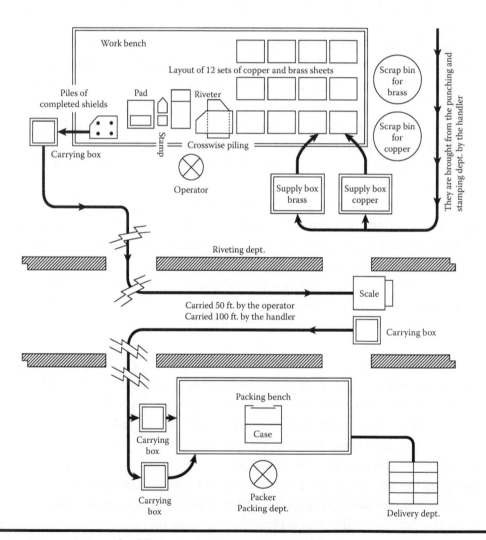

Figure 6.4   Current method layout.

Examples of material handling work on this job include bringing the sheets from the punching and stamping department to the supply boxes. The copper and brass sheets had to be carried to the workbench, and the completed shields had to be transported from the bench to the scale and then to the packing section. Examples of machine work include the use of the riveter and scale. There are also several examples of hand work in this operation. The sheets had to be laid on the bench and then stacked crosswise in a pile. They had to be aligned (before riveting) and stamped. At the very end of the process, the completed shields had to be counted and packed.

This sample job has been demonstrated to companies around the world, and the postdemonstration comments are telling. Indeed, what most observers notice when looking at Figure 6.4 suggests that this sample job is ripe for improvement. Typical comments follow:

- Flow of material is long and complicated
- Considerable amount of material handling
- A lot of walking
- Too much picking up and putting down of sheets
- A lot of stress and fatigue

Although a few people remarked that work is no longer done so inefficiently, the overwhelming majority of trainees shook their heads and acknowledged that, in many cases, this is still "how it goes."

Microwave Shield Sample Job: Proposed Method

Let's look at a better way of doing this job. Using the JM four-step method, Anne Adams, the supervisor in this department, in cooperation with the operator Bob Burns, proposed a new method.

First, they had the copper and brass sheets delivered directly to the workbench by the material handler, who claimed that this change would not require any extra work on his part. It didn't make any difference to him whether he delivered the sheets to the supply boxes or to the workbenches since, at the end of the day, he still had to deliver the same amount of material, regardless of the destination. Initially, these sheets were delivered to the opposite side of the workbenches from where the operators were seated and were still not in a convenient location. To make it easier to pick up the material, the stacks were brought even closer to the operators, within arm's reach.

When the material handler first brought these materials to the benches, the stacks were pretty high and operators could easily knock them over while they were working. To prevent this, Anne Adams came up with a jig (similar to a cartridge magazine with three sides) to hold the piles and keep them from falling over and allow operators to take the sheets off the pile from the one open side.

Because the sheets were as thin as paper, however, they were still difficult to pick off the pile one at a time. Bob Burns, the operator, came up with the idea of attaching an angle arm inside the jig at 45°, which would let operators fan the sheets out in the pile. Thus, the edge of the top sheet now stuck out just a little from the sheet below it. This way, the operator could easily separate each sheet from the pile and pick up one at a time (Figure 6.5).

In the CM, each operator used only one riveter. Anne felt this was inefficient, so she took one more riveter from one of the other workbenches so two spots could be riveted at one time. This new setup had one big drawback. In the CM, with only one riveter, the operator held the assembled shields in one hand and used the other hand to operate the riveter to rivet the shields together. Trying to rivet two spots at the same time, the operator found the riveters on the table moved around, making it very difficult to line up the two machines just right to rivet the two holes. Anne devised a fixture that would hold the riveters in place, in exact alignment with each other, so the two rivets could be made in the proper places (Figure 6.6).

The job of aligning the two sheets correctly was extremely tiring and a concern in terms of both product quality and long-term worker injury. Anne came up with a guide that she had built right into the riveter fixture. By sliding the two sheets into this guide, operators could easily and automatically line up the sheets to the proper tolerance level of 5/1000 inch, as shown in Figure 6.6 (the black area on the top of the fixture). Originally, this was the part of the process that

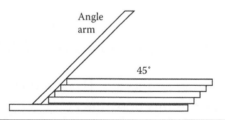

Figure 6.5 Angle arm used inside jig at 45° so sheets would be fanned out.

Figure 6.6 Fixture with riveters.

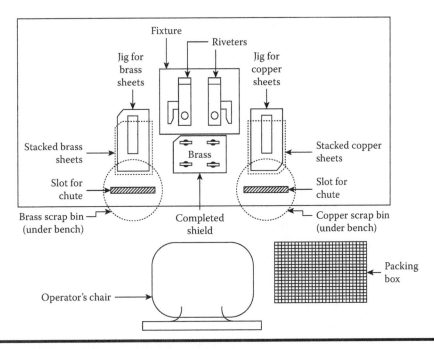

Figure 6.7   Workbench layout after improvement.

required skill and experience. With this adjustment, even an unskilled person could fill in, do the work, and meet the strict requirements of the job.

In the CM, whenever a defective sheet was found, the operator had to go around the end of the workbench where the scrap bins were located to place it in the proper bin. To avoid this, both scrap bins were brought directly under the workbench, on either side of the operator's legs. Bob Burns felt that this was still awkward because he would have to bend over to look under the bench to see the scrap bin. He suggested cutting slots right into the workbench in front of each stack of sheets and attaching chutes from these slots to the two scrap bins under the bench. This way, the operator could simply put a defective sheet into the slot and it would slide down the chute into the proper scrap bin.

Finally, Anne decided to eliminate the carrying box and have the material handler bring the packing case directly to the right side of the operator. In this way, the operator could place the finished shields directly into the packing case. Figure 6.7 shows the layout of the workbench with all of these changes in place.

Microwave Shield Sample Job: How the New Job Process Works Using the New Method

Under the new arrangement, the operator is seated at all times. He picks up, at the same time, a single brass sheet in his left hand and a single copper sheet in his right hand. He inspects both sheets, front and back, and if he finds a scratch or a dent, he puts that sheet down the slot directly in front of the pile of sheets. He then places the sheets together, brass on top, and slides them into the guide and onto the fixture. He uses both hands to operate the two riveters at one time and rivets the top two corners of the shield, turns the shield around, and then again uses both hands to rivet the bottom two corners of the shield. After the shield is complete, he places the finished shield directly in front of the fixture.

One other improvement Anne Adams came up with was to make the height of the fixture the exact same height as 20 completed shields stacked on top of each other. When the height of the pile reaches 20 pieces, it is level with the height of the fixture; without counting, the operator knows he has completed 20 shields and can then place them directly into the packing box to his right. Repeating this process 10 times, there will be 200 completed sets inside the box. After the box is filled, another box is placed on top of it and the operation continues. When four or five boxes are filled, the material handler picks them up and takes them to the packing section.

Figure 6.8 shows the layout of the workflow with these improvement ideas in place. If you compare this figure to Figure 6.4, it is easy to see how the new method has improved the operation.

Supervisor Team Exercise: Have each team member compare the before and after improvement layouts (Figures 6.4 and 6.8) and then discuss as a team the differences found. In what ways has the work improved? What are the areas of major benefit from the changes? As a team, try to estimate how much improvement was made by implementing the new method in terms of (1) production, (2) machine use, and (3) scrap. The actual results are given in the "Results in Improving the Microwave Shield Job" section.

After comparing the two methods, most observers note the following improvements:

■ Less material handling of the sheets and the completed shields
■ Walking has been eliminated
■ More streamlined and efficient process with the operator using two riveters and packing the shields directly into the case

You may have noticed that something has been eliminated by the new method: the operators are not using a scale to weigh the shields or stamping the word *TOP* on the assembled shields. Chapter 7 explains how these were handled in the application of the JM four-step method. For now, let's just look at the results achieved by this improved method.

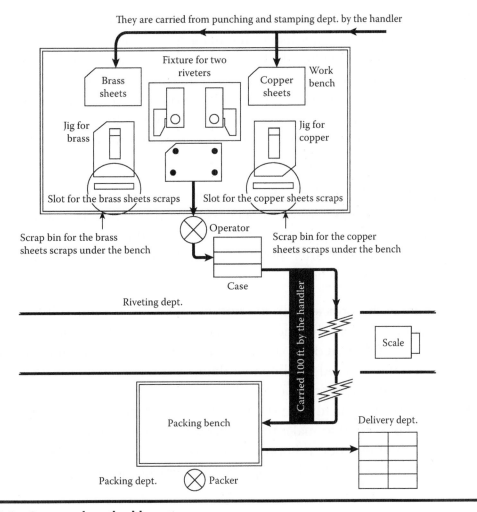

Figure 6.8   Proposed method layout.

Results in Improving the Microwave Shield Job

It goes without saying that the new method increases production for this job. In fact, Anne found that the one operator's production level tripled. The output per machine also went up, but not in the same proportion. This is easy to understand if you recall that Anne took a riveter from one of the other workbenches, so that one worker is now doing on one bench the work that was done previously on two benches by two people. While the total output increased three times, one operator is now using two riveters instead of just one. There are still four riveters, so the output per each machine is half of 3 times (or 1½ times)—a 50% increase.

In this job, it was critical that the operator did not scratch or dent the thin and delicate copper and brass sheets. Under the CM, when the operator found a defective sheet or the packer found a defective finished shield, these were discarded, creating a lot of scrap. Because the new method drastically reduced the number of times the operator had to pick up and put down each sheet, the potential for damage was greatly reduced. As a result, scrap decreased from 15% to less than 2%.

This improved plan for doing the work of assembling and packing the micro-wave shields resulted in better use of the manpower, machines, and materials now available—the ultimate goal of Job Methods. Using the new method, operators did *not* have to work harder or faster. This is important when you consider that people who work in a hurry seldom do good work. Simply speeding up the job often creates more waste—the very thing we are trying to eliminate. *In any application of JM, you should absolutely never speed up the work of any operator.*

> **TWI note:** Improving job methods creates good work. You increase production by eliminating the unnecessary parts of the job and making the necessary parts easier and safer to do. A good piece of business advice says, "Work smarter, not harder," and that is exactly what the JM four-step method teaches you to do.

You can apply the principles of job improvement demonstrated by Anne Adams to any work that includes material handling, machine work, or hand work. In fact, hundreds of other jobs in Anne's plant were improved in the same way, and this method has been working at countless plants, offices, and service sites around the world for decades.

Chapter 7 uses the microwave shield example to show how Anne Adams used the JM four-step method to make these improvements and to help you learn how to use the method in order to improve your own jobs. Team members will also apply the JM four-step method to improve their practice jobs.

Chapter 7

Four Steps of Job Methods Improvement

As discussed in Chapter 1, embedded in the Job Methods (JM) improvement plan are some of the fundamental tenets underlying continuous improvement (kaizen), quality circles, proposal systems, and many other concepts that developed in Japan after World War II and have become the principles of today's Lean manufacturing. Specifically, JM is a four-step method that helps supervisors develop an improvement plan *to produce greater quantities of quality products in less time by making the best use of the manpower, machines, and materials **now** available.* Furthermore, JM applies to the scope of each supervisor's responsibilities, which should be the target of improvement efforts.

Many supervisors resist improvement efforts that focus on producing more in less time without growing manpower because they believe that increasing productivity leads to layoffs. As good supervisors, they have invested time and effort into building good relationships with employees and feel it is their duty to protect employees' jobs and livelihoods. However, maintaining old and inefficient modes of work puts the entire company at risk. Companies that cannot compete in the global marketplace fold and disappear. To avoid this fate, a company must stay profitable and continually produce higher quantities of quality products and services at lower prices. It is the duty of the supervisor to help increase and sustain the production efficiency that makes this possible. Supervisors who understand this know that the best thing they can do for employees is to lead them in this effort. If they are successful, the company will prosper and expand, jobs will improve, and employees will be promoted to these new and improved jobs.

> **TWI note:** The Training Within Industry (TWI) developers stated that the objective of Job Methods is to produce greater quantities of quality products in less time by making the best use of the manpower, machines, and materials *now* available to you, which means

JM is *not* about investing large amounts of money in new technologies, infrastructure, and so on. It is about what you can do better with what you have right now. Of course, there is an important role for specialized staff to work on broader-scale improvements, for example, waste-free process flow throughout the entire production system. As supervisors, though, you don't have to wait for those big investments to begin making real improvements to your jobs right now.

While there are many ways to increase production efficiency, the most effective way is through improving Job Methods. Most of the affordable products that consumers enjoy today are a result of improvement in production methods. It did not take long for the first cell phones, with few makes and models costing several hundreds of dollars, to be replaced by myriad options, with the cheapest ones practically being given away. This kind of rapid progress comes from countless improvements developed and applied by practical production supervisors. JM is a practical method that accomplishes this quickly and easily.

This chapter uses the microwave shield sample job from Chapter 6 to take you through the four steps of the Job Methods improvement (JM four-step method). In the team exercises, each team member will apply three of the four steps to his or her practice job to develop a new method. In Chapter 8, which discusses ways in which to make and sell your improvement proposal to management, team members will practice the fourth and final step on their practice jobs.

Supervisor Team Exercise: Return to Chapter 2 and review Table 2.1, "Five Needs Model for Good Supervisors." Discuss the difference between knowledge and skills. Remember, just because you know about a job or understand a process doesn't mean you have the skill to teach the job or improve it, which is why you practice the TWI four-step methods. Discuss the kinds of knowledge about the work you and your team need to implement improvement. Then discuss what skills you think you will need to develop in order to find improvements.

To understand the Job Method improvement plan, you need to learn and follow the JM four-step method, which is on the JM pocket card (Figure 7.1). You should have this pocket card with you every time you implement improvement. These four steps were all that supervisor Anne Adams used to improve the microwave shield job discussed in Chapter 6. In this chapter, each of these steps will be applied to this sample job to show just how she used the JM four-step method. In Chapter 8, you will read about an improvement proposal from another company to see how a supervisor adapted this method to his own work.

HOW TO IMPROVE
Job Methods

A practical plan to help you produce *greater quantities* of *quality products* in *less time* by making the **best use** of the **manpower, machines, and materials now available**.

Step 1: Break down the job

1. List *all* details of the job *exactly* as done in the *current method*.
2. Be sure details include everything:
   – Material Handling
   – Machine Work
   – Hand Work

Step 2: Question every detail

1. Use these types of questions:
   WHY is it necessary?
   WHAT is its purpose?
   WHERE should it be done?
   WHEN should it be done?
   WHO is best qualified to do it?
   HOW is the 'best way' to do it?
2. Question the following at the same time: Materials, machines, equipment, tools, product design, workplace layout, movement, safety, housekeeping

Step 3: Develop the new method

1. **ELIMINATE** unnecessary details
2. **COMBINE** details when practical
3. **REARRANGE** details for better sequence
4. **SIMPLIFY** all necessary details
   To make the job easier and safer to do:
   – Put materials, tools, and equipment into the *best position* and *within convenient reach* for the operator
   – Use *gravity feed hoppers* or *drop delivery chutes* whenever possible
   – Make effective use of *both hands*
   – Use *jigs* or *fixtures* instead of hands
5. Work out your ideas *with others*
6. *Write up* the proposed new method

Step 4: Apply the new method

1. *Sell* your proposal to the *boss*
2. *Sell* the new method to the operators
3. Get *final approval* of all concerned on Safety, Quality, Quantity, Cost, etc.
4. *Put* the new method *to work*. Use it until a **better** way is developed
5. Give *credit* where credit is due

Figure 7.1   JM four-step method.

Step 1: Break Down the Job

Making a job breakdown (listing all the details of how a job is currently done) is the starting point of all JM improvements. A job breakdown creates a complete record and an accurate picture of how a job is executed. It gives the supervisor the opportunity to review forgotten details or details so familiar they are performed almost unconsciously. Inevitably, it also lets the supervisor see if something needs to be improved. The more detailed and accurate the breakdown is, the more complete and effective the improvements will be. *Details* mean, quite literally, *every single movement that is done in the job.* Obviously, this includes material handling, machine work, and hand work. But it also includes inspections or even delays.

Applying Step 1 to the Microwave Shield Sample Job

Let's take a look at the microwave shield job and make a breakdown for the current method (CM) of doing the work, the way the job was done before Anne Adams made any improvements. What happened first? Bob Burns walked over to the supply box for copper sheets, which was 6 feet away from his workbench. The first detail is *walk to the box of copper sheets—6 feet.* He then picked up 15–20 of the copper sheets. The second detail is *pick up*

15–20 copper sheets. What happened next? He had to walk back to the bench, again 6 feet. The third detail is *walk to the bench—6 feet.* When he got back to the workbench, he inspected and laid out each of the 12 copper sheets on the workbench. The fourth detail is *inspect and lay out 12 sheets.* He threw defective sheets into the scrap bins. Then he walked back to the supply box, 6 feet away, and replaced the extra sheets. The fifth detail is *walk to the box and replace extra sheets—6 feet.* Continuing in this way, you can capture everything that is done in the job, detail by detail. Table 7.1 shows a breakdown of the entire job.

Pat's Exercise: How Many Buttons on a Shirt?

In our TWI classes, we pick out a trainee (usually a man) who is wearing a button-down long-sleeve shirt, the kind where even the collar buttons down, and ask him how many buttons there are on his shirt. Usually the trainee will say 9, although some will get daring and say 12. Then we ask him to count them and he immediately gets flustered when he realizes that the cuffs have two buttons, not just one, to adjust for people with thick or thin wrists. Someone in the group then points out that there might be a little button halfway up the forearm sleeve— that one counts, too. Typically, the person is aware of the buttons on the collar, but doesn't remember that there is also a button at the top of the shirt, which is there if you want to wear a tie. Finally, we ask if the shirt has any "spare" buttons at the bottom. The trainee, now embarrassed, pulls the tails out of his pants to find another two or three. In all, there are usually 17 to 19 buttons. The point of this exercise is to show that when we carefully observe even the things we are familiar with, we discover many more facts and details than we assumed we knew.

Now consider how long it would take you to think of the first five details as outlined above? Probably not more than a minute or two. At that pace, you can do a breakdown for the entire job in less than 15 minutes. This may not be the most exciting part of your day, but it is time well invested because it lets you see what can be improved.

Notice that Table 7.1 includes a column for remarks. This space is used for recording anything that might be useful to know about any particular detail: distances, tolerances, waste, defects, safety, time taken, and so forth. It can also be used for comments about actions that are important but are not details. For example, when the operator inspected and laid out sheets, he threw defective sheets into the scrap bin. Anne noted this in the "Remarks" column rather than in the "Details" column because this did not occur every time the operator performed the detail.

Notice that this breakdown is very different from the breakdowns for JI, which listed only the important steps. In JM, each important step may include quite a number of details. For JI, important steps include only the most important things

Table 7.1   Current Method Breakdown Sheet of Microwave Shield Sample Job

		Remarks	
	(Current)/Proposed Method Details	Distance	Time/Tolerance/Rejects/Safety
1	Walk to the supply box containing copper sheets	6 ft.	Already been carried by the material handler
2	Pick up 15–20 copper sheets		
3	Walk to the bench	6 ft.	
4	Inspect and lay out 12 copper sheets		Rejects with dents and scratches go into the scrap bin
5	Walk to the supply box and replace extra sheets	6 ft.	
6	Walk to the supply box containing brass sheets	3 ft.	
7	Pick up 15–20 brass sheets		
8	Walk to the bench	6 ft.	
9	Inspect and lay out 12 brass sheets		Rejects with dents and scratches go into the scrap bin; place them on top of copper sheets
10	Walk to the supply box and replace extra sheets	6 ft.	
11	Walk to the bench	6 ft.	
12	Stack 12 sets near the riveter		
13	Pick up a set of sheets with the right hand		
14	Line sheets together and position them in riveter		Lineup tolerance is 5/1000 in.
15	Rivet the top left corner		
16	Slide sheets to the left and rivet top right corner		
17	Turn sheets and position them in the riveter		
18	Rivet the bottom right corner		
19	Slide sheets to the left and rivet bottom left corner		
20	Turn sheets around as you lay them on the bench		
21	Stamp *TOP* and stack them on the workbench		Stamp on the bottom right corner
For items 13–21, repeat the process 11 times			

(Continued)

Table 7.1 *(Continued)* Current Method Breakdown Sheet of Microwave Shield Sample Job

		Remarks	
	Current /Proposed Method Details	Distance	Time/Tolerance/Rejects/ Safety
22	Put 12 sets of shields in the carrying box		
23	Carry the full box to the scale and weigh it	50 ft.	From bench to scale
24	Fill out a measuring slip and place it in the box		Total weight: 75 lb
25	Take the carrying box to the packing area	100 ft.	Carried by the material handler
26	Unload the shields from the box		Unloaded by the packer
27	Put 200 sets of shields into the packing box		Inspection; packing box handled by packer
28	Enclose the box and fill out the address slip on it		
29	Fill out a delivery slip		
30	Store it until it is delivered		Empty boxes are returned by material handler

that advance the work; anything that is common sense or clear to the operator is not included. For JM, *you must list all details because you cannot omit anything in the search for improvement.*

Supervisor Team Exercise: Each team member should select a real job that his or her own department is currently doing. You can use the same practice job used for JI or some other simple job—preferably, something that is giving you trouble. Print out a blank copy of the JM breakdown sheet (from the TWI Institute website) and create a current method breakdown sheet. Go to the actual worksite and list all of the details in the job exactly as it is currently done down the left-hand-side column. Remember that a detail means *every single movement that is done*, including inspections and delays. Record any remarks concerning the details in the "Remarks" column. Compare your breakdown sheet with those of other team members and evaluate whether breakdowns are complete. Did you get all of the details? Did you remember to list all movements or delays?

The best place to do a job breakdown is at the job site. Don't rely on your memory. Make sure you actually go and see the details. Get complete and accurate facts. At the worksite, if you are observing other people performing the job, tell them what you are doing and why you are doing it. Show them your job breakdown sheet and ask for their help. Tell them about the JM program and show them the JM four-step method pocket card so they can work with you as you go through the method. In most cases, when workers understand the purpose and technique of JM, they become very enthusiastic about participating.

Step 2: Question Every Detail

Your success in improving an operation will depend on your ability to question everything about that operation. In step 2, question every detail of the job that you broke down in step 1. Use the five W's and one H presented below.

Five W's and One H	
1.	*Why* is it necessary?
2.	*What* is its purpose?
3.	*Where* should it be done?
4.	*When* should it be done?
5.	*Who* is best qualified to do it?
6.	*How* is the best way to do it?

The answers to these six questions have taught us practically all we know now about the world around us and are very useful for JM. They are most useful when they are asked in the order presented. There is a very good reason for this. When you ask, "How should we improve this detail?" before you ask, "Why is it necessary?" you may waste time improving something and then find out that the detail was not necessary.

It is important *not* to act on any answer in this sequence prematurely. When an answer gives you an idea for improvement, it is often tempting to put that idea into effect immediately. Resist the temptation and continue the questioning process. When you do get a good idea for something, just *write it down* on the breakdown sheet. Ask all of the questions, in the right order, for each detail before proceeding to the next detail. Do not act until you have questioned all of the details.

Asking the Five Ws and One H

Let's look at each of these questions individually. "*Why* is it necessary?" is the most important question. Asking this question first (for each detail) helps you distinguish between necessary and unnecessary details. "*What* is its purpose?" is a check question for "*Why* is it necessary?" It lets you see if the detail has any useful purpose or if it adds quality or value to a product or service. In other words, it confirms that a detail is necessary or allows you to see that it is not.

If you decide that a detail is necessary, continue asking questions. "*Where* should it be done?" helps determine the *best place* to do each detail: In which department or section? On which machine, bench, or equipment? "*When* should it be done?" helps determine the *best time* to do the detail: First or last? In what order? Before or after some other detail(s)? When will the necessary people, machines, materials, equipment, or tools be available? "*Who* is best qualified to do it?" determines the *best person* for this detail in terms of knowledge, skill level, experience, physical strength, or availability. "*How* is the best way to do it?" is the last question in the sequence because it should only be answered when the answers to all of the other questions are in place and show that improvement is actually needed. Usually there is a better way when we think about it.

Questioning Other Important Items Regarding the Overall Job

In addition to questioning every detail of the job process in step 2, you must take into consideration and question a list of important items for the overall job. This list is shown on item 2 of step 2 on the JM pocket card (Figure 7.1) and includes *materials, machines, equipment, tools, product design, workplace layout, movement, safety,* and *housekeeping*. Questioning these items at the same time you question the details of the job helps you develop a complete improvement plan. For example, materials, machines, equipment, and tools can be expensive and hard to get, so improving their usage can make a dramatic improvement in output. Making a small change in the design of a part or product often leads to big improvements in quality, productivity, or safety. Even minor changes in the movement of people, parts, or materials or in the layout of a work area can save on unnecessary effort and floor or bench space. Because poor safety and housekeeping habits can lead to injuries or inefficient work, you must consider them when analyzing the details of the job procedure itself.

Applying Step 2 to the Microwave Shield Sample Job

Now that you understand what questions to ask, why to ask them, and in what order to ask them, it is time to review how Anne Adams applied these questions to the details of assembling and packing the microwave shields. For this process, Anne used the breakdown sheet presented in Table 7.2.

The left-hand columns of the table show the details and remarks obtained in step 1. To the right of these are columns for the questions. Notice that "Why?" and "What?" are combined in one column. Next, is a column for ideas. (The columns at the far right are used in step 3 of the process and are discussed later in this chapter.)

Because the answers to the W and H questions stimulate new ideas and suggest improvements, Anne Adams questioned each of the details, one by one. Comments illustrating her thinking process are listed under each detail.

Table 7.2 Current Method Job Breakdown Sheet Using Steps 1–3 of the JM Four-Step Method

| Product: Microwave Shields | | | Made by: Anne Adams | Date: 5/20/20XX |
| Operations: Inspecting, Assembling, Riveting, Stamping, and Packing | | | Department: Riveting and Packing | |

	Current/Proposed Method Details	Remarks: Distance	Remarks: Time/Tolerance/Rejects/Safety	Why–What	Where	When	Who	How	Ideas: Write Them Down; Don't Try to Remember	Eliminate	Combine	Rearrange	Simplify
1	Walk to the supply box containing copper sheets	6 ft.	Already been carried by the material handler										
2	Pick up 15–20 copper sheets												
3	Walk to the bench	6 ft.											
4	Inspect and lay out 12 copper sheets		Rejects with dents and scratches go into the scrap bin										
5	Walk to the supply box and replace extra sheets	6 ft.											
6	Walk to the supply box containing brass sheets	3 ft.											
7	Pick up 15–20 brass sheets												
8	Walk to the bench	6 ft.											
9	Inspect and lay out 12 brass sheets		Rejects with dents and scratches go into the scrap bin; place them on top of copper sheets										

(Continued)

Table 7.2 (Continued) Current Method Job Breakdown Sheet Using Steps 1–3 of the JM Four-Step Method

Product: Microwave Shields
Made by: Anne Adams
Date: 5/20/20XX
Operations: Inspecting, Assembling, Riveting, Stamping, and Packing
Department: Riveting and Packing

	(Current)/Proposed Method Details	Remarks: Distance	Remarks: Time/Tolerance/Rejects/Safety	Why–What	Where	When	Who	How	Ideas: Write Them Down; Don't Try to Remember	Eliminate	Combine	Rearrange	Simplify
10	Walk to the supply box and replace extra sheets	6 ft.											
11	Walk to the bench	6 ft.											
12	Stack 12 sets near the riveter												
13	Pick up a set of sheets with the right hand												
14	Line sheets together and position them in riveter		Lineup tolerance is 5/1000 in										
15	Rivet the top left corner												
16	Slide sheets to the left and rivet top right corner												
17	Turn sheets and position them in the riveter												
18	Rivet the bottom right corner												
19	Slide sheets to the left and rivet bottom left corner												
20	Turn sheets around as you lay them on the bench												

(Continued)

Table 7.2 (Continued) Current Method Job Breakdown Sheet Using Steps 1–3 of the JM Four-Step Method

Product: Microwave Shields

Operations: Inspecting, Assembling, Riveting, Stamping, and Packing

Made by: Anne Adams

Department: Riveting and Packing

Date: 5/20/20XX

	(Current)/Proposed Method Details	Distance	Remarks — Time/Tolerance/Rejects/Safety	Why–What	Where	When	Who	How	Ideas — Write Them Down; Don't Try to Remember	Eliminate	Combine	Rearrange	Simplify
21	Stamp *TOP* and stack them on the workbench		Stamp on the bottom right corner										
	For items 13–21, repeat the process 11 times												
22	Put 12 sets of shields in the carrying box												
23	Carry the full box to the scale and weigh it	50 ft.	From bench to scale										
24	Fill out a measuring slip and place it in the box		Total weight: 75 lb										
25	Take the carrying box to the packing area	100 ft.	Carried by the material handler										
26	Unload the shields from the box		Unloaded by the packer										
27	Put 200 sets of shields into the packing box		Inspection; packing box handled by packer										
28	Enclose the box and fill out the address slip on it												
29	Fill out a delivery slip												
30	Store it until it is delivered		Empty boxes are returned by material handler										

Detail 1: Walk to the Supply Box Containing Copper Sheets

Why is it necessary?

"To get the copper sheets. But is it necessary to walk 6 feet?"

"Right! If the sheets are located closer to the workbench, then it's not necessary."

By questioning the need to walk 6 feet for the sheets, Anne concluded that it wouldn't be necessary if the sheets were in a different location, nearer to the bench. In the "Ideas" column, Anne wrote, "No, if sheets nearer bench" (Figure 7.2).

She also put a checkmark in the "Why" column because the idea she got for this detail came from answering the question "Why?" Since she thought she could eliminate the detail, she didn't bother asking the remaining questions and moved on to the next detail.

Detail 2: Pick Up 15–20 Copper Sheets

Why is it necessary?

"Necessary to assemble the shield."

What is its purpose?

"We have to pick up the sheets to assemble them. So this detail is necessary."

Where should it be done?

"How about doing it closer to the riveter?"

In the CM, the operator had to walk to the supply box 6 feet away. But if the sheets were delivered to the workbench, the operator could pick them up right at the riveter. Anne wrote, "Close to riveter" in the "Ideas" column and put a checkmark in the "Where" column. Then she continued questioning detail 2. Figure 7.3 shows how Anne recorded her ideas on the breakdown sheet after finishing all of the questions for this detail.

	Why–What	Where	When	Who	How	Ideas			
						Write them down, don't try to remember.			
No. 1	✓					No, if sheets nearer bench.			

Figure 7.2   Detail No. 1 on the breakdown sheet.

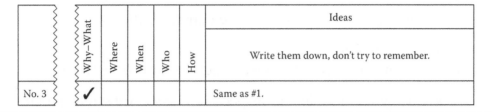

	Why–What	Where	When	Who	How	Ideas
						Write them down, don't try to remember.
No. 2		✓			✓	Close to riveter. Better way.

Figure 7.3 Detail No. 2 on the breakdown sheet.

	Why–What	Where	When	Who	How	Ideas
						Write them down, don't try to remember.
No. 3	✓					Same as #1.

Figure 7.4 Detail No. 3 on the breakdown sheet.

Detail 2: Pick Up 15–20 Copper Sheets (More Questions)

When should it be done?
  "Any time before assembly. This is the same as in the current method."

Who is the best person?
  "The riveter. This is also the same as in the current method."

How should it be done?
  "Mmmm … there must be a better way."

Detail 3: Walk to the Workbench

Why is it necessary?
  "If it's not necessary to walk over, then it's not necessary to walk back either."

Here Anne had the same idea she got in the first detail: placing the sheets near the operator's bench. She wrote, "Same as #1" in the "Ideas" column and put a checkmark in the "Why" column (Figure 7.4).

Detail 4: Inspect and Lay Out 12 Copper Sheets

In this detail there are two distinct activities. Anne first captured them as one detail because the operator performed both activities at the same time, as one combined action. On closer inspection, however, she decided that inspection and laying out sheets are two separate activities. To make it easier to question this detail, Anne drew a line down the center of the row for this item on the breakdown sheet and divided it into two details: 4a (inspect) and 4b (lay out).

Detail 4a: Inspect

Why is it necessary?
"Necessary to maintain the quality of the finished product."

What is its purpose?
"To ensure that the finished part functions properly. So this detail is necessary."

Where should it be done?
"At the riveting bench. Same as in the current method."

When should it be done?
"The best time to inspect the sheet would be just before assembly."

When questioning the best time to inspect the sheets, Anne remembered that the sheets were delicate and were sometimes damaged between inspection and assembly. The idea here was to cut the time between these activities to prevent damage. She wrote, "Just before assembly" in the "Ideas" column and put a checkmark in the "When" column. Then she continued questioning the detail.

Detail 4a: Inspect (More Questions)

Who is the best person?
"The riveter. No change."

How should it be done?
"There must be a better way."

Anne felt that the CM was not the best way of doing this work and noted this in the "Ideas" column and put a checkmark in the "How" column.

Detail 4b: Lay Out

Why is it necessary?
"This detail is not necessary because it adds no value to the product if the sheets are moved closer to the bench."

Anne felt that the only reason the sheets were laid out on the workbench, which had just enough room for 12 sheets, was because they had to be carried from the supply box. If the sheets were delivered directly to the bench, the operator could handle them one at a time. There would be no need for the lay-out, which did not add quality or value to the product. She wrote, "Same as #1" in the "Ideas" column and put a checkmark in the "Why" column for this detail. (Figure 7.5 shows Anne's comments on detail 4.)

Detail 5: Walk to the Supply Box and Replace Extra Sheets

Why is it necessary?
"If there is no need to walk to the box, why do I need to walk back?"

	Why–What	Where	When	Who	How	Ideas
						Write them down, don't try to remember.
No. 4			✓		✓	(4a) Inspect: Just before assembly. Better way.
	✓					(4b) Lay out: Same as #1.

Figure 7.5   Detail No. 4 on the breakdown sheet.

Detail 6: Walk to the Supply Box Containing Brass Sheets

Why is it necessary?
    "If there is no need to walk for the copper sheets, why walk for the brass sheets?"

The answer to "Why is it necessary?" for both detail 5 and detail 6 was the same as the answer for detail 1. For each, Anne wrote "Same as #1" in the "Ideas" column and put a checkmark in the "Why" column.

Detail 7: Pick Up 15–20 Sheets

Why is it necessary?
    "Necessary to assemble the shield."

Detail 8: Walk to the Bench

Why is it necessary?
    "Is there a need to walk?"

Because the work in detail 7 was the exact same work as in detail 2, Anne wrote, "Same as #2" in the "Ideas" column and put checkmarks in the "Where" and "How" columns. Because the activity in detail 8 had already been found useless in detail 1, she wrote "Same as #1" in the "Ideas" column and put a checkmark in the "Why" column.

Detail 9: Inspect and Lay Out 12 Sheets (Brass)

Work in this detail is exactly the same work done in detail 4 (copper). Anne divided the row into two parts, as she had done with detail 4. For detail 9a, she wrote, "Same as #4a" in the "Ideas" column and put checkmarks in the "When" and "How" columns. For detail 9b, she wrote "Same as #4b" in the "Ideas" column and put a checkmark in the "Why" column (Figure 7.6).

Detail 10: Walk to the Supply Box and Replace Extra Sheets

Why is it necessary?
    "More walking to replace sheets."

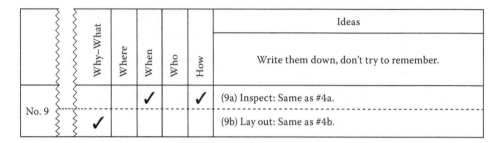

Figure 7.6   Rows for detail Nos. 9a and 9b on the breakdown sheet.

		Why–What	Where	When	Who	How	Ideas
							Write them down, don't try to remember.
No. 12		✓					No, if no layout.

Figure 7.7   Detail No. 12 "Ideas" column: "No, if no layout."

Detail 11: Walk to the Bench

> *Why is it necessary?*
> "More walking!"

The answer to "Why is it necessary?" for both detail 10 and detail 11 was the same as the answer to detail 1. For each, Anne wrote, "Same as #1" in the "Ideas" column and put a checkmark in the "Why" column.

Detail 12: Stack 12 Sets near the Riveter

> *Why is it necessary?*
> "If the layout is not necessary, then this detail is not necessary either."

Anne realized that the only reason the combined sets of copper and brass sheets were stacked crosswise was because they were initially spread out on the workbench. She also realized that it was easier to pick up the combined sets for riveting if they were stacked up on one pile near the riveter. If, however, there was no need to lay them out, then there would be no need to stack them up either. She wrote, "No, if no layout" in the "Ideas" column and put a checkmark in the "Why" column (Figure 7.7).

Details 13–20: Riveting Details

Anne also questioned **details 13–20**. In each case, she felt that there must be a better way of doing the riveting work. For each detail, she wrote, "Better way" in the "Idea" column, putting corresponding checkmarks for each in the "How" column.

	Why–What	Where	When	Who	How	Ideas
						Write them down, don't try to remember.
No. 21	✓					Find out.

Figure 7.8   Detail No. 21 "Ideas" column: "Find out."

Detail 21: Stamp TOP *and Stack Them on the Workbench*

Why is it necessary?
 "The specifications call for it."

What is its purpose?
 "This is questionable. Can find no good reason for this detail.
Let's find out why."

The work instructions for detail 21 clearly stated that stamping the shields was part of the job. In cases like this, supervisors are tempted to think, "This is the way you are supposed to do it." This is when the check question *"What* is its purpose?" comes into good use. You cannot simply accept the CM. You have to find the purpose for the work. Anne wondered whether stamping the word *TOP* on the shield added any value to the part itself or to later operations. She wrote, "Find out" in the "Ideas" column and put a checkmark in the "Why" column (Figure 7.8).

Details 22–30: Packaging Details

Anne also questioned **details 22–30**. For detail 23 (carry the full box to the scale and weigh it) and detail 24 (fill out a measuring slip and place it in the box), she wrote, "Not necessary to weigh" in the "Ideas" column and put checkmarks in the "Why" column. For detail 22 (put 12 sets of shields into the carrying box) and details 25–30 (taking the shields to the packing area and packing them for delivery), she wrote, "Anytime, anywhere, anyone, after riveting" in the "Ideas" column and put checkmarks in the "Where," "When," and "Who" columns.

Supervisor Team Exercise: Get out the JM breakdown sheets you used in step 1 for your practice job. For step 2, use the six basic questions (5Ws and 1 H) to question every detail in your breakdown, just as Anne Adams did in the sample job. From the answers to these questions, write down any ideas you get in the "Ideas" column, being sure to check off which question triggered the idea in the question columns. Really question each detail and don't just accept the current method as the best way to do the job. While rooting out wasted activities, keep the bigger picture in mind and consider the best places, times, and people to do each detail. (Do not forget to consider other departments or other time frames.) Remember that you are just recording your ideas and not doing anything yet. Compare these ideas with those of others on the team. This may lead to even more ideas.

(**Note:** If you can't find any ideas for this job, pick another job and return to step 1 and break it down.)

Table 7.3 shows the completed breakdown sheet for this job. While Anne was questioning each of these details and getting definitive answers, she wrote down her ideas and did not take any immediate actions. In this way, she was able to generate a thorough and complete analysis of the entire job. As a result, she discovered that certain ideas opened up the door to additional, complementary ideas. She was now ready to move on to step 3, develop the new method.

Step 3: Develop the New Method

In the previous part of this chapter, you learned to apply a questioning process to each detail of a job to discover ideas that can help improve an operation. The next step is to formulate those ideas into a clear development plan for the new method. Step 3 of the Job Methods program provides tools that will easily and quickly lead you to a better way to do the work.

Companies increase production or service output when they begin to *eliminate, combine, rearrange,* and *simplify* the details of each job. When you find opportunities to accomplish these four things, there is no question that you will improve the efficiency of your operations. This step will show you how questioning each detail in step 2 leads directly to the development of the new method using these four elements of improvement.

Four Improvement Elements

1. *Eliminate* unnecessary details.
2. *Combine* details when practical.
3. *Rearrange* details for better sequence.
4. *Simplify* all necessary details.

Notice that there is a definite order to these four items. If you eliminate a detail after spending time and effort to simplify it, you waste time. Likewise, before you rearrange a set of details into a better sequence, check to see if there are any opportunities to combine those details and do them all at the same time. Eliminating is a 100% improvement because you don't have to do the detail at all. Combining two or more details is a 50% improvement. Although you still have to

Table 7.3 Completed Current Method Job Breakdown Sheet Applying Steps 1–3 of the JM Four-Step Method

Product: Microwave Shields									Made by: Anne Adams		Date: 5/20/20XX		
Operations: Inspecting, Assembling, Riveting, Stamping, and Packing									Department: Riveting and Packing				
	(Current)/Proposed Method Details	Remarks		Why–What	Where	When	Who	How	Ideas	Eliminate	Combine	Rearrange	Simplify
		Distance	Time/Tolerance/Rejects/Safety										
1	Walk to the supply box containing copper sheets	6 ft.	Already been carried by the material handler	✓					No, if sheets nearer bench	✓			
2	Pick up 15–20 copper sheets				✓			✓	Close to riveter. Better way			✓	✓
3	Walk to the bench	6 ft.		✓					Same as #1	✓			
4	Inspect and lay out 12 copper sheets		Rejects with dents and scratches go into the scrap bin			✓		✓	(4a) Inspect: Just before assembly. Better way.			✓	✓
				✓					(4b) Lay out: Same as #1	✓			
5	Walk to the supply box and replace extra sheets	6 ft.		✓					Same as #1	✓			
6	Walk to the supply box containing brass sheets	3 ft.		✓					Same as #1	✓			
7	Pick up 15–20 brass sheets							✓	Same as #2			✓	✓
8	Walk to the bench	6 ft.		✓					Same as #1	✓			

(Continued)

Table 7.3 (Continued) Completed Current Method Job Breakdown Sheet Applying Steps 1–3 of the JM Four-Step Method

Product: Microwave Shields

Operations: Inspecting, Assembling, Riveting, Stamping, and Packing

Made by: Anne Adams

Department: Riveting and Packing

Date: 5/20/20XX

	Current/Proposed Method Details	Distance	Time/Tolerance/Rejects/Safety	Why–What	Where	When	Who	How	Ideas (Write Them Down; Don't Try to Remember)	Eliminate	Combine	Rearrange	Simplify
9	Inspect and lay out 12 brass sheets		Rejects with dents and scratches go into the scrap bin; place them on top of copper sheets			✓		✓	(9a) Inspect: Same as #4a.			✓	✓
				✓					(9b) Lay out: Same as #4b	✓			
10	Walk to the supply box and replace extra sheets	6 ft.		✓					Same as #1	✓			
11	Walk to the bench	6 ft.		✓					Same as #1	✓			
12	Stack 12 sets near the riveter			✓					No, if no layout	✓			
13	Pick up a set of sheets with the right hand							✓	Better way				✓
14	Line sheets together and position them in riveter		Lineup tolerance is 5/1000 in.					✓	Better way				✓
15	Rivet the top left corner							✓	Better way				✓
16	Slide sheets to the left and rivet top right corner							✓	Better way				✓
17	Turn sheets and position them in the riveter							✓	Better way				✓

(Continued)

Table 7.3 (*Continued*) Completed Current Method Job Breakdown Sheet Applying Steps 1–3 of the JM Four-Step Method

Product: Microwave Shields

Operations: Inspecting, Assembling, Riveting, Stamping, and Packing

Made by: Anne Adams

Department: Riveting and Packing

Date: 5/20/20XX

	(Current)/Proposed Method Details	Distance	Remarks: Time/Tolerance/Rejects/Safety	Why–What	Where	When	Who	How	Ideas: Write Them Down; Don't Try to Remember	Eliminate	Combine	Rearrange	Simplify
18	Rivet the bottom right corner							✓	Better way				✓
19	Slide sheets to the left and rivet bottom left corner							✓	Better way				✓
20	Turn sheets around as you lay them on the bench							✓	Better way				✓
21	Stamp *TOP* and stack them on the workbench		Stamp on the bottom right corner	✓					Find out	✓			
	For items 13–21, repeat the process 11 times												
22	Put 12 sets of shields in the carrying box				✓	✓	✓		Anytime, anywhere, anyone after riveting		✓		
23	Carry the full box to the scale and weigh it	50 ft.	From bench to scale	✓					Not necessary to weigh	✓			
24	Fill out a measuring slip and place it in the box		Total weight: 75 lb	✓					Not necessary to weigh	✓			
25	Take the carrying box to the packing area	100 ft.	Carried by the material handler		✓	✓	✓		Anytime, anywhere, anyone after riveting			✓	

(Continued)

Table 7.3 (Continued) Completed Current Method Job Breakdown Sheet Applying Steps 1–3 of the JM Four-Step Method

Product: Microwave Shields

Operations: Inspecting, Assembling, Riveting, Stamping, and Packing

Made by: Anne Adams

Department: Riveting and Packing

Date: 5/20/20XX

	Current/Proposed Method Details	Remarks: Distance	Remarks: Time/Tolerance/Rejects/Safety	Why–What	Where	When	Who	How	Ideas (Write Them Down; Don't Try to Remember)	Eliminate	Combine	Rearrange	Simplify
26	Unload the shields from the box		Unloaded by the packer		✓	✓	✓		Anytime, anywhere, anyone after riveting		✓		
27	Put 200 sets of shields into the packing box		Inspection; packing box handled by packer		✓	✓	✓		Anytime, anywhere, anyone after riveting		✓		
28	Enclose the box and fill out the address slip on it				✓	✓	✓		Anytime, anywhere, anyone after riveting				
29	Fill out a delivery slip				✓	✓	✓		Anytime, anywhere, anyone after riveting				
30	Store it until it is delivered		Empty boxes are returned by material handler		✓	✓	✓		Anytime, anywhere, anyone after riveting				

do all of the operations, you can do them at the same time instead of separately. Rearranging the order of several details produces less dramatic results, but if doing so reduces backtracking and repetition, it is more efficient than what you are doing now. Simplifying an operation to make it easier and safer (only after you are sure it cannot be eliminated, combined, or rearranged) is an incremental improvement that fine-tunes the way the work is done. Let's look at these items individually, using Anne Adams's breakdown sheet for step 3.

Improvement Element 1: Eliminate Unnecessary Details

The goal is to eliminate details to avoid the unnecessary use of manpower, machines and equipment, and materials. If you have determined, by asking the question "Why?" in step 2, that a detail serves no useful purpose, there is a good chance you can eliminate it without losing any added value to the job.

Anne's notes on Table 7.3 showed that she decided that details 1, 3, 5, 6, 8, 10, and 11 could all be eliminated. All of these details have to do with the walking to get sheets from the supply box area and can be eliminated if the sheets are delivered closer to the bench. By making this one change, Anne was able to eliminate seven details of the job. As you can see on the breakdown sheet, she put a checkmark in the "Eliminate" column for each of these details.

Details 4b, 9b, and 12 involved laying out and stacking the sheets on the workbench. Anne found there was no added value or quality to the work and eliminated them.

Anne found out that detail 21, stamping of the word *TOP* on the assembled shields, was also unnecessary. Before making this decision, she consulted the engineering and inspection departments. When she asked why the stamp was necessary, the response was "Are you guys still doing that?! Didn't you get our email?" She learned that the sheets had been redesigned: the upper left-hand corner of the sheets had been cut off to make the distinction between top and bottom, and the stamp should have been eliminated 6 months ago when the design was changed. Obviously, there had been a breakdown in communication, only one of many factors that can keep alive an activity that has outlived its usefulness. The moral of the story is to emphasize how important it is to ask "Why?" about every detail of a job.

Finally, details 23 and 24 (carrying and weighing the shields) were also eliminated because they served no useful purpose. The shields, once sold by weight, were now sold by count. Bob Burns and the other operators had continued to weigh them because they were unaware of the change. They had been carrying 75-pound boxes all day long for no good reason. It is very common for a practice to continue long after the reason for that job has gone away, such as when a temporary countermeasure is put in place. The countermeasure continues even after the problem has been resolved.

Improvement Element 2: Combine Details When Practical

The answers to the questions "Where?" "When?" and "Who?" can help you find details that may be combined or done simultaneously. In the microwave shield assembly and packing improvement plan, Anne Adams found she could combine details 22, 26, and 27, which involved loading the completed shields into carrying boxes and the packing cases, by bringing the packing cases closer to the workbench. With this change, the operator (not the packing person) would pack the finished shields directly. Asking "Where?" and "When?" and "By Whom?" the shields should be packed, she decided that the best person for this activity was the riveter, who could pack the shields into the packing box right at the workbench and right after finishing the assembly. The riveter could do these three details at one time. Anne could not eliminate the packing of the shields, but she was able to improve the efficiency of the overall operation by combining details.

One opportunity for combining details is in a job that entails separate assembly and inspection processes. Typically, one person assembles a particular part, and another person checks to see if the assembly was done properly. You can often combine these two functions by having an operator self-check the work as it is being done. This does not eliminate the need for a thorough inspection later in the process, but it can reduce the total number of inspections and catch errors early in the process.

Improvement Element 3: Rearrange Details for Better Sequence

Rearrange, the third improvement element in step 3, is a good option to consider if it is impossible or unpractical to eliminate or combine details. Here again, the answers to the questions "Where?" "When?" and "Who?" suggest details that can be rearranged into a better sequence. Rearranging the order of details can help you save unnecessary movement of parts or materials and reduces backtracking and picking up and putting down motions.

Let's look at the details that Anne Adams rearranged. Because she changed the location of the supply boxes for the copper and the brass sheets by having these materials delivered directly to the workbench, she had to rearrange the details of picking up both kinds of sheets (details 2 and 7). Furthermore, because she decided not to lay the sheets out on the bench, she also had to rearrange the inspection details (details 4a and 9a). The operator would still be picking up and inspecting both the copper and brass sheets, but would now perform these activities directly before assembly. Because it would no longer be necessary to carry the boxes to the scale and because the operator would pack the shields directly into the packing cases at the workbench, Anne had to rearrange the delivery of the cases to the packing department (detail 25).

By checking off which details were to be eliminated, combined, and rearranged (on the breakdown sheet in Table 7.3), Anne could easily see what was going to change and how. This put her in an excellent position to begin writing up the proposed New method. But first she had one other very important element to review.

TWI note: A common error in step 3 is to think you have eliminated a detail because you have moved it to another area or department. If you decide to move a detail, even though you will not have to do that detail in your own area, you did not eliminate it. It still has to be done, and what you have changed is to rearrange the location of the detail and the sequence of when it is performed.

Improvement Element 4: Simplify All Necessary Details

The fourth improvement element of step 3 is to simplify details to make them safer and easier to do. It is facilitated by the question "How?" The JM pocket card (Figure 7.1) lists some specific principles that can help you find ideas for simplifying work details. Let's look at how Anne applied these principles to the sample job.

The first principle under simplify is *put materials, tools, and equipment into the best position and within convenient reach for the operator.* Everything the operator needs to use is easy to pick up, within arm's reach, and placed at the job site ahead of time on shelves or holders or racks. Keep in mind that this space is a semicircle radiating from the center of the body and varies according to a person's arm length. The second principle is *use gravity feed hoppers and drop delivery chutes.* Coffee bean or candy dispensers at the supermarket and mail or laundry chutes are common examples of this principle. The third principle is *make effective use of both hands*, a commonly overlooked commonsense improvement.

Finally, the last principle for simplifying the work is *use jigs and fixtures instead of hands.* A jig is a *movable* mechanical holding device such as a clamp, a template, or a guide. A fixture is a *fixed* mechanical device usually used in connection with a machine. The terms are often used interchangeably because each of these devices is made to hold materials, parts, or tools in place, freeing the hands to move. Without them, operators have to hold parts in one hand and use the other hand to do an operation. It is difficult, unwieldy, and often unsafe to do work this way. (Just imagine maneuvering a part into a secure position with one hand while turning down a screw, bending a corner, attaching a piece, or doing whatever the operation calls for with the other.)

Anne Adams applied these principles to details 2, 4a, 7, 9a, and 13–20. Following the first principle (*put materials within convenient reach*), she had the sheets placed directly on the bench. Because the operator had to reach to the opposite side of the workbench to pick them up, this was still not the best position, so she brought them closer, right in front of the operator. When the sheets were delivered, they were in high stacks and could accidentally be knocked over. Anne applied the principle of *using jigs and fixtures instead of hands* and made a jig to hold the tall pile of sheets, but Bob Burns found it was still difficult to pick up the thin and delicate sheets one by one. Based on his suggestion, Anne found that a 45° angle arm could be used to improve this. With this new arrangement, she also applied the principle of *making effective use of both hands*—the operator could now pick up a sheet in each hand. She applied this principle again when she added a second riveter to the workbench. With this change, both hands could be used to rivet two spots at one time.

In changing this detail, Anne also followed the principle of *using jigs or fixtures instead of hands*. Because the two riveters moved about on the workbench, she devised a fixture that held them in place. In addition, she attached a guide to the fixture to align two sheets automatically to the proper lineup tolerance of 5/1000 inch. She also made the height of the fixture equal to the height of 20 completed shields when they were stacked together so that it would no longer be necessary to count the shields.

Anne found an additional way to apply the principle of *putting materials, tools, and equipment within convenient reach of the operator*. She placed the scrap bins that were originally on the right side of the bench directly under the bench so that the operator would not have to walk around them to dispose of defective sheets. Realizing that the operator would still have to lean over to look under the bench to be sure the shield went into the scrap bin, she used another idea suggested by Bob Burns. Applying the principle of *use drop delivery chutes*, Anne and Bob cut slots into the bench and made chutes to guide the defective sheets directly into the scrap bins. Placing the packing case right next to the operator made it easier to pack the shields and was another application of the principle of *putting materials, tools, and equipment in the best position within convenient reach of the operator*.

In making these improvements, Anne applied all but one of the principles (*using gravity feed hoppers*). In each case, she was able to simplify the details of the job.

Step 2 leads us directly to the development of the new method in step 3. The answers to the questions "Why?" and "What?" identify unnecessary details that we can *eliminate*. The answers to the questions "Where?" "When?" and "Who?" lead us to areas we can *combine* or *rearrange*. And the answers to the question "How?" give us hints for developing the one best way to do the job when we *simplify* the details. Steps 2 and 3, then, are like two sides of the same coin because they work together as one. The model in Figure 7.9 shows the relationship between them and is incorporated into the breakdown sheet as a tool for moving quickly and decisively from step 2 to step 3.

Supervisor Team Exercise: Discuss with the team any further improvement opportunities in the sample job that Anne and Bob may have missed (e.g., a more efficient way to operate the riveters). Then, using your breakdown of the practice job, identify which details you feel you will be able to eliminate, combine, rearrange, or simplify. Check off the appropriate columns at the right side of your breakdown sheet. Discuss the improvements with the team, specifically noting how answering the five W's and one H led to identifying improvements for the details.

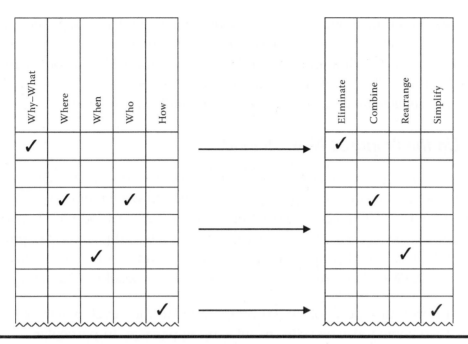

Figure 7.9   Relationship between steps 2 and 3.

Work Out Your Ideas with Others

The last two items in step 3 are critical to developing the new method. The fifth item, *work out your ideas with others*, means that you have to get other people involved in your improvement activity. Recognize that you can get good ideas from others (the boss, fellow supervisors, or operators). In the sample job, Anne Adams got important ideas from her operator, Bob Burns.

> **TWI note:** When the Japanese began bringing their concepts of quality and productivity back to the United States in the 1980s, many people in American industry felt that it was a revolutionary idea to get operators involved in the management of their own work. However, the original TWI training manuals from the 1940s show that this concept was originally an American idea.

Getting the workers involved in improving their own jobs may be the most significant thing that affects the success of your improvement plan. After all, it is the worker who will be implementing the new and improved methods you are developing. Involving workers in the improvement process motivates them to use the new method when it is completed. A wise adage for leadership is "No involvement, no commitment." People involved in developing a new idea will commit themselves to making it work. This, in the long run, may be more important than the idea itself.

In training JM across the United States, we have found that many supervisor trainees have been hesitant to go to the shop floor and work with their people. They are anxious about resistance to change, concerned that workers may question their methods, and wary about damaging relationships they have built. Almost without fail, these supervisors find that their people are eager to get involved, once they see the purpose and the mechanics of JM. In some cases, trainees have actually complained that the operators get too excited about the process and suggest more ideas than they can handle at one time.

Write Up the Proposed New Method

The last item in step 3 is to *write up the proposed new method*. Many ideas are never put into action because supervisors have failed to write them down. You need an accurate written record explaining what the new method will do and how it will work. A complete, written summary of your ideas and proposed improvements can be used to sell your ideas to management and as a tool for implementing your work. (We will discuss this written proposal in detail in Chapter 8.)

> **TWI note:** All aspects of the JM program led to the development of what we know today as Lean manufacturing practice. In particular, "work out your ideas with others" and "write up the proposed new method" were especially influential because they led directly to the development of small group activities and proposal systems, two of the critical steps in the evolution of Lean tools.

Step 4: Apply the New Method

Needless to say, improvements are of no value unless you put them into use. Step 4, *apply the new method*, ensures the success of improvements because it turns ideas into action. Many a frustrated supervisor has been heard saying, "Nobody listens to my ideas!" These supervisors see their improvement plans and ideas go nowhere because they failed to apply step 4 of JM, which places the responsibility squarely and unequivocally on the supervisors to implement their improvement plans. The five vital elements of step 4 are outlined below.

Item 1: Sell Your Proposal to the Boss

Whether you call the person who approves your work your boss, your superior, or your manager, this is the person who will (or will not) approve any changes that you want to make. For this reason, you will need to sell your ideas to this person. The best way to do this is to give him or her a short but complete summary of the idea, with supporting facts, in writing. The proposal should contain breakdown sheets, samples, data, sketches, and pictures, along with anything else that will aid in illustrating your improvement plan. This written record, which you made in step 3, will give the reader confidence that you have "done your homework" and understand the process in question well enough to know how to make it better. Table 7.4 shows the proposed method breakdown sheet

Table 7.4   Proposed Method Breakdown Sheet of Microwave Shield Sample Job

	Current/⟨Proposed⟩ Method Details	Remarks	
		Distance	Time/Tolerance/Rejects/Safety
1	Pile copper sheets onto the right jig		Materials are placed on the bench by handler
2	Pile brass sheets onto the left jig		
3	Pick up the copper sheet with right hand, brass sheet with the other		
4	Inspect both sheets		Rejects with dents and scratches go into the scrap bins through slots
5	Position both sheets in the riveter		The guides in the fixture will automatically align the edges and holes. The brass sheet goes on top
6	Rivet bottom two corners		
7	Turn sheets around and position in riveter		
8	Rivet upper two corners		
9	Place the shields in front of the fixture		
	For items 3–9, repeat the same process 19 times		
10	Place 20 finished sets of shields in packing box (1 full box contains 200 sets)		The box is carried by the handler
11	Take the full box to the packing area	100 ft.	The handler uses a pushcart
12	Pack and put address on it		
13	Fill out a delivery slip		
14	Store it until it is delivered		

for the microwave shield inspection and assembly process using the improvements Anne Adams developed following the JM four-step method.

Compare this breakdown sheet with the CM breakdown (Table 7.3) and you will recognize that the proposed method suggests a much better way to do the work. So will the boss. The presentation in this format is clear and compelling and makes it quite easy to sell your ideas. When you explain in your written proposals the increases and better uses of manpower, machines, materials, space, equipment, quality, safety, and so forth, the point is already made.

Item 2: Sell the New Method to the Operators

To get the full benefit of the improvement, you need the support and cooperation of the operators who will actually be using the new method. Sometimes,
people resist change. Your people may become defensive, especially if they
perceive your ideas as criticism of their work. For these reasons, it is vital to take
the time to gain the support and cooperation of the operators who will be putting the plan into action. The best way to get this support is to involve workers at
an early stage, just as Anne Adams did when she worked with Bob Burns. When
you get people to take part in the process of putting the new method together,
they take ownership and commit themselves to carrying out the new method
properly.

With operators who do not take part in the Job Methods improvement exercise, be sure to explain that the purpose of the improvement is to constructively
seek better ways to increase production and output. You can explain how the
new method makes the work easier and safer to do, emphasizing that it is not a
form of speeding up the process. Point out the areas of waste that you are eliminating and explain the principles you are using to streamline and simplify the
operation. Knowing that you have their best interest in mind will make it easier
for them to trust the new method.

Whenever you instruct the new method to an operator, follow the JI four-step
method, being sure to get the person interested in learning the job. Remember
that using proper JI technique helps operators learn the new method quickly,
conscientiously, and correctly.

Item 3: Get Final Approval of All Concerned
on Safety, Quality, Quantity, and Cost

Remember that other related departments have a stake in how the work is done
in your departments and may need to approve any changes you make in methods for a job. The quality department needs to be sure that the work is being
done in a way that satisfies the final customers. The safety people need to be
sure that no one is being injured or hurt in the process. The cost accounting
department needs to be sure that you are doing the work within the budget.
And the production and planning departments need to be sure that the work
you do fits into the overall production and output plans. In some cases, even the
customers that you supply may need to approve new work procedures. Getting
approval from everyone beforehand will prevent trouble and misunderstandings.

It is a big part of the supervisor's responsibility to know what authority or function will be needed to approve the improvement plan (either in full or in part).
Different proposals will need different approvals depending on the content. Be
sure to follow your company's organizational procedures and policies. Your best
asset will be your written proposal because this can be copied, passed around,
reviewed, marked up, revised, and signed by any and all interested parties.

Item 4: Put the New Method to Work—Use It until a Better Way Is Developed

Amazingly, even with full approval and support, supervisors sometimes place improvement plans in a drawer and forget them while they deal with pressing things that need immediate attention. Don't wait. Put your plan into action as quickly as possible. Your plan is an investment in the future. It will pay for itself with interest. You cannot afford to be too busy when your improvement plan can solve the very problems that are eating up so much of your time.

Never allow yourself to think that this is the end of your improvement activity for this job. Use your improved process until a better way is developed. Never assume that all of the improvements have already been found. Always remember that improvement is a continuous process.

> **TWI note:** Continuous improvement is the bedrock principle of good Lean practice, and it came from this one line of the JM four-step method: *use it until a better way is developed*. We must keep searching for further improvements because there will always be a better way.

Item 5: Give Credit Where Credit Is Due

As suggested throughout the process of developing your improvement plan, you should get ideas or advice from other people and incorporate these into your final proposal. Do not forget to give these people credit and show your sincere appreciation for their contributions. Not doing so can provoke resentment, and one "stolen" or unacknowledged idea can come back to haunt you. Showing gratitude is not difficult and can take many forms. At the very least, you should include the names of the people who assisted you in your final proposal. The more credit you give, the more people will contribute ideas.

Closing

As you saw with the microwave shield assembly and packing example, the principles of Job Methods improvement are all that you need to make substantial and vital improvements to your work. People from around the world have used these principles to make countless improvements in the many decades since their development. Today, whether in mass production facilities or in job shops, in service industries or in medical institutions, the Job Methods improvement plan is a simple but effective method to introduce and sustain the process of continuous improvement. In this era of Lean thinking, JM is invaluable.

In Chapter 8, we will look in more detail at item 6 in step 3 for writing effective proposals that you can sell to your boss. Team members will examine an improvement proposal example using the JM method, practice writing a draft proposal, and consider a strategy for applying the new method.

Supervisor Team Exercise: Print out another blank copy of the JM breakdown sheet from the TWI Institute website. You will create a proposed method breakdown sheet of your practice job similar to the one in Table 7.4. Start by reviewing the right-hand columns of your current method breakdown and identify the details marked to eliminate, combine, or rearrange. Based on that plan, record the details as done in the new method. Have each team member explain to the group both the current and the new job procedure for their practice job, highlighting the ideas that led to the new method. Also, explain any ideas for simplifying the job. Have the group comment on each demonstration and provide additional ideas.

Chapter 8

Writing and Selling the Improvement Proposal: Example

In Chapter 7, you applied the first three steps to your practice jobs, an exercise designed to provide a clear understanding of the purpose of the Job Methods (JM) improvement plan. That purpose is *to help you produce greater quantities of quality products in less time by making the best use of the manpower, machines, and materials now available.* The focus of this chapter is step 3, item 6 (write up the new proposed method) and step 4 (apply the new method). To help team members write and use the improvement proposal, the chapter includes an example from one of our JM classes. Figure 8.1 provides a quick, high-level overview of the JM four-step method that will help you develop the written proposal.

Proposals: Write It Down and Work Out the Numbers

Many improvement ideas fade away before they are ever put into practice simply because people do not write them down. The best idea for doing a job better, even if you tell other people about it, is useless until it is implemented. Until you get it down on paper, you cannot act on it. Furthermore, ideas should be written in a format that can be passed around for others to review, understand the contents, and make notes and corrections. In this format and sequence, your idea becomes a written proposal that everyone can agree upon, giving you the freedom to implement it. As discussed in Chapter 7, you can use a written proposal as a tool to explain the development of your improvement ideas and then use it to sell these ideas to your boss and other individuals or departments with a vested interest in the job you want to improve.

Be sure to include in your written proposal your completed current method breakdown sheet and your proposed method breakdown sheet. This shows

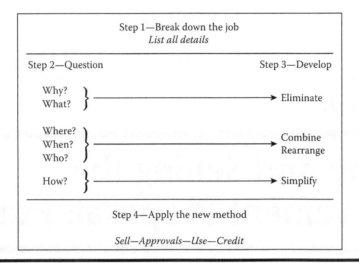

Figure 8.1   Overview of JM four-step method.

interested parties that you really understand the current process and how to improve it. The same worksheets that helped you through the JM four-step method will serve double duty by helping others understand the details of the job and see the research that went into your ideas for the new method. You should include any additional diagrams, photographs, charts, or drawings that illustrate your improvement ideas.

If you compare the current and proposed improvement breakdowns of the microwave shield assembly and packing process (Figures 7.3 and 7.4), you can easily see that the improved method is a much better way of doing this work. Because the breakdown is clear and logical, Anne's boss will have no difficulty understanding and approving the proposed changes.

Supervisor Team Exercise: Look at your current method breakdown sheet and proposed method breakdown sheet for the practice job you did in Chapter 7. Is there significant improvement? Do the before and after improvement breakdowns tell a compelling story that promotes the new method? If not, double-check your work. Remember, even a small improvement can add up to significant results. Discuss with the group the potential benefits of each member's suggested improvements.

The most important thing that your written proposal needs to show is the expected results from implementing your improvement ideas. It is very important to explain *concretely* and, whenever possible, *quantitatively*, how the manpower, machines, and materials are going to be utilized better. These before improvement and after improvement parameters will make the most compelling case for selling your proposal.

TWI note: From the very beginning, the TWI program of comparing before and after improvement results had a huge influence on the success of the Japanese manufacturing practice; the improvement proposal is a benchmark of good improvement practice today. This format is also the genesis of the famous proposal systems, or *teian seido*, that most Japanese manufacturers promote and that Toyota still uses energetically. In 2001, employees at Toyota's Georgetown, Kentucky, plant generated $18 million for the company from the ideas that came from their proposal system.

Improvement Proposal Sheet for the Microwave Shield Sample Job

Table 8.1 shows the improvement proposal sheet that Anne Adams submitted for the microwave shields. At the top of the sheet, she noted who is submitting and who is receiving the report and what the report covers. The first part of the report is a *summary* of the main thrust of the improvement. Below the summary are sections outlining the *results* and the detailed *content* of proposed changes. The results show expected quantitative benefits. The content highlights what functions and operations will improve with the new method and in what way. The sheet is easy to read and understand. It prompts the reader to refer to the completed breakdown sheets (attached to the proposal) to see what inspired these ideas. Note that the proposal also gives credit to Bob Burns for his assistance in this process.

Expressing Results Quantitatively for Greatest Impact

The most important part of this improvement proposal sheet (the section that will do the most to help sell your proposal) is the "Results" section. As Table 8.1 shows, Anne increased the production of the microwave shields by 300% (from 800 sets before improvement to 2400 sets after improvement). In addition, by having each operator use two riveters, she reduced the number of operators needed for the job from four skilled people to two nonskilled people, making better use of the machines and increasing total production. By reducing the number of times operators handled the delicate materials, the reject rate decreased from 5% to less than 0.5%, and the volume of scrap decreased from 15% to less than 2%. The proposal sheet shows precisely how Anne's new method will produce greater quantities of quality products in less time by making the best use of the manpower, machines, and materials now available.

The "Results" section in Anne's proposal works well because she expresses the results numerically, avoiding vague statements, such as "production will be more and the reject rate less." If a proposal does not specify exactly how much something will improve, it is impossible to judge whether the improvement is worthwhile. Always express the results quantitatively and calculate what the new values will be. If you cannot assign a precise numerical value, give your best estimate. Trying out the new method or taking measurements of areas to be improved can help you do this.

Table 8.1   Improvement Proposal Sheet Submitted by Anne Adams

Submitted to: Sam Johnson, Manager	
Made by: Anne Adams, Supervisor	**Dept.:** Riveting and Packing
Product/part: Microwave shields	**Date:** May 20, 20xx
Operations: Inspecting, assembling, riveting, and packing	

The following are proposed improvements on the above operations.

1. Summary

We worked on improving the assembly and packing process for the microwave shields. Our analysis shows that there is too much walking and handling of the product that leads to wasted effort and material. By rearranging the layout of the work and devising jigs to automate the assembly, we were able to make dramatic improvements.

2. Results

	Before Improvement	*After Improvement*
Production (one worker per day)	800 sets	2400 sets
Machine use (one machine per day)	3200	4800
Reject rate	5%	Below 0.5%
Number of operators	4 skilled	2 nonskilled
Other—scrap	15%	Less than 2%

3. Content

1. Operators will no longer have to walk to the supply box if the material handler brings the sheets to the designated area on the workbench.
2. Placing two riveters inside a fixture and the guides on it to align the sheets will enable two holes to be riveted simultaneously.
3. Having two jigs with sheets on top and placing them near the fixture will enable workers to use both hands to pick up the sheets.
4. Stamping *TOP* operation will be eliminated since it's not necessary.
5. Empty packing boxes next to the bench will enable the operator to install the completed shields directly into the box (by number, not by weight).
6. Having two slots on the bench will enable operators to drop defective sheets easily into the scrap bins. (Refer to the attached breakdown and layout sheets.)

This proposal was made with the cooperation of Bob Burns.

Note: Explain exactly how this improvement was made. If necessary, attach present and proposed breakdown sheets, diagrams, and any other related items.

Anne, for example, set up and simulated the new method, timing how long it took to complete the assembly of the shield compared with the current method. By dividing the time it took to make one shield into the total number of minutes and seconds in a day, she calculated the number of shields that could be made in a day using the new method. She performed similar calculations to quantify the amount of scrap and assess defects, finding that the operator caused many of them while making the shields.

It is important to emphasize that being thorough in your approach and looking at the bigger picture can nearly always produce some bottom-line quantitative result for the improvement. The following example illustrates how this can be done. What if you made a job easier to do, but it did not necessarily increase the output or reduce the cost of doing it? How can you express the improvement quantitatively? Certainly, the morale of the worker doing the job will increase because you simplified the job or reduced the strain involved. If the worker does not need to focus on complicated operations anymore or is more comfortable performing the work, he or she can pay more attention to the quality of the work or have more time to spot other problems. In addition, by looking at defects (kind and number) that occur during a process, you may be able to estimate how many and what kinds of these can be reduced with your improvement and put a number to it.

Another example that illustrates this point is reducing the amount of weight someone has to carry. This improvement may seem difficult to quantify, but you can tailor your proposal to include the numeric reduction in the total weight being carried and a numerical estimate of savings in potential medical costs because the improvement will decrease back strain or other injuries. You can supplement this estimate with data on current claims and what they cost the company. Such quantitative results are particularly useful for selling a proposal to human resources, safety, and cost departments.

If you cannot show a dramatic change on a daily basis, calculate small improvements over a longer period. For example, placing tools and materials close to the point of usage can save a minute or two every time they are used. In the long run, this change can save as much as 30 minutes a week or 26 hours over an entire year. If you know the hourly rate of the employee involved (including benefits and taxes), show the savings of those 26 hours in dollars and cents.

In the end, your goal is a proposal that shows how effective and valuable your improvements will be. This is the whole point of your Job Methods improvement activity.

Improvement Proposal Example: Reduction of Workers on the Handset Assembly Line

An example of a practice demonstration, presented by one of our TWI trainees at a plant in Mexico, contains ideas a supervisor found by using the JM four-step method. Pay close attention to how JM was used in this process.

A large electronics assembly plant used mass production assembly lines to make cordless phones for the home. Each of the company's five lines turned out as many as 25,000 telephones per day on two shifts. The plant hired many

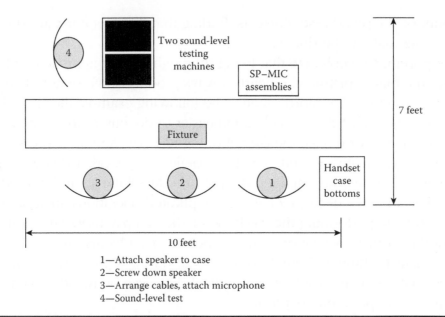

1—Attach speaker to case
2—Screw down speaker
3—Arrange cables, attach microphone
4—Sound-level test

Figure 8.2   Before improvement layout for handset assembly line.

operators to do this work (there were as many as 100 operators on a single line). Because turnover was high, people were always in demand. The line speed was about 10 seconds, so each operation had to be done in that amount of time or less. There were a multitude of different operations and a wealth of opportunity to find improvements.

The JM trainee studied the line upstream, where handsets (the part of the phone you pick up and talk into) were made for one of the phone models. In this upstream section of the line, operators took the bottom half of the handset case and inserted the speaker–microphone assembly, which included wires that had to be arranged properly inside the case. Then they put this subassembly into a testing machine that checked the sound level of the components. Four people worked on this part of the operation. Because of the long cycle time, two machines did the testing. Figure 8.2 shows the layout of the worksite.

Step 1: Break Down the Job

The supervisor felt that this part of the line was giving him the most trouble. By going to the line and studying the actual assembly and testing process, the supervisor was able to find and list the details for this work on the current method breakdown sheet (Table 8.2). The three fundamental types of work (material handling, machine work, and hand work) were performed in the area, and each presented opportunities for improvement to the current process. As for material handling, because all four of the operators worked while sitting at a conveyor line, their work involved a lot of picking up and putting down of parts and product. Machine work included the automatic screwdriver and

Table 8.2 Current Method Breakdown Sheet

	(Current)/Proposed Method Details	Distance	Remarks — Time/Tolerance/Rejects/Safety	Why	Where	When	Who	How	Ideas — Write Them Down; Don't Try to Remember	Eliminate	Combine	Rearrange	Simplify
1	Pick up 1 handset case bottom		From plastic container			✓			At same time as picking up SP–MIC assembly		✓		
2	Place in front		Directly on conveyor					✓	Better way				✓
3	Pick up 1 speaker–microphone (SP–MIC) assembly		From white foam container				✓		Same person who screws it down		✓	✓	
4	Place SP–MIC assembly in case bottom		Presetting speaker in position			✓	✓		Same time as case bottom; same person who screws it down		✓	✓	
5	Pass to next operator	24 in.		✓					No, if done by same person	✓			
6	Pick up case bottom with SP–MIC assembly			✓					Same as #5	✓			
7	Place in fixture		Fixture specially fitted to case	✓					Same as #5	✓			
8	Pick up screwdriver					✓			Just after inserting speaker			✓	
9	Screw down speaker to case		2 screws			✓			Just after inserting speaker			✓	

Product: Handset

Operations: Assembly, Testing

Made by: Saul Sanchez

Department: Production FA

Date: July 12, 2004

(Continued)

Table 8.2 (*Continued*)   Current Method Breakdown Sheet

Product: Handset

Operations: Assembly, Testing

Made by: Saul Sanchez

Department: Production FA

Date: July 12, 2004

	(Current)/Proposed Method Details	Distance	Time/Tolerance/Rejects/Safety	Why	Where	When	Who	How	Ideas	Eliminate	Combine	Rearrange	Simplify
10	Pass to next operator	24 in.		✓					Write Them Down; Don't Try to Remember	✓			
11	Pick up case bottom with SP–MIC assembly			✓					Same as #5	✓			
12	Place in front		Directly on conveyor	✓					Same as #5	✓			
13	Straighten out wires		Inserting along edge of case				✓		Same person who inserts speaker			✓	
14	Insert microphone		Snapping into place			✓	✓		Same time as speaker; same person who inserts speaker		✓	✓	
15	Pass to next operator	24 in.		✓					Same as #5	✓			
16	Pick up case bottom with SP–MIC assembly			✓					Same as #5	✓			
17	Place in #1 testing machine fixture				✓				At top of line, one machine on each side of line			✓	
18	Start #1 machine												

(Continued)

Table 8.2 (Continued)   Current Method Breakdown Sheet

Product: Handset — Made by: Saul Sanchez

Operations: Assembly, Testing — Department: Production FA — Date: July 12, 2004

#	(Current)/Proposed Method Details	Remarks: Distance	Remarks: Time/Tolerance/Rejects/Safety	Why	Where	When	Who	How	Ideas	Eliminate	Combine	Rearrange	Simplify
19	Hold buttons		While die closes on case					✓	Better way (use safety cover with switch)				✓
20	Take out handset from #2 testing machine												
21	Place on conveyor												
22	Pick up second handset						✓		Done by other operator			✓	
23	Place in #2 testing machine fixture						✓		Done by other operator			✓	
24	Start #2 machine						✓		Done by other operator			✓	
25	Hold buttons		While die closes on case				✓	✓	Done by other operator; better way			✓	
26	Wait 10 seconds		While machines cycle	✓					No, if operator is doing assembly while machine cycles	✓			

the sound-level testing equipment. Hand work included insertion of the parts into the case and the arrangement of the wires.

The work of the first three operators was straightforward. Each of them picked up the handset case bottom and did something inside of it: operator 1 picked up the speaker–microphone assembly and inserted the speaker into the case, operator 2 screwed the speaker into place, and operator 3 arranged the wires inside the case and snapped the microphone into place. Of course, each operator had to pick up and put down the handsets one by one during the process. Operator 4's work was a bit different because she handled two handsets at the same time. Because the cycle time of the machine was slower than the line speed, she used two machines. While one handset was being checked, she unloaded and loaded the other machine. Even with the loading and unloading of two machines, she still had 10 seconds of waiting time for the completion of two sets.

Although these details account for just one part of the entire line, this part of the line can be studied independently because all of the assembly operations culminated in the sound check inspection of the speaker and microphone. Obviously, it is important to keep the bigger picture in mind, but what makes continuous improvement possible is breaking down the line into smaller sections. Doing this lets you apply each step in the JM four-step method on a manageable scale. Trying to improve the entire line all at once can be discouraging because you may not have time to handle the complexity of the task. You can use Pareto charts, line-balance analysis, cause-and-effect diagrams, or similar tools to identify the parts of the process that would be the most beneficial to work on first.

Step 2: Question Every Detail

By using the five W and one H questions (Why? What? Where? When? Who? How?), the supervisor was able to collect concrete ideas for improving almost all of the details (Table 8.2). When he questioned *why* the handset had to be picked up and put down so many times, he got the idea to eliminate this wasted motion by having the same person do all of the assembly operations. Because there were two sound-level check machines, which had a fairly long cycle time and caused the operator to wait, the supervisor asked *why* the operator could not use that waiting time to do the assembly process. By asking *who* and *when*, he discovered that it was more productive and less time-consuming for one operator to perform certain operations. For example, the operator could assemble the speaker and the microphone in the same operation instead of picking them up twice and handling them separately one by one. The supervisor asked *where* to determine the best location for the testing equipment and to evaluate the workplace layout (one of the nine items we also question in item 2 of step 2). This gave him the idea to place each of the two machines on a different side of the line. With this change, two operators could manage the machines separately while doing assembly work at the same time the machines were operating.

By questioning *how* the operation was done, the supervisor noticed that operators were struggling to get the parts and the wires correctly into the case bottoms that sat directly on the conveyor. He decided that there must be a better way of inserting the parts. He also determined that there must be a better way of operating the sound-level testing machines. For safety reasons, the operator had to use both hands to hold down two buttons while the top half of the machine came down on the handset and closed it to make a tight seal. Each time the operator started one of the machines, she was prevented from doing anything else for a few seconds.

When he began this exercise, the supervisor was not exactly sure where his ideas for improvement would come from. He was pleasantly surprised to find that his intuition about where to start was correct and that there was, in fact, much more opportunity for making the process better than he had expected. By making better use of the waiting time for the machines, he was able to come up with the idea to split the work between two people and combine all of the other operations into one.

Step 3: Develop the New Method

Table 8.2 shows that by having one operator do all of the assembly operations within the line speed, the supervisor was able to *eliminate* most of the picking up and putting down details (details 5–7, 10–12, 15, and 16) that occurred between operations. He was also able to *eliminate* detail 26, the 10-second waiting time during the sound-level check, by having the operator do the assembly while the machine performed the test.

The supervisor's decision to *rearrange* the work so that two operators did all of the same assembly operations in tandem made it possible to do all of this work while keeping up with the speed of the conveyor. Rearranging details 3, 4, 8, 9, 13, and 14 so they were performed sequentially made it possible for each of the two operators to assemble the same number of sets it had previously taken three operators to assemble. With this change, he was now able to *combine* details 4 and 14 and have the operator attach both the speaker and the microphone at the same time, one with each hand. With these changes, the supervisor found there was still a little extra time for the operator to work the testing machine. Because most of the time spent handling these machines was waiting time, he rearranged details 22–25 so they could be done at the same time as the assembly.

The key to this new arrangement was placing both testing machines at the front of the line and having the operators sit on each side of the line (Figure 8.3). The new arrangement took less overall space from the line, a valuable benefit because the remaining operations were packed tightly together all the way down the line.

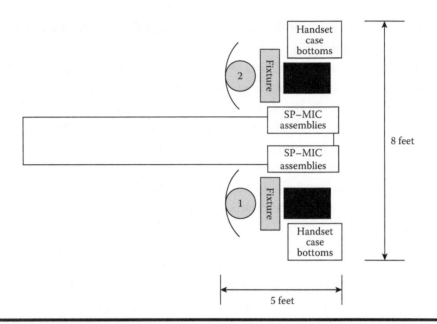

Figure 8.3   After improvement layout for handset assembly line.

In the current method, operators arranged wires and inserted parts into the handsets directly on the conveyor. They could only use one hand at a time to do the work because the other hand was needed to stabilize the case. To improve this, the supervisor made use of the principle of *jigs or fixtures* to facilitate the effective use of *both hands*. By placing the case into the fixture right from the start, the supervisor *simplified* the work. Because the case was firmly held in place, it freed up two hands to do the work.

The supervisor also used *jigs or fixtures* to improve other aspects of the operation. Plexiglas safety covers, which slid up and down with a start switch attached, were installed on the testing machines. Operators could now simply pull down this cover to start the machine. They no longer had to wait for the machine to close or worry about getting fingers or hands caught inside.

Incorporating all of these changes, the supervisor wrote up the proposed method as shown in Table 8.3. A comparison of the proposed method breakdown and the current method breakdown (Table 8.2) shows a dramatic improvement. Work on this part of the line was reduced from 26 details to 12.

By implementing the proposed method, you can expect the following results:

■ Reduce the number of operators from four to two
■ Reduce the amount of space on the line from 70 square feet to 40 square feet
■ Move the other two operators to other areas where people are needed and train them in different work
■ Spread out the downstream line a little, alleviating crowding

As for output, the supervisor calculated that, in the current process, four operators working together could turn out a maximum of 2500 sets in

Table 8.3   Proposed Method Breakdown Sheet

	Current/~~Proposed~~ Method Details	Remarks	
		Distance	Time/Tolerance/Rejects/Safety
1	Pick up one handset case bottom		From the plastic container
2	Place in the fixture		
3	Pick up one SP–MIC assembly		From the white foam container
4	Place speaker and microphone in case bottom		Using both hands
5	Grab the automatic screwdriver		
6	Turn down 2 screws		Using the screwdriver
7	Straighten out wires		Inserting along edge of case
8	Open test machine cover		
9	Take out finished handset		Check if passed test or not
10	Place on conveyor		If defect, place in defect container
11	Place new handset in test machine fixture		
12	Close test machine cover		

a single shift (625 sets per person per shift). Timing a single operator using the new method, he found that two operators could turn out 2000 sets (1000 sets per person in a shift). While the per person rate increased, the total number of sets completed on a shift went down by 500 sets. Because his production schedule for the next month required maintaining only a pace of 2000 sets per shift on this line, he could meet the current schedule using the new method. However, he would have to continue looking for improvements so that he can increase the capacity of the two operators should the production totals increase.

The supervisor then wrote up the proposed new method (item 6 of step 3). He detailed all the changes and results for the new method using the improvement proposal sheet (Table 8.4). He also attached copies of the before and after improvement breakdown sheets (Tables 8.2 and 8.3) and diagrams of the layout of the line—what the current state was and what the future state would look like after implementation of the improvement ideas (Figures 8.2 and 8.3).

Step 4: Apply the New Method

The supervisor was excited about putting his ideas to work. It was easy for him to *sell* the new method to his boss and to the operators using his proposal.

Table 8.4   Improvement Proposal Sheet

Submitted to: Ken Suzuki, Production Manager	
Made by: Saul Sanchez, 2nd Shift Production Supervisor	**Dept.:** Production FA
Product/part: Handset	**Date:** July 12, 2004
Operations: Assembly, testing	

The following are proposed improvements on the above operations.

1. Summary

We worked on improving the assembly and testing process for the beginning part of the handset line. Our analysis shows that there is too much picking up and putting down of the product that leads to wasted time and effort. By having one operator each do all of the processes and by rearranging the layout of the work, we were able to make dramatic improvements.

2. Results

	Before Improvement	*After Improvement*
Production (one worker per day)	625/shift	1000/shift
Machine use (one machine per day)		
Reject rate		
Number of operators	4	2
Other—space on line	6.6 m^2	3.75 m^2

3. Content

1. Operators will no longer have to pick up and put down the handset if they place it directly into the jig and have one person do all of the assembly operations.
2. By having one person do all of the operations, we can keep the case bottom in the jig so that the operator will be able to do the work more easily using two hands to insert components and arrange the wires.
3. By taking out this wasted time and simplifying the method, we can get the assembly done by two people instead of three.
4. By moving the sound-level testing machines up to the front of the line, we can use the cycle time of the machines and have the two assembly operators work these machines at the same time they do the assembly work. This eliminates the need for this fourth operator.
5. We can make the job of starting the machines easier and save a few seconds by making a Plexiglas cover with the machine start switch attached. By simply closing the cover, the operator does not have to wait for the die to close before being able to use her hands to do something else. (There is no concern about getting hands caught in machine.)
6. By combining these operations, the total output will be lower, from 2500 to 2000 sets per shift. However, since the current month's schedule calls for 2000 sets per shift, we can keep up using the new method. But we will have to continue improving the process to get back up to the 2500 sets per shift level.

This proposal was made with the cooperation of Victor Chavez.

Note: Explain exactly how this improvement was made. If necessary, attach present and proposed breakdown sheets, diagrams, and any other related items.

The expected results prompted everyone to agree quickly that these changes would benefit the entire line. However, because this entailed rearranging the line and moving machinery, he had to convince the other departments that the work was worth the effort. He talked with the people concerned and used his proposal to explain what would make these changes possible and, in particular, how he would maintain the output and quality of the work after making them. He was able to get *final approval* and *put the new method to work* quickly, making sure it was implemented properly. Finally, though he was the architect for the major ideas for change, he remembered to *give credit* to his assistant manager and to all four operators on the line for helping him to understand the process and for cooperating with him in making and implementing his proposal.

> **TWI note:** Each step in Job Methods contains a major function that moves the process forward, and if done completely and in order, these four steps will take you toward the incremental improvements that, over time, make Lean's continuous improvement a reality.

As this example shows, the supervisor came a long way. He began the assignment not knowing exactly what kind of changes he could make. He had a notion that there was room for improvement in this part of the process, but it was only when he began sequentially applying the JM four-step method that he generated improvement ideas. Then these ideas took shape as a new method, culminating in a written proposal that he could sell to the appropriate people in the company. This kind of improvement activity should be a regular part of every supervisor's daily work. An organization that endorses and promotes a continuous improvement culture will achieve the greatest benefits from this process.

Supervisor Team Exercise: Print out the improvement proposal sheet from the TWI Institute website. Each team member should complete items 5 and 6 in step 3 for the practice job. Item 5 is work out your ideas with others. Each member should get real feedback from other parties in the company regarding improvement ideas, especially the operators who do the work and the departments the ideas will affect. At a minimum, extrapolate what some of the concerns or issues of others might be.

Now write your improvement proposal, attaching types of documentation discussed in this chapter. Have team members read their proposals and discuss the pluses and minuses of each, highlighting the ones that show the most compelling reasons for implementation and why. Was the proposal well documented and clear? Did it show dramatic differences between the before and after processes? Did it show results quantitatively?

Finally, each team member is ready to follow the items in step 4 and apply them to the new method. This will entail returning to your worksites and selling your proposal to the boss, selling the new method to the operators, getting final approval of all concerned, and then putting the new method to work and giving credit to those who helped advanced your efforts. Discuss with the group your strategy for getting these things done. Then put your proposal into action.

JOB RELATIONS

Chapter 9

Job Relations: Working with and through People

When a machine or new piece of equipment is installed in your department, it comes with a user's manual or handbook, directions on how to keep it in good operating condition, and a troubleshooting guide on what to do when it breaks down. There may be special training on how to operate it, a technician specially qualified to operate it, a help-line phone number, and at the very least, some sort of guarantee or warrantee.

Supervisors hire or acquire new people all the time, but none of these people come with handbooks even though all of them are more complicated than any machine. So how can a supervisor keep these new people working well and in top form? And what can a supervisor do if they do not perform to expectations?

Few people realize just how complex a supervisor's job really is. Company management demands output and quality, but to achieve this, the supervisor needs the dedication and cooperation of the people who are actually doing the work. Often, supervisors find these are hard to come by. Sometimes they have no one but themselves to blame for this. The following points show why and how this happens.

- *Unwilling to delegate work.* Supervisors who now manage work they used to do themselves are often tempted to continue doing much of that work instead of assigning and teaching it to others.
- *Unwilling to be the boss.* New supervisors often feel uncomfortable telling others what to do since only recently they used to be "one of them."
- *Overcoming the lack of experience with the work.* Supervisors often direct workers who know more about the technical aspects of the job than they do. These people will question the supervisor's judgment because the supervisor does not have the background, experience, or the detailed knowledge of the work.

- *Handling veteran workers.* Supervisors directing the work of people with more years of service than themselves may have difficulty in getting these workers to take orders or listen to instructions from someone who has less experience. This is especially true in plants where operators have worked continuously for 20 or 30 years.

- *Unable to teach or mentor inexperienced workers.* Supervisors, both new and experienced, have trouble teaching and managing people who have never worked before or who have never had steady work. When people have little experience working, it takes time for them to adjust to the discipline of an organization and its rules.

- *Handling work habits from a different company culture.* People who have worked in a different company environment or culture may expect things to be the same everywhere. When they change companies, they have to not only learn the new rules and adapt to the new culture, but also unlearn all of the old ways of doing work. Supervisors need to be aware of this and know how to help these transplanted workers take root and grow.

To overcome and manage these various complexities, supervisors need to develop skill in leading people, and this means *working with and through people.* Leadership is a skill you learn through practice; when applied regularly, it will help you solve and even prevent problems. This is the purpose of the Training Within Industry (TWI) Job Relations (JR) program.

This chapter gives an overview of some of the characteristics of good supervision. In Chapter 10, you will use the JR pocket card to go through the JR four-step method of handling people-related problems. In Chapter 11, you will use the reverse side of the pocket card to discuss some foundations for good job relations that prevent problems from happening in the first place.

What Is Good Supervision?

There are many models, programs, and "how to" books that define good supervision. However, when dealing with people, there is never an easy fix or secret formula to success. The JR method, like all of the TWI programs, goes back to basic principles learned and passed down to us by countless generations of good supervisors. It is in their experience and knowledge that the real wisdom of working with people lies. To appreciate the value of this, you need to remember just one thing: social norms and technology change; human nature does not.

The TWI founders developed the following paradigm of good supervision: *good supervision means that the supervisor gets the people in the department to do* **what** *the supervisor needs done,* **when** *it should be done, and the* **way** *the supervisor needs it done, because* **they** *want to do it.* In other words, as a member of the company's management team, the supervisor knows the demands being placed on the company—what orders are due and by when—and must divide and delegate the work in order to meet these demands. Moreover, the supervisor must see to it that the work is done according to standards that ensure the work is done in a way that meets customer expectations in terms of performance, quality, safety, durability, and so forth. By far the most difficult task for a supervisor is motivating people to do that work in a way that makes them want to accomplish the what, when, and how of the work.

> **TWI note:** TWI's Job Instruction (JI) and Job Methods (JM) programs also cover many of these aspects of leadership and getting people involved in their work. In JI, when you teach a job, you take the time to get the person interested in learning the job by showing them the importance and value of the work. And by getting operators involved in all aspects of the JM improvement activity, you get them to generate ideas and suggestions and become committed to owning and using the new method.

How do we get people to work "because *they* want to do it?" The essence of leadership is to work with people in a way that gets them to take charge or ownership of the requirements of the work. Defined this way, a leader is a person who has followers, not simply a boss who issues orders about what to do, by when, and how. People who work under this kind of boss are not being led; they are simply being told what to do. They also instinctively dislike the boss who fits this description. Being boss does not invite dedication or cooperation. Leadership, on the other hand, does. Leaders get people to understand the importance of their work and motivate them to do the work because they want to do it. This is the essence of JR.

Supervisor Team Exercise: Conduct a general discussion around what is good supervision and how effective each team member is at getting the people in the department to do *what* needs to be done, *when* it should be done, and the *way* it should be done, because *they* want to do it. Review the aforementioned six bullet points on obstacles to getting people's cooperation and have each team member identify his or her tendencies. Has this behavior hindered your ability to motivate people? What effect has that had on your production results?

Supervisor's Relationship with People

TWI defines a supervisor as *anybody who is in charge of people or who directs the work of others.* There are many titles for people with this kind of responsibility.* Regardless of your actual title, as long as you direct the work of others (even if they do not organizationally report directly to you), you are the one who has

---

* Titles can include, among others, director, manager, assistant manager, foreperson, superintendent, line leader, group leader, team leader, and working lead.

the important role of leading people toward good work that creates successful results. As companies flatten their organizational structures, cutting out layers of management, who is in charge of whom becomes less obvious. As noted above, a person who is a boss is not necessarily a leader. Conversely, a person who is a leader may not always be a boss. Organizations today want people who can make things happen without necessarily holding all the baggage that comes with the superior–subordinate relationship. This is all the more reason to develop and utilize leadership skills.

As a supervisor in charge of getting work done, you answer to your supervisor for a variety of things. *Production* (that is, whatever work gets done in your department) is one of these things. You also have to make sure that what you are producing has the required *quality* to meet the customer's demands. And since your customers want the best price for that quality product or service, supervisors are also responsible for the *cost* of the work that gets done or for making sure that costs meet budget. To produce quality products at the right cost, supervisors are responsible for *training* their people to quickly remember to do jobs correctly, safely, and conscientiously. If you work in a production setting where machinery is in use, you are also responsible for the *maintenance* of that equipment and the *safety* of the people operating it. If you do mainly office work, you are most likely responsible for *reports* and, what is more, the *accuracy* of those reports. It goes almost without saying that supervisors everywhere are always responsible for *schedules* and *deadlines*.

These are some examples of the main responsibilities of supervisors. There are more. Nevertheless, there is a common denominator that connects all of these responsibilities—people. Are people involved with production? Of course. This is true even for an automated factory. People have to program the robots, make sure they are stocked with materials and parts, attend to the machines if they break down, and adjust the tooling when models change. Whom do we train to do this work? People. Who makes a quality product? Who is responsible if a defective product is produced? When it comes to safety, who gets hurt? People also have a direct impact on the cost of the product or service depending on the level of their skill and attention to the work. And people who directly handle equipment have a great impact on how well that equipment is maintained. Even when you collect data for a report, the accuracy of that report depends on the people giving you the data. And, for all these things, you depend on people in order to meet your deadlines. There is no part of the supervisor's job that does not involve people. Therefore, the supervisor *always works with and through people.* Figure 9.1 illustrates how people are at the center of the supervisor's responsibilities. The blank segment represents all of the other responsibilities not shown.

To meet all of these responsibilities successfully, a supervisor must have a relationship of some kind with each of his or her people. When you look carefully at this relationship, it is by no means a one-way street. It is a two-way relationship that affects the kinds of results you will get when striving to meet your responsibilities. Good relationships will give you good results. Poor relationships will give you poor results. Figure 9.1 illustrated that people are at the center

Figure 9.1 People are at the center of a supervisor's responsibilities.

of a supervisor's responsibilities. Figure 9.2 adds a Job Relations line to show that there is a two-way relationship between the supervisor and the people who, for better or worse, affect these responsibilities.

When you experience difficulties with people or when trust is strained, the Job Relations line will bend—a signal that you need to deal with a situation. When trust is high, people give you the benefit of the doubt because they feel you have their best interests in mind and they believe you will do right by them. When that trust is missing, however, you will find yourself "drowning in a puddle," struggling over the most minor details and unable to move forward on even simple issues. The goal, then, is to keep this Job Relations line as *straight*, as *strong*, and as *correct* as possible. This chapter provides an overview of relationship principles; specific strategies that will help maintain smooth relations and keep the Job Relations line strong are covered in Chapter 11.

People Must Be Treated As Individuals

The word *people* has appeared quite a few times in this chapter, but it is important to remember that no two people are alike. As obvious as this may seem, the JR pocket card reminds supervisors that *people must be treated as individuals*. So what makes one employee different from another? When you look at the people at the center of your responsibilities and try to understand this, you will find similarities and differences. One thing your people have in common is the need to work or making a living. Look beyond that, however, and you will see there are a number of factors that make each of your people unique. Your employees can be married or single, have children, or live at home with mom

Figure 9.2   Job Relations line: good supervision is a two-way relationship between the supervisor and his or her people.

and dad. They may come from a rural community or a big city. Some are well educated, some are not. One person is strong or athletic, while another is weak or prone to illnesses. These factors, and many others, make each person unique. They also affect an individual's performance on the job. Figure 9.3 shows four critical factors that shape and define the individuals who work at your plant or office each day. A fifth segment of the figure represents other factors.

Most people don't leave personal concerns or problems at the door when they enter the workplace. One thing or another concerning a person's family, background, health, and so forth, comes through the door with him or her each day. And because individual circumstances change constantly, they may not bring the same things through that door from day to day. For this reason, supervisors have to maintain a steady relationship with each individual to keep up with his or her changing life and attitudes. This may seem daunting and difficult, but when it comes to building strong relationships with people, this effort is necessary and worthwhile. Strong relationships help you make good decisions that take individual differences into account. The goal and purpose here is not about changing people—that is impossible. The goal is to recognize each person's uniqueness and how this affects performance and to act wisely based on this understanding.

Some supervisors question whether it is right, or even legal, to pry into an employee's personal business. This is a delicate issue. There are many areas of a person's life that are off limits, such as medical history, religion, ethnic background, and age. It is also not polite or advisable to intrude on anyone's privacy. You can, however, in the normal course of friendly conversation, learn many

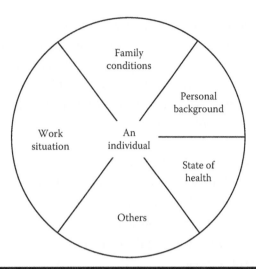

Figure 9.3   Factors that make individuals unique and affect their work.

things about the people who work with you. People generally share information about themselves, especially if they trust you, and trust is something that you are trying to build. They may, for example, tell stories about children, trips, school, relatives, health issues, their house or car, or sports. Take the time to listen and show an interest. This will help you relate to them as individuals.

Keep confidential information confidential. When you do this continuously and reliably, you will earn the trust of the people who confide in you. Some people find this difficult and do not want to be responsible for information they cannot share. Some, in fact, see this as such an unwelcome burden that they turn down promotions. Good supervisors, however, recognize this as one of many responsibilities that come with the territory. More information about this issue, along with some useful suggestions, is provided in Chapter 10.

Supervisor Team Exercise: Using the four common factors that shape individuals, discuss how well you know the employees in your department (without revealing confidential details or private information). Are you familiar with the family situation, background, or health status of your people? How many do you really know well? How many times have you attempted to get to know them better? Do they appear to be open with you or withdrawn? Why do you think this is the case? If an employee is unapproachable, do you know why? Consider how these factors affect your employees' productivity and performance on the job.

What Is a Problem and How Do You Solve It?

A problem is *anything the supervisor has to take action on* when not doing so will have a negative impact or influence on the overall results of the operation. Keeping the Job Relations line straight, strong, and correct is critical here because it is often "people problems" that get in the way of the supervisor's efforts to produce good results. Often it is hard to define just what the problem is. Because people are at the center, it may not be easy to understand or fix.

Participants in TWI classes around the world, when asked what problems they have had with people in their departments, never found it difficult to compile a long list. The list provided here is typical.

- An employee loses interest in the job.
- A person continually fails to come to work on time.
- A person wants to change jobs all the time.
- Plant safety regulations are not followed.
- There is a drop-off in an individual's output.
- Friction between shifts exists.
- There are arguments between individuals.
- New workers do not get along with long-term employees.
- A person is lazy and goofs off on the job.
- There is poor communication between the office and the shop floor.
- A person doesn't follow orders.
- A couple who has broken up but still work together don't get along.
- A person's poor personal hygiene angers coworkers.

These are real issues that surface on a regular basis. To resolve any of these problems and continue meeting his or her responsibilities, a supervisor needs to understand individuals, size up situations, and work with people to resolve them. All supervisors need to have or develop the skill to do this.

Handling a Problem

There are good ways and bad ways to handle people problems. The example below provides some useful insights.

The Joe Smith Problem

Joe Smith was a good worker and his earnings were high. The department was busy and was working regular overtime hours. Some time ago, Joe had fallen into the habit of calling in sick on Mondays. The rush of work was so great that his being out held up a lot of work. The supervisor had spoken to Joe about it several times, but Joe just said that he was making more money in 4 days than he used to make in 2 weeks. The supervisor tried to appeal to Joe's loyalty, but did not get anywhere.

Then Joe got married and he started working five full days regularly. The supervisor decided that the extra money now looked good to Joe, and that was why he came to work regularly. Joe kept up the good record for several months.

Then, one Monday morning, a general salary increase was announced. On Tuesday, Joe failed to come to work. The supervisor decided that the extra money had again brought Joe to the place where he could get along on 4 days' pay. He decided that he was going to teach Joe a lesson, and that the only way to get to Joe was to show him how it would feel to lose 5 days' pay.

When Joe came in on Wednesday, the supervisor was waiting for him on his way to the locker room and shouted out, "Hey, Joe! Don't bother changing. I talked to my boss and I'm suspending you for a week. That'll give you a chance to think over what's in your paycheck. Maybe you'll decide it won't be so bad to get 5 days' pay next time."

This supervisor certainly had a problem. How do you think he handled it? What was the supervisor trying to accomplish? It's pretty clear that what he wanted was for Joe to come to work regularly. Instead, he sent him home with a 1-week suspension.

The supervisor made no attempt to find out why Joe didn't come to work on that particular day. He jumped to the conclusion that Joe, in spite of his apparent change, was after all just an irresponsible person and that he would never be able to count on him. He thought that money was the only thing that mattered to Joe. Another important factor supervisors must take into consideration is the effect a disciplinary action has on the other people in the department. What do you think their reaction was to Joe's supervisor's action? How about the Job Relations line in this department now?

Here's what happened next:

The Joe Smith Problem (continued)

The supervisor suspended Joe. A few days later, at lunch, another supervisor came up to him and said he'd heard he had been pretty hard on Joe Smith. Joe's father had been hurt in an accident the previous Monday night. Joe had left word with the night watchman that he was called out of town, but the guard forgot to report it. When Joe went back to the plant on Wednesday, he didn't know that his supervisor hadn't heard about what had happened.

Do these additional facts throw more light on the situation? Joe had a good record for a while, but the supervisor had decided that the wage increase was the reason for his not coming to work. But Joe's failure to come to work had been for a good reason, and he thought his supervisor had been notified. Let's consider the consequences of the supervisor's actions from three angles.

1. *How does Joe feel toward his supervisor?* Without a doubt, Joe is bitter about being punished for behavior that is valued by all of society, taking care of a parent. How do you think this will affect Joe's job performance in the future?

2. *How do the other people in the department feel about the way Joe was treated?* Word spreads fast in an organization, especially when something happens that affects the people that work there. Other people in the department must feel uneasy, perhaps even angry, about the action taken against Joe. They may worry about what might happen to them if they have to take off work suddenly due to an emergency in the family. The supervisor misunderstood what was happening with Joe. Could the same thing happen to them?

3. *What did this supervisor's action do for production?* If the work in the department was delayed by Joe's being out just 1 day of the week, it would certainly be delayed that much more by his being out for a full 5 days. Did the supervisor's action help production or hurt it? Will this have an effect on the company?

The supervisor was wrong on all three counts. Because the Job Relations line between the supervisor and Joe was not *straight, strong,* and *correct,* the supervisor now finds himself working with people who do not trust his judgment and certainly will not be very cooperative. Moreover, he has created an atmosphere of fear and anxiety instead of trust and respect. Below are four steps that might have made the supervisor handle this situation differently. Every supervisor should follow these steps when trying to handle a people problem:

■ Step 1: Get the facts. Be sure you have the whole story. These facts will form the basis of what you do to resolve the problem.

■ Step 2: Weigh and decide. Weigh the facts carefully and then decide what to do. Resist the temptation to jump to conclusions.

■ Step 3: Take action. Carry out your decision. Don't pass the buck to others. Do not make the human resources department or higher level management responsible for the situation. You are responsible.

■ Step 4: Check results. Follow up to see if your decision and action worked out. Did they help production?

By following the above JR four-step method, there is an excellent chance that you will take the correct action that best solves the problem and avoid the kind of trouble Joe's supervisor created. More information about this JR four-step method is provided in Chapter 10.

Supervisor Team Exercise: Each team member should discuss actions taken with employees that backfired because he or she did not have all the facts or jumped to a wrong conclusion. Were any of these bad decisions caused by miscommunication or incorrect assumptions on either party's side? Discuss how those situations played out after you took the action and what effects they had on production and on employees' attitudes toward you and their work.

Chapter 10

Four Steps of Job Relations

The Job Relations (JR) method, just like the other two Training Within Industry (TWI) programs, uses a four-step method as shown on the JR pocket card (Figure 10.1). This handy tool contains everything you need to follow when applying the JR method, and you should keep it with you at all times.

This chapter revisits the Joe Smith problem and the action his supervisor took. It provides a thorough explanation of the four steps of JR and includes team exercises that you can use to practice the method on one of your own "people problems." The chapter also presents an additional case study to give you further insight on how to apply the JR four-step method.

Supervisor Team Exercise: Review the list of people problems in Chapter 9. Have each team member bring in a people problem that was recently handled or a current problem that needs to be handled. Your problem must involve you and the people you supervise—don't work on someone else's problem because you will not have all the facts or know all of the individuals involved. A recent problem is good because you can remember the facts. You will help the team if you take up a problem that didn't turn out just right because this will create opportunities for the team to look at why things turned out the way they did. A problem you haven't taken action on yet is also good because it is fresh in your mind and pressing.

Have one person describe his or her problem briefly *without telling the action taken or the results*. Remember that the contents of these real problems are confidential and the discussions should never go beyond the team. Make sure everyone on the team agrees to this condition before continuing. Never use real names when telling your story. (You can say "Mr. A," "Ms. B," "Mr. C," etc.)

After hearing the problem, write down (in one sentence) the outcome or solution you envision. How does this compare with what other team members thought? While going through the four steps of

---

HOW TO HANDLE A PROBLEM

Determine Objective

Step 1: Get the facts

- Review the record
- Find out what rules and customs apply
- Talk with individuals concerned
- Get opinions and feelings

Be sure you have the whole story

Step 2: Weigh and decide

- Fit the facts together
- Consider their bearings on each other
- What possible actions are there?
- Check practices and policies
- Consider objective and effect on individual, group, and production

Don't jump to conclusions

Step 3: Take action

- Are you going to handle this yourself?
- Do you need help in handling?
- Should you refer this to your supervisor?
- Watch the timing of your action

Don't pass the buck

Step 4: Check results

- How soon will you follow up?
- How often will you need to check?
- Watch for changes in output, attitudes, and relationships

Did your action help production?

Did you accomplish your objective?

Figure 10.1 JR four-step method pocket card: back side.

the JR process, team members will continue to analyze this particular people problem. The remaining members will have a chance to practice the same process on their own people problems in the last exercise of this chapter.

Get the Objective

You can begin solving a problem without knowing what you want the outcome to be. You may even successfully resolve the issue. But this approach means that you probably didn't get to the root of the problem. To solve a problem well, you need to have a clear idea of where you want to end up so that you can take the appropriate steps to get there. In other words, before beginning the JR four-step method, you need to determine the objective that you want to achieve and create a thesis statement that defines your objective.

TWI note: The objective is something to shoot at and hence may be difficult to determine. Moreover, it may have to be changed in the course of handling the problem. But be sure it is not shortsighted or too narrow in scope. Asking these kinds of questions can help:

- What makes this a problem?
- Just what are you trying to accomplish? What do you want to have happen here?
- What effect is this having on production?
- Are any other people in the department involved or concerned?
- What results do you want to get out of this?

Step 1: Get the Facts

In the problem discussed in Chapter 9, Joe's supervisor did not have the facts, and this led to a bad decision and poor action. Collecting facts effectively is the basis of any successful resolution to a problem, but this means having *all* relevant facts. Supervisors often make the mistake of thinking that the facts include only data and details from physical evidence. But because we are dealing with people, you also need to include what people think and how people feel about the situation.

Item 1: Review the Record

To understand a current problem, the supervisor needs to review the employee's previous record on job performance, career, achievement, attendance, problems, disciplinary actions, and so forth. Companies typically keep such records on file in the form of attendance sheets, performance appraisals, disciplinary reports, and so on. Not all records are paper records. A review of the record includes looking at what the supervisor knows. Joe's supervisor recalled vividly Joe's previous poor record (when Joe had regularly called in sick on Mondays), but he overlooked or ignored Joe's more recent good record (Joe's attendance for several months after he got married). Also keep in mind that a review of the record means looking at all behavior, not just unacceptable or inappropriate behavior.

Item 2: Find Out What Rules and Customs Apply

When supervisors deal with any problem, they invariably run into something covered by company rules and customs. These guidelines help maintain fairness and equality in the workforce. Rules are written standards in the company's policy manual or handbook that everyone needs to follow. A company's customs, on the other hand, are not necessarily in a policy manual; they are precedents set by many accumulated cases that were handled in a fixed way. At Joe's plant, for example, it was apparently a custom for people to call in and let someone know they were not coming to work. Such unwritten customs are just as important as (and sometimes even more important than) written rules.

Item 3: Talk with Individuals Concerned

If supervisors don't talk with the people involved, they may never discover the critical elements that caused the problem in the first place. Joe's supervisor did not take the time to do this. He took action without even asking Joe why he had not come to work the day before. On some levels, this is understandable. Dealing with people problems usually entails uncomfortable situations for supervisors, and there is a strong temptation to avoid confronting people directly about difficult issues. Some supervisors feel it is more appropriate or easier to have someone more experienced handle these problems, someone from human resources, for example. However, if you are to build strong relationships with your people and strengthen the Job Relations line, you must embrace this communication role, no matter how unpleasant, and take responsibility for getting the facts from the people involved. By doing this, you build trust and respect.

Item 4: Get Opinions and Feelings

When you talk with the key individuals concerned, you should be looking for their opinions and feelings. Joe's supervisor didn't think at all about how Joe felt. He focused only on his own preconceived notions about Joe and on his own feelings. Many supervisors, in fact, disregard feelings because they are not based on fact. A key point in JR is that *what a person thinks or feels, whether right or wrong, is indeed a fact to that person, and we must consider it as such.*

For example, some people feel their supervisors do not like them. This may or may not be true. Supervisors are people and, like other people, don't always show what they feel. Nevertheless, if a person *feels* disliked, this feeling is a fact to that person. It is an important piece of information. You cannot understand the real gist of what is happening in a situation without knowing the personal emotions involved.

Caution Point: Be Sure You Have the Whole Story

This is a caution point for the whole of step 1. The more facts you gather, the better the judgment you make. The better the judgment you make, the more likely the action you take will be correct and successful. We pointed out that Joe's supervisor did not have the whole story.

Whenever you deal with a problem concerning people, it is easy to think you understand everything based on your own experiences and then incorrectly assume everyone has had similar experiences. But each person's situation is unique, and it is up to you to get this unique story before taking any action on a problem.

Supervisor Team Exercise: Have the lead member quickly list all the facts to the people problem presented in the previous exercise. The order is not important; just write them down as you think of them based on the story told. Then, to make sure you haven't missed any of the facts, go over each of the four items in step 1 and pick out which facts listed belong with each item. For example, which facts have to do with the record? Was anything missed? If so, fill it in. What information was gathered from talking with the person involved? Was anything missed? Fill it in. Team members can then ask questions about the story, which might bring out additional facts. When the team members feel they have all the facts, ask, "Do you think we have gotten the whole story?"

Step 2: Weigh and Decide

This step consists of two activities, analyzing the facts and determining what you will do to resolve the problem. These two processes are interwoven, and you must do them at the same time. TWI uses the word *weigh* because with people problems, the issues are not always black and white or easy to understand. So you want to weigh the facts and try to determine meaning from what you know, even if you have contradictory facts or are missing pieces to the overall picture. Only after this thorough analysis and review do you decide on the best course of action.

Item 1: Fit the Facts Together

Once you list all the facts concerning a problem, you fit these facts together in a logical pattern (by content, time sequence, subject, etc.) and begin looking for gaps or contradictions. For example, in Joe's case, Joe's father being hurt was an important gap in the facts. If the supervisor had known about this, he might have taken a different course of action.

Many times when we fit the facts together, we also find that certain facts contradict each other. Joe's failure to come to work that day contradicted his recent behavior (coming to work regularly for the past several months). Contradictions can tell you a lot about the real nature of a problem. For example, one person sees an employee's aggressive actions as coercive and threatening, while another views them as a positive attitude of "getting the job done". This underscores the fact that different people see things in different ways. Your job is to see the contradictions and figure out the reasons behind them.

Item 2: Consider Their Bearings on Each Other

Once you begin fitting the facts together, you can consider what bearing they have on each other. A good way to understand this process is to examine the difference in meaning between facts and information. Facts are just the raw data. By themselves, they don't really mean anything. You obtain information when you take these facts and give meaning to them. By taking the facts gathered in step 1 and looking at what bearing they have on each other, you can turn them into useful information that you can act on.

Putting facts side by side may reveal something you may not have realized up front. For instance, if today is the first day of hunting season and half of your team has called in sick, you can put those two facts together, consider their bearings on each other, and deduce that team members are not really sick but out hunting. (Some companies deal with just this situation by making the first day of deer season a paid holiday.) Joe's supervisor looked at the wage increase and Joe's previous bad record. He decided that these two facts accounted for Joe's absence and came to the conclusion that all Joe cared about was money. If he had looked at Joe's recent good record, he might have seen that some other fact had a bearing on what had occurred.

Item 3: What Possible Actions Are There?

Joe's supervisor thought that there was only one option for his situation. This is a common perception among supervisors facing people problems. Because supervisors depend so heavily on their own experiences, they often fall back on what has worked for them in the past and believe that this is the one and only way to fix a problem. One of the most important lessons to learn from JR is that *when you carefully weigh all of the facts in a case, there is usually **more than one** possible action to resolve the problem.*

Take a person who is not performing up to standard. You might simply warn that person to "get up to speed." But a careful look at the reasons for this problem might suggest other possible actions. If, for example, the person is having trouble doing the work, you can provide additional training. If a health problem is involved, you can suggest medical attention or some time off to rest. If marital problems are involved, you can suggest some form of counseling. You might even discover that the problem may be somewhere else further up the line and that the person's performance might improve if that problem is fixed.

Some supervisors (especially those in plants with a long history of employee strife) strongly resist the idea of looking for more than one possible action. These supervisors have learned from the "school of hard knocks" that if they don't rigorously apply a well-defined set of rules and consequences, they will not be able to handle the people doing the work (e.g., if you don't call in when you're out, you're suspended—no exceptions). There are many reasons for this draw-the-line and one-size-fits-all mentality, but it is counterproductive. It is *not* the best way to handle people.

The JR method *does* take into account company practices, policies, and customs to make sure that every possible action complies. It advocates, in all cases, a fair application of all company rules to all employees. But it also advocates that supervisors consider the complexity of people and make a concerted effort to understand that each individual has different motives for his or her actions and behavior. It follows that the corrective action should reflect the particular set of circumstances and people involved. People must be treated as individuals. Listing several possible actions presents the opportunity to weigh the merits of each, picking the one that is best suited to solving a particular problem with a particular person.

What about the case when the employee has broken a no-tolerance policy? When it comes to issues such as critical safety violations, violence in the workplace, or sexual harassment, it is important and appropriate for companies to enforce strict rules regardless of the individual circumstances. In these situations, there may be only one course of action. However, it is still a failure of leadership because these problems did not start when the employees broke the no-tolerance rules. They began as smaller issues that, through supervisor neglect, were allowed to escalate until an unfortunate action was taken. When problems are small, before any egregious acts have taken place, many avenues will be available to prevent them from growing and getting out of hand. In Chapter 11, we will see how supervisors can recognize and get into problems early when there are still many possible actions that can be taken to solve them.

Item 4: Check Practices and Policies

Your possible actions must comply with the company's practices and policies or else they are, quite simply, not possible. A supervisor has to know the ground rules by which the company operates and know whether a possible action falls within those rules. Like long-established customs, practices built and developed over a long period constitute the way things are done in a company, even if they are not written down or formalized in a company's policy manual. If a company has established a practice that there is no excuse for not calling in when you fail to come to work, then that practice has to apply to everyone in the plant. You may also have to follow standards that society sets, many of which are dictated and controlled by state and federal laws. In Joe's case, it would seem unreasonable to most people for the company to penalize him for his actions. Moreover, even though he failed to contact his supervisor, it would seem fair to take into consideration that he made a positive effort to do so.

Item 5: Consider Objective and Effect on Individual, Group, and Production

This item is the evaluation part of step 2, in which you look at each of the possible actions and consider whether they are viable. In JR, you make that decision by checking whether a possible action will meet the objective. Then you consider what effect that possible action will have on the following factors:

1. The individual who is the target of the action
2. The group that will be indirectly influenced by whatever action is taken
3. The production of the department and the company overall

What Joe's supervisor really wanted was for Joe to come to work regularly. This was the supervisor's objective in resolving the problem. When he decided to suspend Joe for a week, he did not consider whether that action would meet *any* of these criteria.

In TWI classes, one of the possible actions that invariably comes up during a review of actual problems is to fire the worker. Sometimes, this is indeed the best thing to do. However, the objective we started out with in solving the problem is usually some variation on "Make Joe (or Mary) a good worker." If you check to see if firing the worker meets this objective, the answer is an emphatic no. Good supervisors who use the JR method know you should always consider if there is anything else you can do to help make an employee a better worker before taking this final option.

If the possible action will help meet the *objective* and have a positive effect on the *person*, the *group*, and *production*, then it is probably worth pursuing. Occasionally, the possible action may be a mixed bag that cannot have a positive effect on all three of these. Say you changed a person's job and the department approved because that person's poor performance was causing everyone to struggle. However, the job change, if perceived as a demotion or a lack of confidence in the employee's work, might demoralize the individual and lead to new problems. In situations like this, someone (or something) benefits and someone (or something) does not, and you have to weigh such options very carefully.

Caution Point: Don't Jump to Conclusions

It is pretty clear that Joe's supervisor jumped to a conclusion when he assumed money was the only reason for Joe's absence. He jumped to the conclusion that he was not going to be able to count on Joe—that Joe was just an irresponsible person. It is very easy to fall into this mode and, because of human nature, very difficult to resist doing so. Because JR emphasizes knowing *all* the facts before drawing conclusions, this caution point is extremely important.

Supervisor Team Exercise: Have the group look at the lead member's people problem and weigh the facts listed by looking for gaps and contradictions and considering their bearings on each other. Then, have *team members* consider possible actions for resolving the problem. Each member who proposes a possible action should identify which facts he or she used to make that decision (this confirms how they fit the facts together). The *lead member* should state whether the proposed possible action violates any practices and policies in his or her department. If so, it should be discarded.

After considering four or five possible actions, the *lead member* should tell the group whether each of them meets the stated objective.

The *lead member* should also identify what effect each would have on (1) the individual, (2) the group, and (3) production. The lead member is the only person qualified to make these judgments. All team members can then discuss times they jumped to conclusions and what the consequences were.

Step 3: Take Action

Sometimes taking action means making someone unhappy or causing emotional upset, so it is understandable to want someone else to do the task. This is a mistake. It is imperative that you directly and personally handle this very important responsibility and handle it well.

Item 1: Are You Going to Handle This Yourself?

The first question to ask when taking action is whether you are *responsible* for handling this problem. This has to be decided by the supervisor. Joe's supervisor, in spite of his other flaws, understood that dealing with Joe's failure to report to work was his responsibility. If you determine that you are the right person to take action on a problem, then it is your responsibility to take the appropriate measures to deal with the problem. (In some cases, the problem may be outside of a supervisor's area of responsibility—e.g., a problem with an outside vendor—and has to be referred to another authority.)

Item 2: Do You Need Help in Handling?

This JR item addresses your *ability* to handle the problem well. This does not mean you pass off the problem to someone else. It simply means that you take action with the help of someone who may be a specialist or someone from a department that specifically handles certain aspects of personnel issues. For example, you may not have the knowledge, experience, or expertise to deal with legal, medical and psychological, or financial aspects of a particular problem and you need assistance from these specialists.

You can also turn to many other people for help in providing solutions to problems, not the least of which may be the person who is the target of that action. As you will see in the Tina problem later in this chapter, this approach may have a better chance of addressing the real cause of a problem. Other people in the department may also be good sources of assistance because they are indirectly affected by any action you take. In either case, when people involved in a problem take a part in its solution, there is a better chance that the action will have good results. Additionally, you may get good assistance from other supervisors who have faced or are facing similar situations.

Item 3: Should You Refer This to Your Supervisor?

Many supervisors like to take action and then inform the boss so that he or she is aware of the situation should it come up again. But if your action is beyond your own *authority*, then you will need approval before you act. Before acting, you need to determine whether your action is within your own authority or if you need your superior's approval. For many day-to-day situations, you may not need to bother your boss; for other issues, you may want approval or to make sure the boss knows what is happening. (Recall that Joe's supervisor informed his boss and got approval to suspend Joe.)

Some supervisors claim, with some frustration, that they have no authority to act when it comes to dealing with people. Keep in mind, though, that **recommending action** *is an action in itself and an important responsibility of supervisors.* The better you get at sizing up situations and recommending good actions, the more confidence your own superiors will have in you.

Item 4: Watch the Timing of Your Action

Joe's supervisor didn't waste any time in suspending Joe after he failed to show up for work, but was this the time for him to act? As with most things in life, timing actions aimed at resolving people problems is critical and influences the effectiveness of the action taken. Even a good action can be spoiled if the timing is inappropriate. Someone who is upset, for example, will have difficulty seeing past emotion. No matter how rational your action is, this person is not likely to understand or agree at this time. On the other hand, if people are aware of a problem and you wait too long to act, they may get discouraged. This is especially critical when morale, safety, or even legal issues are involved. If you do not act quickly, these issues will only fester and grow. As a rule, the most effective way to handle people problems is to deal with them early, when they are still manageable, or to anticipate them and prevent them. Timely actions are one way of maintaining a strong Job Relations line with your people.

Caution Point: Don't Pass the Buck

This caution item does not need much of an explanation as everyone reading this already knows it is bad form to push a "dirty job" onto someone else. Joe's supervisor, to his credit, did not do this. Neither should you.

Supervisor Team Exercise: Have the lead member now tell what action he or she took, write it down, and point out which facts were used to come to that decision. If the action is pending, just write, "Pending action."

Apply the four items in step 3 to the problem. Was the member the appropriate person to handle the problem? Did he or she get any outside or professional help and was that appropriate? Was it necessary to refer the action to the supervisor? Was the action taken at the appropriate time? As each question is answered, ask "Why?" and try to get answers that emphasize *responsibility, ability,* and *authority.* If this is a pending problem where no action has been taken yet, ask the above questions in the future tense ("When you take action, will you get any outside help?"). If the team member passed the buck in this case, discuss the consequences.

TWI note: The TWI philosophy of learn by doing stresses practicing the method and not solving any one individual problem. In these exercises, then, the team is not trying to pass judgment on the action taken by the person giving the problem, nor is it trying to decide whether the action taken was good or bad. The member giving the problem is the only person in the position to get all the facts and to take action on it. For everyone else on the team, the purpose in dealing with these problems is solely to practice using the JR four-step method.

Step 4: Check Results

When you take action on a people problem, it is always necessary to see if you succeeded in resolving that problem. An action that was successfully used with one person in the past will not necessarily work on another person, even if the problem is similar. Joe's supervisor never even considered checking the results. It was only when another supervisor made him aware of what had actually happened that he discovered that his action was incorrect. This is not unusual. Even when supervisors follow the first three steps of JR, they often fail to *follow up* on the results of their actions. This step lets you see if the action worked and will also help you learn to make even better decisions in the future.

Item 1: How Soon Will You Follow Up?

When it comes to implementing solutions to people problems, you need to make your first check as soon as you can reasonably expect results, and not before. This sometimes calls for a waiting period, especially when people's feelings are involved. You may need to give them some time to let their emotions run their course. On the other hand, if urgent issues, such as quality or safety, are involved, you may need to check right away to prevent defects or accidents.

Item 2: How Often Will You Need to Check?

You can settle some problems quickly and decisively, but with most people-related issues, you may need to keep an eye on the situation for quite some time to be sure that it doesn't recur. Moreover, you should be aware that an action you have taken can cause other problems. Although this is generally not intentional, it does occur, and it is something you need to watch out for. Solutions to people problems are almost never a slam dunk. Most supervisors, in fact, find that they have to continue checking on many of their actions indefinitely because of the possibility that the problem will resurface.

Item 3: Watch for Changes in Output, Attitude, and Relationships

When you go to check on the results of your action, just what is it that you will be looking for? First, you look to see if your actions have improved or adversely affected the *output* (the work of the person involved). This is a quantitative issue. Your role as a supervisor is to help the company stay profitable. If your efforts are impeding this, you are not doing your most basic job.

When dealing with people and people problems, however, you cannot check results by looking only at objective figures, such as production totals or defect quantities. You have to observe people's behavior, and this will be an indication of the success of your action. Checking the *attitude* of the person involved will let you see whether that person has accepted your actions. Even if a person does not like the action you took, experience shows that most people will accept an action as long as they feel that you treated them fairly. If you have built a strong Job Relations line with each of your people, they are more likely to accept the action because they trust you and believe you are trying to represent the best interests of everyone concerned.

The third thing to look for is the effect your action had on the overall group. Even when other people in the department are not directly involved in the problem, their ideas and opinions are important because the outcome will most likely affect them or their jobs. When you examine the *relationships* among people in the department—Are they getting along? How are they treating the person who was the subject of the action? Do you detect any resentment between them?—you will know if your actions are working by how they are behaving.

Caution Point: Did Your Action Help Production?

In spite of the best intentions, supervisors often take actions that have a negative impact on production. Because Joe's supervisor didn't get the facts, he chose an action that gave him poor results. Suspending Joe for a week hurt the production of the entire plant. Regardless of what your company produces, whether it is a product or a service, you need to be sure that what you do as a supervisor contributes in a positive way to that overall effort.

Did You Accomplish Your Objective?

You begin the JR four-step method by determining what the objective of your problem-solving effort will be, and you end it by questioning whether you achieved that objective. If you have a clear vision of the end results you want, you can determine how successful you were in handling the problem. There will be times when you will not achieve your objective, but your efforts will give you invaluable experience analyzing where you went wrong and how to avoid these failures in the future.

There is no recipe for handling people, nor is there ever only one way to respond to a people problem, but the JR four-step method will serve as a steady guide for leading your efforts in the right direction. Combining the method with your own *common sense and judgment*, which you develop through experience, you are certain to achieve good results.

The exercise below will help you see how well you have grasped the JR four-step method so far. The three case studies that follow will help you gain experience in applying JR. The Tina problem in this chapter stresses step 1 (get the facts), the Mike problem in Chapter 11 stresses step 2 (weigh and decide), and the team leader problem, also in Chapter 11, stresses steps 3 and 4 (take action and check results).

Supervisor Team Exercise: Discuss the lead member's people problem, applying the three items in step 4. When did the lead member make the first check, and how long did he or she continue checking up on the action? What affect did the action have on the person's output and attitude and on the relationships between people in the department? Was this action beneficial to the overall production of the company? If this is a pending problem where no action has been taken yet, discuss these items in the future tense (e.g., "How long will you wait after taking action before you do your first check?"). Revisit the *original* objective you wrote down in the first team exercise. Did you achieve it? If not, why not and what could have been done differently?

Applying the JR Four-Step Method to the Tina Problem

As we saw in both the Job Instruction (JI) and Job Methods (JM) sections, the best way to understand the four-step method is to see how to apply each item of each step to a real problem in a workplace. The Tina problem is a common people problem that supervisors face every day: poor performance from an employee who brings a problem from home to work.

Because the success of steps 2–4 depends on getting all the facts, the Tina problem case study focuses on step 1. More specifically, it shows how to obtain personal opinions and feelings to get at the whole story. We want to know what the supervisor said and how she said it to learn her technique, so most of the case study is presented as a dialog.

The Tina Problem

The supervisor was out in the shop one day when she noticed Tina, an operator, reaching into a machine. She called out to her in a stern and loud voice, "Tina, I've told you to shut off that machine when you take the guard off!" The supervisor was angry. Apparently, she had warned Tina about this before.

Tina then yelled back, "If you want to fire me, why don't you say so instead of harassing me all the time!" Tina was angry, too.

Supervisor: "Take it easy. I don't want to fire you, Tina. I just don't want you to fire yourself by getting your hand mashed. The number of times that machine has to be adjusted makes me think there must be something wrong with it."

Tina: "Well, stop harassing me!"

The supervisor was certainly facing a problem here, and before she took any action, here is what went very quickly through her mind: "Now, let's see. I've known Tina a long time. She's been one of the best people in the department. She says I've been harassing her, but she's been careless about safety. Yesterday, I had to talk to her about quality. And it hasn't been so long since I had to tell her that her line wasn't keeping up with the rest. What's happened to Tina? I guess I have been on her back a lot. But, it was always something that had to be done. I can't have her taking chances the way she does."

The supervisor suggested that they meet later on that day to talk things over. She told Tina that she would let her know when she could get someone to relieve her.

*Why do you think the supervisor didn't talk to Tina right then and there, when the problem occurred? They were both angry, and any discussion they would have had would have been overshadowed and drowned out by their emotions. It wouldn't have done any good to stay there and **argue** with Tina on the plant floor or while they were both angry.*

That afternoon, Tina came to the supervisor's office.

Supervisor: "Hello, Tina. Please, sit down. Now, Tina, I guess you think I've been after you. I don't mean to do anything like that. A couple of times I felt I had to stop you because you were doing something dangerous. And there have been a couple of times lately when your work hasn't been quite up to par. I'm used to quality work and plenty of it from you. Every time I see you taking a chance that might cause trouble, I've got to stop you. When your work isn't up to standard, I've got to say something about that, too."

"Now, is there something the matter with the machine? I know you're always raising the guard and reaching into it. If there's something wrong with that machine, I want to get it fixed."

The supervisor is trying the obvious thing first—to see if the trouble is connected with the machine. It's a straightforward observation to which only Tina knows the answer and a good way to get the discussion started without focusing directly on Tina and her work behavior.

Tina: "Well, if you think I'm going to run over to that switch, pull it, and hang the 'Don't Touch' sign on it, you're just crazy. You're yelling now about how little I get done. If I had to spend half of my time turning that switch on and off, I wouldn't get anything done. And the other day, you said the parts were below standard. Well, if I didn't fix that machine, they'd all be below standard."

*Tina wasn't going to make it easy. The supervisor could have cut in there and told her it wouldn't take half of her time to turn off the switch. She could have argued as Tina vented her frustration with a lot of unreasonable claims. But she had told Tina to come talk and she wasn't going to **interrupt** her.*

Supervisor: "Now, Tina, there's more to it than breaking a safety rule. There's a reason behind that rule. You could get your hand crushed."

Tina: "And that would cost the company money, wouldn't it?"

*With this comment of Tina's, the supervisor might **jump to the conclusion** that Tina was angry at the company about money. But was that how Tina really felt? The supervisor did not fall into that trap.*

Supervisor: "Oh, sure it would cost the company money, but have we made you think that's all we're interested in?"

Tina: "Well, that's all that counts with some people." Tina was bitter about something.

Supervisor: "It would cost us a good person. And that's a harder thing to replace than money."

Tina (letting out a sigh and more quietly): "Well, not everybody feels that way." It looked like she was thinking about the importance of money to some people.

Tina had been pretty hard to talk to up to this point, but this gave the supervisor something to follow up on: Was that what Tina really thought—that money was the only important thing to some people?

Supervisor: "Why are you so uptight about money? You're doing all right that way, aren't you? Didn't you tell me last spring that you were planning to buy a house? You're going to need two people to get that house together, aren't you?"

Tina: "House? Yeah, we were. Except that all our savings was in the stock market. It's all gone now. Banks don't care about you if you don't have a down payment. Since then, it seems all my husband and I do is fight—mostly over money."

Supervisor: "I'm sorry, Tina. I didn't know. I just wanted to get you thinking about what an injury to you might mean to somebody else."

Tina: "Well, it doesn't mean anything anymore. Ten years of savings down the drain. There's no way we could save enough to get the bank to give us a loan. Nobody cares about what happens to us anyway. And I don't need to try to make any more money or save it either. It changes a lot of things."

*This kind of problem takes careful handling on the part of the supervisor. She doesn't want Tina to have an accident and wants to get the production in the department back to normal. She also wants to stay on good terms with Tina and is in a very delicate situation because Tina is vulnerable and emotionally exposed. She had a chance here to make a speech and tell Tina that everyone goes through hard times like she is facing now, but that things always work out in the end. However, she is disciplined in her approach with Tina and is going to **listen** to her and **not do all the talking herself**.*

Supervisor: "That's really a shame, Tina. And I don't have an easy answer for your problems. But I can tell you one thing, and that is I need you. I need you to help me figure out why this line isn't running well. I can see why you've gotten a bit careless about taking chances. But I know you wouldn't be taking those chances unless something else had been wrong. Now, is the machine worn? Does it need overhauling? How are the tools?"

There seems to be two things to look at here. The first is the person, and that is the most important thing. The second is the machine.

Tina: "No, it isn't the machine. The parts aren't coming through the same as they used to. There's a burr left on them, and after so many have gone through, well, I just have to clean the machine out. That's why I had to take off the guard, and I just forgot to put it on again."

The story isn't finished, but at this point, you can begin to apply the JR four-step method to the Tina problem. Refer to the JR pocket card (Figure 10.1), "How to Handle a Problem," so you can see how the supervisor used the four steps.

The first thing the supervisor did, before applying the steps and before talking to Tina, was to *determine the objective*. The question here is, "Just what was Tina's supervisor trying to accomplish?" What did she want from Tina?

Remember when the problem broke out and she took a few moments to gather her thoughts, she considered that she didn't want Tina to have an accident and wanted her to be a safe worker. At the same time, she was struggling with production and quality problems, so she wanted to get production back up to where it was supposed to be. Putting these all together, she determined that her objective was *to make Tina a safe worker and get production back to normal.*

Notice that the objective is a simple, clear, and direct description of the desired outcome of the problem. It gives Tina's supervisor something to shoot for as she goes through the problem-solving process using the JR four-step method. Now, let's look at how the supervisor used each of the four steps and the items under each step to get all the facts and find a good solution to this problem.

Step 1: Get the Facts on the Tina Problem

Below are the facts that the supervisor listed after talking to Tina and looking closely at the situation.

- Was a good worker.
- Quality and quantity down.
- Broke safety rule.
- Careless.
- Warned before.
- Talked back.
- Failed to buy a house.
- Felt nobody cared.
- Burrs on parts.

She just quickly wrote down these facts as she remembered them. She didn't number them or use bullets or any other type of notation because she simply wanted to get them on paper without any special emphasis or meaning, without any premature judgment or any preconceived notions. As she goes through the items of step 1, she will be able to determine if she missed anything in her initial listing of the facts.

Item 1: Review the Record

The supervisor looked at Tina's previous record in terms of performance, career, achievement, and so on. The facts she already listed for this item were that Tina was a good worker, was being careless, and had been warned before, and quality and quantity were down. These facts all relate to things that had happened prior to the problem and may or may not have been part of the written record. The supervisor also included what she knew about Tina, in this case that Tina had been a good worker but was now being careless about her work. The supervisor looked at these facts and tried to see if these helped her to remember any similar facts concerning Tina's record that she may have missed. After careful review, she felt that she had gotten them all.

Item 2: Find Out What Rules and Customs Apply

In reviewing the second item, the supervisor had already listed the following facts: Tina broke a safety rule and talked back. In breaking a safety rule by reaching into the machine without turning it off, Tina was breaking a written rule. Talking back to her supervisor was most likely breaking a custom set by precedent. While not necessarily written down in the rulebook, the custom had the same force as a rule. It was obviously not an accepted practice, so Tina's supervisor put it down as a pertinent fact in this case. The supervisor reviewed the facts under this item and couldn't think of any others.

Items 3 and 4: Talk with Individuals Concerned and Get Opinions and Feelings

The most important individual in this problem was Tina, and the supervisor got several important facts because she took the time to talk with Tina and get her opinions and feelings: Tina failed to buy a house, felt nobody cared, and burrs were on parts. (Just how she got these facts will be discussed in more detail at the end of this chapter.)

The final item under step 1 is the caution point for the whole step: *be sure you have the whole story.* By reviewing the record, rules, and customs, and because she made the effort to talk with Tina to get her opinions and feelings, the supervisor got all of the pertinent facts and felt she had the whole story.

Step 2: Weigh and Decide on the Tina Problem

To *weigh* the facts in Tina's problem and put some order and meaning to certain individual facts or groups of facts, the supervisor used the first two items under step 2. She began looking for gaps and contradictions and considering the relationships between the facts.

Items 1 and 2: Fit the Facts Together and Consider Their Bearings on Each Other

The goal of the first two items is to take the raw facts and turn them into meaningful information that helps a supervisor understand a situation clearly and come up with good possible actions. Tina's supervisor saw there was a contradiction between the facts that Tina had been a good worker and now she was being careless. She also connected related facts to see what meaning she could draw from those relationships. The fact that Tina felt nobody cared about her helped to explain why she was being careless and why she broke a safety rule, even after she had been warned about it. The fact that there were burrs on the parts helped to explain why the quality and the quantity of the production were suffering and why Tina was reaching into the machine—to clean out the burrs.

Item 3: What Possible Actions Are There?

To *decide* what to do about Tina's problem, Tina's supervisor began considering possible actions. Initially, she came up with the following:

- Warn Tina about safety rules.
- Report bad parts.
- Tell Tina a house isn't everything.
- Give Tina a penalty suspension.

The supervisor was not yet ready to act. This was a brainstorming process during which she entertained *all possibilities* without judgment before drawing conclusions and taking action. The supervisor knew that the more possible actions she could list, the better the likelihood that she would come up with an effective solution.

> **TWI note:** One of the advantages to entertaining a variety of possible actions is that one idea, however unreasonable or even nonsensical, can lead to discovering possibilities not noticed before. In a Job Relations class demonstration once, someone suggested, "Hang a diaper over his head" as a possible action because he felt the employee in question was acting like a baby. This silly suggestion led to a discussion over why the employee was acting childishly, and the supervisor admitted that he, in fact, might have been treating the employee like a child. This led to other, more serious possible actions to resolve the problem, such as "Treat him with more dignity."

Item 4: Check Practices and Policies

As previously noted, you may not be able to implement some of the possible actions because they break a company practice or policy. In warning Tina about the safety rules, the supervisor would not go against any policies. The next possible action, reporting the bad parts, was also proper and good practice. Consoling Tina by telling her that owning a house isn't everything in life did not go against any written policies, but the supervisor knew it might not be a good practice to give employees personal advice on investments. Finally, Tina's supervisor looked at the possible action of suspension. She realized that she would have to check into the policy on suspensions before taking such a harsh action because certain conditions would have to be met first.

Item 5: Consider Objective and Effect on Individual, Group, and Production

Applying this item to *each* of the possible actions helps determine which possible actions might give the best results for meeting the objective. In this case, the objective was to make Tina a safe worker and get production back to normal. The supervisor asked herself, "Would warning Tina about the safety rules help meet the objective?" The answer was no. She's been warned before, but she doesn't seem to care whether she's fired or even hurt. She also felt that warning Tina again might only aggravate her situation and make her feel more defensive. On the other hand, she considered the effect of a warning on the group. Other employees in the area may be aware that Tina is break-ing the rules and might not be happy she's getting away with that, so hear-ing her being warned might have a positive effect on the group. Finally, she considered what effect a warning would have on production. She decided this would still not resolve the problem of why Tina had to keep opening up the machine—the burrs on the parts.

Tina's supervisor had to question each of the possible actions while keeping in mind this step's caution point, *don't jump to conclusions*, and keep an open mind as she went through the entire weigh and decide process. Questioning each item in this step would help her choose and pursue the best possible action(s). Let's return to the Tina story and see what happened next and what action Tina's supervisor finally took.

The Tina Problem (continued)

Supervisor: "I can see why that [burrs on parts] would cause you trouble. Suppose we go down and take a look at those parts. Now, I feel bad about your money problems, but I do thank you for helping me. And I must tell you that we cannot tolerate any more breaking of the safety rules."

*Throughout the entire process, the supervisor had listened sympathetically to Tina and had **encouraged her to talk about the things that were important to her**.*

As soon as the supervisor got something specific to work on, the bad parts, she immediately went to the shop floor to check on this. After returning to her office, she called her own boss.

Supervisor: "Jim, can I come up a minute? I want to talk to you about the parts we're getting from the punch press department. They're not coming through clean. I have a good operator on our line, and it's interfering with her work and slowing down our output."

That's the end of the story. The supervisor looked at all of the facts and felt she had the complete story. She found out why Tina was always trying to catch up with production and why she was careless about breaking the safety rules. The story has an obvious moral: sometimes the addition of just one more fact may suggest or preclude a possible action.

Step 3: Take Action on the Tina Problem

As you can see below, Tina's supervisor did a combination of things; the order in which she did them is important. Here are the action items:

- Told Tina she was sorry.
- Asked for Tina's help.
- Warned Tina about safety.
- Checked parts.
- Reported faulty parts.

These action items were all based on the facts that the supervisor got in step 1 and weighed carefully in step 2. In order to take these actions effectively, she had to apply the four items in step 3. Let's see how she did this.

Item 1 is "Are you going to handle this yourself?" This was a simple decision. Tina's problem was the supervisor's problem because Tina worked in her area. Therefore, she had the *responsibility* to ensure Tina's safety on the job and the proper output of quality product from the department. Item 2 is "Do you need help in handling?" Tina's help was all that was necessary. The supervisor felt she had the *ability* to carry out each part of her action plan and so did not need the help of specialists or other professionals. Item 3 is "Should you refer this to your supervisor?" The supervisor did refer the problem to her own supervisor, but only for the purpose of getting good parts. She did not mention Tina's troubles because there was absolutely no need to tell anyone else about them. Although she was in a position to deal directly, and confidentially, with Tina's personal issues, she did not have the *authority* to fix the defective parts and needed her boss to work with the punch press department on solving the part problem.

The fourth item, *watch the timing of your action*, is critical. Tina's supervisor did not lose any time in acting, and this made her action successful. Remember that even a good action can be spoiled if the timing is missed. In this case, the supervisor did a good job of listening to Tina and was quick to sympathize with her problems. Then, once she found out about the bad parts, she immediately went to check on them and report the problem to her own boss for correction. The effect of this quick response is easy to see. Tina felt her supervisor understood her situation and took it seriously enough to respond right away. This would not only build trust in the relationship but would motivate Tina to work safely, since she now had proof that someone indeed cared about her situation. In addition, the burr problem was resolved and made production in the department more efficient and safer. The supervisor was also careful to avoid the mistake of ignoring the caution point for all of step 3: *don't pass the buck.* She personally took strong and effective action.

Step 4: Check Results on the Tina Problem

Although the Tina story does not cover this, it is a good idea to look at the four items and determine how Tina's supervisor should follow up with her action. The first of these is "How soon will you follow up?" Because of her concern for Tina's safety and the possibility of a serious accident, the supervisor wanted to check right away. To follow up, when she can reasonably assume the parts problem has been corrected, she will also check on this. The second item is "How often will you need to check?" The supervisor will have to continue checking for some time because Tina's personal and emotional problems may take time to heal. She will want to make sure that Tina's situation has stabilized and she is working safely.

When Tina's supervisor checks on her action, she will follow the third item on the JR pocket card: *watch for changes in output, attitudes, and relationships.* There is a good chance that her action will help in all three of these, but she'll be sure of that when she reviews the caution point for all of step 4: *Did your action help production?* Because she got to the root of the problem, the burrs on the parts, there is no question that her action will help production. At the same time, because she treated Tina as an individual, she has very likely strengthened the Job Relations line between them.

The last item on the JR pocket card is "Did you accomplish your objective?" Tina's supervisor wanted to make Tina a safe worker and to get production back to normal. Along with common sense and judgment, having this clear objective throughout the entire process helped the supervisor apply the JR four-step method to resolve the problem successfully and meet this objective.

> **TWI note:** The TWI developers built the JR method on simple, commonsense principles of human interaction that are easy to understand and apply. Their focus was on treating people as individuals, building strong relationships of trust through good communication and understanding, and maintaining good relations with *all* people on a regular basis. The TWI developers did not try to invent new terminology for old concepts. Nor did they place their focus on only handling people problems. Instead, they made JR easy to master by using the same scientific four-step methodology of the other two TWI programs, JI and JM, while providing insights and techniques on preventing problems before they occur. (Chapter 11 addresses prevention in detail.)

How to Get Opinions and Feelings

One of the main reasons for studying the Tina problem was to see how the supervisor was able to obtain personal opinions and feelings while getting the facts in step 1. This is perhaps one of the most difficult and challenging parts of the method and merits some additional guidance. You can certainly see what might have happened if this supervisor had *not* decided to get more facts before she took action on the problem. She would have been unaware of Tina's personal problems and insensitive to the reasons behind her breaking the safety rules. In addition, without working with Tina on this personal level, she would never have found out about the problem with the faulty parts.

It was only after Tina lowered her resistance and revealed her feelings that she was able to talk about what was really going wrong with the work. This is very common behavior when people are emotional about a situation. The real causes of the problem are buried under personal issues that are foremost in the employee's mind. Because Tina's supervisor took the time to hear her out, Tina was able to see past her own troubles and reveal the true nature of why she broke the safety rule.

Considering all the rules and legalities of obtaining and handling confidential information concerning people, do you think Tina's supervisor was justified in getting Tina to talk about her personal affairs? This, of course, ultimately depends on the individual and the problem. You cannot force people to tell you information that is not directly related to the work itself. In this case, Tina's supervisor mentioned buying the house only after Tina complained about how an accident to her would cost the company money. The supervisor countered that Tina should be doing OK with money because she was saving to buy a house and that an accident to her would cripple her family's ability to pay for one. In this case, Tina's supervisor felt she knew Tina well enough to discuss things she already knew about her. This demonstrates why it is important for supervisors to concern themselves with the feelings of their people—personal issues affect the output of the work they do.

On the other hand, when Tina's supervisor talked to her own boss, she did not reveal any of the personal information she had about Tina. She could have said, "I have a girl down here who lost her shirt in the stock market!" Instead, she said, "I have a good worker down here." Good supervisors take their roles and responsibilities seriously and never reveal personal information to others without permission. This is one important way to keep the two-way Job Relations line strong. Below are six tips that will help you work effectively with people to get the whole story. They are specifically connected to Tina's story, but you can easily use these tips in developing your own skill set for JR.

Six Tips to Get Opinions and Feelings: Tina Example

- *Tip 1: Don't argue.* Do you ever satisfactorily settle anything by an argument? When emotions are charged, the mind is clouded, and arguing doesn't lead to the real causes of the problem. Tina's supervisor arranged to meet Tina later on in the day at a specified time.

- *Tip 2: Encourage the individual to talk about what is important to him or her.* It took a lot of encouragement to get Tina to talk about what was important to her—her struggles with money and buying a home. The supervisor had to help her to say what was wrong by following up on her comments about the importance of money to some people.

- *Tip 3: Don't interrupt.* When you are telling a story and someone interrupts you, do you feel like continuing? Tina, because she was upset and defensive, made many wild claims, and it would have been easy for the supervisor to cut in and tell her she was being unreasonable. But after Tina started talking, the supervisor did not interrupt and let her speak her piece.

- *Tip 4: Don't jump to conclusions.* The supervisor could have spoiled everything by jumping to the conclusion that Tina was just angry at the company about money when she claimed an accident to her would cost the company money. She avoided the temptation to do this.

- *Tip 5: Don't do all the talking yourself.* The supervisor had many opportunities to make a speech—on the importance of safety or on how things always work out in the end. It is very tempting to want to try to fix other people's problems, thinking that we know what's wrong with them based on our own experiences or background. However, because each person is unique, we cannot assume that we know all the answers.

- *Tip 6: Listen.* Finally, we can certainly say that Tina's supervisor was a good listener. Good communicators are always good listeners, and the supervisor knew that the best way to get facts about Tina's feelings and opinions was to listen.

Supervisor Team Exercise: Now is the time for all of the other members of the team to review their people problem with the team. Have each member present his or her problem, covering all four steps and following the instructions from the previous team exercises at the end of each step. Be sure not to use real names when describing the problem. Have the presenting member give the objective to the problem and see if the group agrees. In step 1, list all the facts, checking the card to be sure you haven't missed any. Let the group join in with questions so that additional facts may be brought out. In step 2, let members of the group offer possible actions and state which facts they used to come to their conclusions. The team member presenting the problem should confirm if any practices and policies would be violated and then evaluate each possible action. Then, in steps 3 and 4, let the presenter tell how he or she handled each item of each step and why. If it is a pending action, the presenters should say how they *will* handle each when they actually do take action and follow up on the problem. Confirm if they feel they have reached their objective.

Finally, have each team member discuss the problem in light of the Tina problem and the six tips to get opinions and feelings. While getting the facts to your people problem, in step 1, were you thorough in getting opinions and feelings? Were you able to use any of the tips that Tina's supervisor used so effectively? Did the information obtained play a role in your final action? If you didn't get these facts, and they came up later, would it have changed your action?

Chapter 11

Problem Prevention Using JR's Foundations for Good Relations

Chapter 10 illustrated how the Job Relations (JR) four-step method guides supervisors down a systematic path of problem solving to arrive at actions that solve problems and meet objectives. But what if you could prevent these problems from happening in the first place? Or address problems early, while they are still small? Many supervisors say that most of their big problems result from smaller problems that were neglected or poorly handled. This happens for a reason. In most cases, problems that are big and complicated right from the start tend to get immediate attention. Someone says, "This is a tough one. I'd better deal with it carefully." On the other hand, small problems often get ignored or mishandled. Because such problems seem insignificant, there is a tendency to jump to conclusions and make poor decisions. This occurs because the person dealing with the problem perceives it as minor and does not take the time to get the facts or think them through carefully. Before long, these minor problems grow into big headaches. What started as a small fire that could have been put out with a cup of water becomes a blaze that needs the fire department.

In Job Relations, the old saying "if you take care of the little things, the big things will take care of themselves" is especially appropriate. In most cases, the only reason the big problems exist is because you ignored the little ones. Moreover, *when it comes to people, the little things really are the big things.* Supervisors often complain about people with "attitude problems" who disrupt the work of everyone around them. They are the "troublemakers" who turn every small issue into a crisis and try to convince anyone who will listen that their supervisor is "out to get them" or that there is a company conspiracy to take advantage of the workers. When you engage with these types, you can usually trace their bitterness back to some small episode that the supervisor or someone else handled poorly. Maybe they did not get recognition or thanks for a good or special effort. Maybe they believe they were unfairly criticized or punished for something that was not their fault. Maybe they resent or feel threatened by a recently implemented change in company policy. Maybe they feel they could be doing more in their job and are being held back by a supervisor who is not interested in their potential.

People with these feelings and attitudes can really cause trouble. Implementing techniques and methods for fighting these "problem people" can be a long and difficult process; learning how to handle all of your people correctly and effectively before they "go sour" and cause problems is much smarter. In other words, a method that treats *everyone* fairly and equally can *prevent* problems or catch them *before* they become burning blazes. The purpose of this chapter is to illustrate how this work smarter not harder strategy for human relations works.

How to See Problems Coming

As defined in Chapter 9, a problem is *anything the supervisor has to take action on.* When you understand how problems come up, you can learn to see them coming and take timely action on them. According to Training Within Industry (TWI), there are four ways to see a problem coming.

Four Ways Problems Come Up

1. *Sizing up before it happens.* Sometimes you may be aware of things about to occur that might disturb your people. For example, you know that management may be planning a change in policy, such as a promotion policy based on ability rather than seniority. You have the opportunity to do some preventive work and take action that can help minimize, if not eliminate, the potential problem.

2. *Being tipped off.* If you're attentive to people and on the watch in your department, you'll notice changes in people's work or attitudes. For example, suppose a normally pleasant person suddenly becomes quarrelsome. That is a problem in itself, but it is indicative of something else that, if not addressed, can grow into something more difficult to handle. Effective supervisors get into, and resolve, these kinds of issues early on. This is one reason to build a strong Job Relations line with each of your people. If you know them as human beings rather than just workers, you are more likely to be tipped off when things change.

3. *Coming to you.* Some problems are presented directly to you (e.g., someone asks for a raise or a transfer or someone comes to you with a concern or a question). Good supervisors keep an open door for their people to come to them with their issues, and it is your responsibility to listen and respond to them.

4. *Running into.* Finally, there are the problems that you just run right smack into you. (For example, you tell an employee to do something and he or she refuses, or an employee who has been warned about coming in late keeps coming in late.) On such problems, supervisors must act immediately.

The important thing to remember here is timing, including the timeline you have available for taking action. When you "size up a potential problem" or when you are attentive and tipped off, the real trouble has not yet started, and you have time to deal with the situation before it breaks open. It is much easier to handle a problem in these early stages because you will be closer to the problem's root causes. By the time a problem "comes to you", it is already serious enough for someone to bring it to your attention. If you are "running into" a problem, it is probably in full blaze and has generated additional, new problems. This will make your job of finding an appropriate action even more difficult and time-consuming.

People will swallow a lot of job-related frustration, anger, disappointment, and fear, but the container in which these negative emotions are stored does not have a safety valve. Sooner or later, the whole container explodes. In the early stages of a problem, you may not notice that there is anything wrong because people are in the bottling up emotions stage. Your job as a good supervisor is to understand how problems emerge and escalate and to use your skills to solve them at an early stage.

Making Good Decisions

In this case study, a supervisor had several opportunities to tackle a problem early but failed to do so at each stage. He then took a bad action with poor results. Reviewing this problem will help you understand the four ways problems come up and will also give you a chance to practice the JR four-step method. Pay particular attention to step 2, *weigh and decide*, and refer to the Job Relations pocket card (Figure 10.1).

The Mike Problem

An office supervisor had received several reports about Mike, who had been working in the office for about 7 months. Mike evidently was not fully cooperative with other office members. For example, when the office had its weekly meetings to discuss the progress of current projects and plan future projects, Mike frequently skipped these meetings. When he did attend, he did not participate.

Mike had been a salesperson prior to being transferred to the office. Unfortunately, he had been involved in a car accident and hurt his foot, so he wasn't able to drive a car for 6 months. Mike was transferred to the office so he could get full pay instead of partial pay under workers' compensation. Mike had been uncooperative since being transferred into the office. Once his foot had healed, he made it known that he didn't like working in the office and that he wanted to return to his former sales position as soon as possible.

The office was quite busy, however, and needed the extra worker. While Mike was not cooperative, he was capable. Moreover, Mike had recently been assigned to a critical 6-month project to be done jointly with one of the other people in the office. Soon after, the team member complained that Mike wasn't putting any effort into the project and had refused to make a required report.

The office supervisor confronted Mike and told him to put more effort into his work. Mike replied that he didn't care one bit about the project or the office and just wanted to get back on the road again. The supervisor was pretty angry about his attitude. People in the department were watching to see what would happen.

The office supervisor decided it was time to take action.

In the JR four-step method, the first thing to do is *get the objective*. What did the supervisor want from Mike? Because the office was busy, it was important for Mike to contribute to the work. At the same time, it was also important for the supervisor to keep in mind the feelings of the other employees in the department. Clearly, the supervisor's objective here was to *get the job done without upsetting the department*.

Step 1: Get the Facts on the Mike Problem

The task here is to list all of the facts you know right now, in no particular order. The following list shows the facts that are currently available:

- In the office for 7 months.
- Not cooperative in the office.
- Foot hurt.
- In office for full pay.
- Foot healed.
- Asked to return to sales.
- Office busy.
- 6-month project.
- Refused to make report.
- Supervisor angry.
- Department watching.

Item 1 is to *review the record* of Mike's previous performance, career, achievement, and so on. This includes most of the facts on the list and combines information from written sources (e.g., Mike's foot was hurt and he was in the office for full pay) with information that came from observing Mike's behavior (e.g., Mike was not cooperative and asked to return to sales). The list also includes facts about conditions in the office (e.g., he had been in the office for 7 months and the office was busy).

Item 2 is to *find out what rules and customs apply*. In this case, the fact that Mike refused to make a report is a clear violation of the company rules for doing work. The next two items are *talk with individuals concerned* and *get opinions and feelings*. The office supervisor did confront Mike to tell him to put more effort into his work. Whether he wanted to or not, he also heard Mike's feelings on the 6-month project. Mike told him that he "didn't care one bit" about the project and just wanted to "get back on the road again." Opinions and feelings are easy to see in this case. The supervisor is angry about Mike's attitude toward his work; that the department is watching shows that people have put up with Mike's negative attitude for some time and want to see some action taken to resolve the issue.

Now it is time to address the caution item under step 1: *be sure you have the whole story*. Since Mike only came into the office 7 months ago, there is virtually no information about his previous work in sales. The whole story on Mike is not available, but because these were all the facts the office supervisor had when he took action, let's go forward with the method using just the known facts.

Step 2: Weigh and Decide on the Mike Problem

The first two items *fit the facts together* and *consider their bearings on each other*.

Look over the facts listed above and take a moment to see if you notice any gaps or contradictions between any of the facts. For example, there is a contradiction in the fact that Mike is not cooperative in the office, even though he was transferred there to maintain his full pay, clearly a benefit to him. Now put related facts together to see if you can find any meaning to the facts. Mike was moved into the office because his foot was hurt; now that it is healed, it would make sense for him to be unhappy about being kept in the office. It is especially important to analyze carefully all the facts you have because this will reveal various possible actions to solve the problem.

What possible actions are there? is the next item. Most participants in live TWI classes respond to this example by suggesting layoff or transfer back to sales. Almost always, a few people suggest, "Make a deal with Mike." The deal is usually a cause-and-effect scenario: if Mike works hard and completes the 6-month project, then transfer him back to his sales position. In any case, you should always list all of the possible actions so that you can evaluate them one by one:

- Lay off Mike.
- Transfer Mike back to sales.
- Transfer Mike after completion of the project.

In JR sessions, it is very common to have someone suggest, "Talk to Mike" as a possible action. The question here is why? If the purpose of talking to Mike is to encourage him to do a better job, it is a possible action. However, if the purpose is to find out more about why he is not cooperating in the work, that is getting more facts, which means going back to step 1, *get the facts.*

> **TWI note:** It is always good to go back and get more facts throughout the entire four-step process when you feel or sense you do not have the whole story. However, be careful not to confuse this with a possible action, which is meant to solve the problem.

The next item is to *check practices and policies* to make sure your possible actions do not break any rules. Laying off Mike might not go against any of this company's practices and policies, considering the fact that Mike has refused outright to do work assigned to him and that he has a history, albeit a short one, of being uncooperative in the workplace. Transferring him back to sales should not go against any practices and policies because he was transferred into the office from sales in the first place. The same would be true for transferring him back to sales after a successful completion of the special project.

You then want to evaluate each of your possible actions to help determine the best course of action. To do this, you use step 2, item 4, *consider objective and effect on individual, group, and production.* Would the first possible action, lay off Mike, help the office supervisor to meet the objective to get the job done without upsetting the department? The reason the office supervisor is keeping Mike, in spite of his uncooperative attitude, is that there is a lot of work to do on important projects, so laying him off won't get the job done and may actually upset the department. The effect on Mike would be negative since he wants to return to his sales position. The effect on the group might be mixed. Some people wouldn't mind seeing him go; others might mind because laying off Mike would leave the department shorthanded and would probably increase workload for everyone. The effect on production would be negative, at least until the supervisor could find someone else to train to do his work.

The second possible action, transfer Mike back to sales, would hardly meet the objective because the job cannot get done without Mike, and the other employees would be upset that he got away with getting what he wanted at their expense. The effect on Mike would be extremely positive, but that would be offset by the negative effect on the group and on production. The third possible action, transfer Mike after completion of the project, seems like a good compromise. Mike can return to his sales position after he helps get the immediate 6-month project completed. Both sides are giving ground, and that seems fair to everyone. Furthermore, the effect on Mike, the group, and production will be positive. The office supervisor will need to prepare for Mike's departure in 6 months time, but now he has some lead time for this additional responsibility.

The caution point for all of step 2 is *don't jump to conclusions.* This will rarely occur if you do a good job of weighing the facts carefully and deciding on the best course of action from a variety of possible options. Now let's look at what actually happened.

The Mike Problem (continued)

The office supervisor reported all this to his own manager and fired Mike. Mike complained to his former sales supervisor. The sales supervisor called up the office supervisor's boss and relayed the following facts, facts that the office supervisor could have obtained by using the caution item about knowing the whole story.

Mike had been with the company for almost 20 years and was a successful salesperson. He liked sales work, even though it meant being on the road most of the time. He did not like office work and did not know he had been brought into the office to maintain full pay.

The office supervisor had not even questioned Mike's former supervisor about his previous record before taking action. It was due to the former supervisor's intervention that these facts came to light. Eventually, Mike was reinstated in his old job with back pay.

As stated earlier, when initially hearing this problem, many people want to know more facts about Mike and his previous record. This instinct is correct— when you are not certain that you have the whole story, you should go back and get more facts. The facts that came up from Mike's former supervisor were as follows:

- With company 20 years.
- Successful salesperson.
- Liked sales work on the road.
- Not advised why in the office—full pay.

Many people question how it was that Mike did not know why he was transferred into the office—so he wouldn't lose money under workers' compensation. Knowing this, Mike would probably have been more cooperative, and his attitude would have been more positive. However, in many companies, certain changes are implemented automatically with no one questioning the purpose or the duration. In addition, the intent and timeline are not necessarily communicated to the employee. It is easy to see that Mike's attitude was affected by what he did not know and just as easy to see that the supervisor had never talked to Mike about why he had been transferred. Let's now look at steps 3 and 4.

Steps 3 and 4: Take Action and Check Results on the Mike Problem

The office supervisor chose to fire Mike. What facts do you suppose the office supervisor used to come to this decision? Probably that Mike was not cooperative in the office and refused to make a report. More importantly, what are the facts the supervisor did *not* consider or use when making this decision? Probably all the facts about why Mike was in the office in the first place—his foot was hurt, he was in the office for full pay, and his foot had healed. In addition, the supervisor ignored the fact that Mike asked to return to sales. The supervisor gave weight to only a very few of the facts that he had as a basis for his decision. If he had weighed *all* the facts that he did have more diligently and more carefully, he probably would not have fired Mike. As it was, he made a bad decision. Let's wrap up this problem by reviewing the items and caution points for steps 3 and 4.

Step 3 is to *take action* with four items, which are listed below with remarks about the supervisor's handling of each. *Don't pass the buck.* On this point, the supervisor did the appropriate thing.

1. *Are you going to handle this yourself?* This was his problem.
2. *Do you need help in handling?* He didn't ask anyone for help.
3. *Should you refer this to your supervisor?* He referred it to his boss in order to fire Mike and his boss went with his recommendation.
4. *Watch the timing of your action.* Was this the time to take action? Even though the people in the department were watching, Mike was still needed because the office was busy.

    Don't pass the buck. On this point, the supervisor did the appropriate thing.

Step 4 is to *check results* with three items:

1. *How soon will you follow up?* The supervisor did not check up at all on the results of his action because he evidently thought that when he fired Mike the problem was solved.
2. *How often will you need to check?* Same as item 1.
3. *Watch for changes in output, attitude, and relationships.* Because of the action he took and the subsequent bad results, it's pretty clear that this supervisor lost standing with the individual, the group, and management.

    Did your action help production? Without a doubt, this action did nothing to help production. Obviously, this supervisor did not achieve his objective.

Four Ways the Mike Problem Came Up

It is time to look at how Mike's problem came up and what might have happened had the supervisor recognized and handled the problem sooner.

The supervisor had ample opportunity to *size up the problem before it happened*. He might have considered Mike's transfer from sales to the office as a potential source of trouble, especially because of the unusual circumstances that led to the transfer (Mike's foot being hurt). He might also have considered the differences between sales and office work. Most changes have the potential to create problems. When you know from past records or experience that a new directive or order has the potential to cause problems, then you must use your position to take preventive action that counters or minimizes that possibility.

Mike's supervisor also failed to act when he was *tipped off* about the problem. If he had taken up this problem when he first got reports of Mike being uncooperative, especially at planning meetings, things might have turned out another way. As it was, the supervisor ignored the first signs of trouble and the problem continued to escalate.

The supervisor also failed to act when the problem *came to him*, when Mike stated after his foot had healed that he did not like working in the office and wanted to go back to sales. Ignoring problems at this stage is inviting bigger troubles because people will feel that you are not listening to them. They may feel they have no choice but to resort to stronger ways of getting your attention.

At any rate, Mike's supervisor waited until the problem blew up in his face and regrettable words were exchanged—Mike refused to do a required report and rebuffed his supervisor's request to put more effort into the work. As a result, we can say the problem came up when he *ran into* it. It had evolved into something he could no longer ignore. A good supervisor would have handled this problem before it got to the point where Mike overtly broke organizational rules and was openly insubordinate. Because of the severity of the offense, the supervisor felt justified in resolving the matter through strict disciplinary procedures. Knowing the background of the case, the missed opportunities, and the end results, you can see how badly this situation was handled.

Supervisor Team Exercise: Return to your people problem and discuss with the team how each problem came up. Were you tipped off because you noticed a change and took action then? Or did you run into it when the problem exploded in your face? Discuss, in each case, if there were any opportunities to get into the problem earlier and, if so, how that would have changed the dynamic of the problem and made it easier to handle and solve?

Foundations for Good Relations

Through practice, you can gain the skills to see problems coming and engage them when they are small and easily handled. An even more important issue to address is what you can do to prevent problems from occurring in the first place.

JOB RELATIONS

**A SUPERVISOR GETS RESULTS
THROUGH PEOPLE**

FOUNDATIONS FOR GOOD RELATIONS

Let each worker know how he or she is getting along
- ■ Figure out what you expect of the person
- ■ Point out ways to improve

Give credit when due
- ■ Look for extra or unusual performance
- ■ Tell the person while it's "hot"

Tell people in advance about changes that will affect them
- ■ Tell them why, if possible
- ■ Work with them to accept the change

Make best use of each person's ability
- ■ Look for abilities not now being used
- ■ Never stand in a person's way

PEOPLE MUST BE TREATED AS INDIVIDUALS

Figure 11.1   JR four-step method pocket card: front side.

In Chapter 9, you learned about the Job Relations line and that, in order to meet any of their responsibilities, supervisors had to maintain a straight, strong, and correct two-way relationship between themselves and their people. Because people are at the center of everything a supervisor does, a key principle in the JR leadership model is that *a supervisor gets results through people*. Experience shows that successful supervisors have learned to use specific foundations for good relations to maintain the Job Relations line and prevent problems. You can compare this to preventive medicine. The key is to understand commonsense rules for working collaboratively with your people and then make up your mind to use them routinely and conscientiously. When it comes to relationships with people, the simple things are often the most important. When you neglect these, you miss important opportunities to maintain strong relationships that can prevent problems down the line.

Figure 11.1, the front side of the JR pocket card, lists the *foundations for good relations*. Ideally, you use these foundations to prevent problems before they surface. Keep in mind, however, that while these foundations will help you reduce the number of problems that might occur, they will not prevent all problems. If problems surface in spite of your efforts to prevent them, you handle them using the JR four-step method.

Let Each Worker Know How He or She Is Getting Along

A strong Job Relations line means telling people on an ongoing basis how they are doing in their work. Imagine, for example, that someone asks one of your employees, "How are you doing at work?" or "How is your job going?" and all he or she has to say in reply is, "I don't know—no one says anything." What this answer really means is that you don't have good job relations with that employee. People's jobs are important to them. They want to know how they are performing. But too often, supervisors are so focused on schedules and deadlines in the course of day-to-day work that they forget to give their people the feedback they need and want. Some supervisors, in fact, give feedback only when the company requires them to do so in yearly evaluations or reviews. The problem with leaving feedback for annual reviews is that many things about work performance are long forgotten by this time. In most cases, the evaluation process is seen as a management tool for salary increases or promotions rather than a tool to provide guidance and support. Maintaining good job relations means regular communication that lets the employee know, on an ongoing basis, what is going well or not so well.

Figure Out What You Expect of the Person

Before you can tell someone how well he or she is doing in performing his or her work, it is important to know beforehand what the person is supposed to be doing. It is equally important for the employee in question to know what this is. When people know what is expected of them, they usually do it. In addition, knowing what the job entails inspires confidence. Setting a standard and clearly communicating up front what you expect someone to do has two benefits. First, it reduces the number of problems. Second, if things do go wrong, you can focus your problem-solving effort on the job itself and the set standard for doing that job instead of blaming the person involved.

Point Out Ways to Improve

It doesn't do much good to say, "That's all wrong!" if the worker is not doing what you expect. This is confusing as well as offensive. A better way to handle this situation is to point out *exactly* what is not being done correctly (chances are it's not *all* wrong) and then suggest how this specific thing can be improved. Again, pay attention to the work and what needs to be done differently to improve performance instead of blaming the worker. By creating a no-blame environment, you motivate the person doing the job to become your partner in getting the job done well.

Give Credit When Due

Maintaining a good Job Relations line also requires giving people credit when they do something well. It is human nature to want recognition for special efforts, and everyone responds well to positive acknowledgments. When people are not recognized for their outstanding efforts, they may feel their efforts and contributions are not appreciated. This can lead to frustration and even bitterness. Companies who value their people recognize this and have a variety of creative ways to make employees know their work is appreciated (e.g., an employee-of-the-month program or a "caught you doing something good" award). Even a handshake or a pat on the back or a heartfelt "Thank you very much!" can go a long way to building a bond and strengthening the Job Relations line.

Look for Extra or Unusual Performance

It is easy to give appreciation to people who hit a homerun and go beyond normal business expectations. But it is important not to forget the person who contributes by being steadfastly and quietly diligent and reliable. Supervisors often tend to overlook such people, and this is a mistake because it is these people who contribute in an extra and unusual way to the overall stability of a department or company and help create a better working environment for everyone. In doing so, they help prevent problems and help supervisors maintain good Job Relations. Because they do not usually broadcast their efforts, their special contributions may go unnoticed. Be conscious about seeking them out and showing appreciation for what they do.

Tell the Person while "It's Hot"

One of the reasons end-of-the-year evaluations are not effective as motivating tools is because they describe a performance that may have occurred some time ago. Expressing your appreciation for something performed long in the past renders it an afterthought or insincere. Giving thanks when it is due is better. If you miss the timing on this, you may miss an opportunity for strengthening a relationship.

Tell People in Advance about Changes That Will Affect Them

It is important to let people know in advance about any change that will affect them. Suppose, for example, your desk or locker is moved to a different place without any prior notice. Chances are, you will not be very happy about this. Now consider something more important (e.g., a big layoff) that will affect employees. In companies where this has occurred with little or no prior notice, employees are justifiably upset. A typical reaction is "It's not *what* they did, but *how* they did it." Most people can accept a layoff; it is never pleasant, but it happens. What causes more distress is when management springs the announcement on employees out of nowhere, leaving them out of the process with no say and no clear understanding of what happened. When you make *any* change that affects your people, it is best to let them know in advance and let them express their opinions about it. A change that is made without prior notice can make your people feel betrayed or even humiliated—strong emotions that will do real damage to the Job Relations line.

Tell Them Why if Possible

Many supervisors feel that people do not need to know or should not know the reasons for certain decisions and should simply follow directions without question. The problem with this is that people tend to resist changes they do not understand. When you give people reasons, and not just arbitrary decisions, about a change, it is easier for them to accept that change, even when they don't agree with it. It also helps to address the concerns they have about what those changes will mean for them.

Work with Them to Accept the Change

Giving people an explanation of what is going on and why will help them understand the changes you are going to make. Working with them means giving them some of your time, whether you spend that time answering their questions and concerns or just letting them vent their frustrations. Change can be like a death in the family where people go through a grieving process: denial, anger, bargaining, depression, and acceptance. Understanding the emotions people go through and helping them work through those emotions while not giving in to their demands is a real skill. Everyone has to adjust to change, but it is the supervisor's job to make the adjustment easier.

Make Best Use of Each Person's Ability

The last item under the foundations for good relations is to make the best use of the ability of all of your people. Every supervisor knows people who lost interest in a job simply because they felt they could do much more than they were asked to do or allowed to do. Most people want to make the best of their own abilities and look for work in companies that promote learning and growth. Good supervisors challenge their workers with jobs that fully utilize and maximize their abilities and potential. When you don't get the most out of each person every day, you are failing to manage the company's most important resource.

Look for Ability Not Now Being Used

Most people have untapped potential, and good supervisors look for it and try to put it to good use. Do you know today exactly what skills exist in your department? Do you look at the possibility of cross-training your people so that they have more than one skill? Do any of your people have skills from a hobby, sport, or some other special interest that you could make use of in the work? These are the kinds of questions you should ask yourself when looking to maximize the abilities and talents of the people in your department.

Never Stand in a Person's Way

One of the reasons supervisors do not challenge their people with new tasks is because they get comfortable having a skilled person at every station and want to maintain this status quo. But failing to provide skills development may prove to be a costly mistake. It won't be long before your best people master their jobs and want to move on to something more challenging. If you don't find that challenging job for them, they will either find it for themselves by moving to another company or lose interest in the jobs they currently hold in your company.

These basic rules, or foundations, for good relations are important to everyone, and using them will smooth job relations and help supervisors meet their responsibilities. They are the groundwork upon which good relations are built. But they will help prevent problems and strengthen the Job Relations line only if you put them to use on a regular basis. Are they the only things that help build strong job relations? Of course there are other important things. For example, these foundations must be used with *good common sense and judgment.* But if used correctly and consistently, on a daily basis, they will go a long way to making your job more manageable and rewarding.

Keep in mind the bottom line on the JR pocket card: *people must be treated as individuals.* As you apply these foundations, always remember that people are individuals and that you should take their unique traits into consideration whenever taking any action.

Supervisor Team Exercise: Return to your people problem and discuss with the team the application of the foundations for good relations. Which of the foundations apply in each problem? Could these foundations have helped you prevent the people problem? How could they have been applied in each case? For example, what opportunities were there to give credit when it was due? Or what expectations could have been put in place in order to let the worker know how he or she was getting along? Discuss points where you succeeded or failed in developing or maintaining a strong Job Relations line.

Taking Preventive Action

Every organization experiences improved productivity, expansion, new products, new technology and production methods, and various other changes. It is the supervisor's responsibility to adapt to and deal with them effectively. The following case study is about a change that is typical in companies trying to get employees from all levels to assume management responsibilities.

The team leader problem will give you another opportunity to practice the JR four-step method. By applying steps 3 and 4, *take action* and *check results*, you will see how the supervisor in the case study took preventive action and followed up to be sure the action was successful. The case study will also illustrate how the supervisor made good use of the foundations for good relations in taking her preventive action. As you go through this problem, refer to both sides of the Job Relations pocket card (Figures 10.1 and 11.1).

The Team Leader Problem

The plant director called Mary Brown, the production manager, into his office and told her that management had decided to change the organization of the plant to put more emphasis on small teams. The manager told Mary to begin asking team leaders to perform certain duties, like job assignments, production reporting, and operator evaluations, which until that time were done by the department supervisors.

The director also told Mary that the team leaders were to have the same authority to carry out these duties as the supervisors had before them. Mary considered this very carefully and reviewed the following facts.

Most of the team leaders were originally good operators who had been asked to help out with a variety of tasks but had no managerial experience. Because they would be taking away responsibilities from the supervisors, Mary anticipated trouble. This was a major change. Some of the supervisors might resent it. Moreover, some of the employees might not like having the team leaders in authority.

This was the problem Mary faced.

Remember that a problem can be spotted in one of the four ways: (1) sizing it up before it happens, (2) being tipped off, (3) coming to you, and (4) running into it. In this case, Mary anticipated trouble from the people involved, who might resent, resist, or in the worst case, sabotage the change. Mary decided she had to make preparations before the change was announced to prevent this kind of trouble. In other words, she sized it up before it happened.

Mary anticipated trouble from the supervisors, who might resent having some of their key responsibilities taken away and given to the team leaders. She was aware that they might even feel threatened by this change because the team leaders would gain more authority. Mary also felt that the operators, who viewed the team leaders as their equals, might not like a change that gave team leaders authority over them. What Mary wanted was to get everyone to accept the team leaders' new responsibilities so that they could perform these new management duties effectively. Her objective then was to *get the team leaders accepted as members of management.*

Step 1: Get the Facts on the Team Leader Problem

The following facts can be listed from the case:

- No prior managerial authority by team leaders.
- Team leaders would perform job assignments, production reports, and evaluations.
- Team leaders would have same authority as supervisors.
- Team leaders had no managerial experience or training.
- Trouble was anticipated from supervisors and employees.

The items under step 1 helped Mary make sure she hadn't missed any of the important facts to the story. Using the first item, *review the record,* Mary looked at the team leaders as one target group and considered the conditions that fit all of them. In this case, the facts concerning the record would be no prior managerial authority by team leaders and no managerial experience or training.

The second item, *find out what rules and customs apply,* was particularly important in this case because a change in the rules was driving the problem. The facts related to this item were that the team leaders would perform job assignments, production reports, and evaluations and have the same authority as supervisors.

The next two items Mary addressed were to *talk with individuals concerned and get opinions and feelings.* In this case, Mary did not want to talk with anyone about the problem; by doing so, she would have revealed the upcoming change and lost the opportunity to take preventive action before the change actually occurred. Just knowing about the decision to give the team leaders additional responsibilities would have set off the problem she wanted to prevent. However, even without talking to the individuals concerned, Mary had a pretty good idea what their opinions and feelings would be, and she noted that as a fact: trouble was anticipated from supervisors and employees.

These are the pertinent facts to the case, and Mary, reviewing the caution point for step 1, *be sure you have the whole story,* felt that she had the whole story. She was ready to proceed to step 2.

Step 2: Weigh and Decide on the Team Leader Problem

The first two items in step 2, *fit the facts together and consider their bearings on each other,* are used to weigh the facts to gain insight into what is really happening. It is clear that the changes in responsibilities and authority, coupled with the fact that the team leaders had no managerial experience before, spelled trouble for Mary's department. By relating these facts and looking for gaps and contradictions, Mary was ready for the next item: *What possible actions are there?* After weighing the facts carefully, Mary looked at several possible actions; here are a few possibilities:

- Call a general meeting.
- Place a notice on the bulletin board.
- Give authority and say nothing.

Mary's possible actions clearly did not contradict the next item, *check practices and policies,* so she moved to the next item, *consider objective and effect on individual, group, and production* to evaluate each of them. She questioned whether calling a general meeting would meet the objective to get the team leaders accepted as members of management and decided that the supervisors would probably be reluctant to give their true feelings and opinions in front of the whole workforce. Then she questioned the effect of a general meeting on the individuals who were the target of the action, in this case the supervisors. She felt sure that the supervisors would be very angry if they heard about their loss of authority to the team leaders at a general meeting in front of everyone. Mary then asked, "How about the group?" Mary decided that although the meeting would make people feel good that they were being told about the change, it would not change the fact that supervisors might harbor resentment against the plan. Mary then considered the effect of the meeting on production, deciding that the meeting would not have a positive effect on production if the anticipated problem with supervisors and other employees still occurred.

Mary decided that the next possible action, place a notice on the bulletin board, would probably not meet the objective. Impersonal written notices rarely address people's feelings and seldom provide a good enough explanation to convince people of the need for the change. The effect on the supervisors would be negative because they would be caught blindsided. The effect on the group might be negative because people would have no chance to voice their opinions. The effect on production would also be negative because the notice would distract workers and might raise negative emotions among supervisors.

The next possible action was to give authority and say nothing. Mary had already determined that there would be trouble once the change was announced. She did not want to wait for it to blow up in her face when she ran into it. She used her JR skills to get into the problem early before that happened.

The caution point for step 2 is *don't jump to conclusions,* and Mary was not going to rely on any assumptions or preconceived notions in her search for a preventive solution to this problem. Below is what Mary did.

The Team Leader Problem (continued)

Mary thought the situation over pretty carefully. Then she talked individually with her supervisors and also talked individually to the operators who were seen as natural leaders. She gave them the facts and asked for their help.

There was quite a commotion—some people said they wouldn't stand for it. Mary gave them a chance to do their talking and blow off steam. Eventually, they agreed to the change. At this point, Mary set up training classes to teach the team leaders how to do reports and evaluations. Mary also talked to the team leaders and told them that because this was a new situation, they might run into difficulties and must not be easily offended. She asked them to do their best because their work would also affect other team leaders and the development of future team leader responsibilities.

By the time the team leaders took over their new responsibilities, things had calmed down. During the first day that the team leaders began their new responsibilities, Mary talked to the supervisors; later that day, she spoke with the natural leaders she had talked to before. They informed her that apparently the team leaders were being accepted and everything was okay. Mary thanked them for their help and, to be sure her preventive action was effective, kept close watch over the situation for some time.

Steps 3 and 4: Take Action and Check Results on the Team Leader Problem

As you can see, Mary's preventive action was quite extensive. Here are the action items she took:

- Gave the facts in advance to supervisors and natural leaders
- Asked for their help
- Let them blow off steam
- Gave training
- Asked cooperation of team leaders

Let's analyze how Mary applied the four items and caution point for step 3 to the team leader problem:

1. *Are you going to handle this yourself?* Mary handled this herself because she felt it was her responsibility and that she was the best qualified to handle it.
2. *Do you need help in handling?* Mary got help from the supervisors and the natural leaders because they were the ones in a position to help everyone accept the change.
3. *Should you refer this to your supervisor?* Mary's supervisor had referred it to her and expected her to take correct action on it.
4. *Watch the timing of your action.* This was a key element to the success of Mary's action. She allowed just the right amount of time for the key players to blow off steam and cool down before letting the team leaders begin their new responsibilities.

Don't pass the buck. Mary could have blamed management for the idea and any bad results if she had done nothing to anticipate and prevent problems. Instead, she took responsibility for the task and handled it.

Now let's analyze how Mary applied the three items and caution point for step 4.

1. *How soon will you follow up?* It was important for Mary to check right away because this change affected the whole plant and she could expect results immediately after announcing the change.
2. *How often will you need to check?* Mary kept close watch on the situation until she was absolutely certain that the change had been accepted.
3. *Watch for changes in output, attitude, and relationships.* Good attitude on the part of the supervisors indicated their acceptance of the change. Good relationships between the team leaders and the employees in the department proved their acceptance as well.
    Did your action help production? Although no specific evidence of this is given in the case study, it can be readily assumed that Mary's preventive action and the training she gave the team leaders before they took on their new responsibilities did help production.

The overarching goal of the JR four-step method is accomplishing your objective. Mary, by making sure that her actions were working and not causing other side effects, achieved this goal. She got the team leaders accepted as members of management.

Mary's Use of the Foundations for Good Relations

To achieve her objective, Mary made good use of the foundations for good relations, discussed here in order of importance. She certainly used the third foundation, *tell people in advance about changes that will affect them*, by speaking with the supervisors and the team leaders. She even spoke with the natural leaders in the group because she reasoned that employees would follow the lead of these "opinion makers" if they advocated acceptance of the change. By giving them the facts up front, including *telling them why*, and by giving them ample time to have their say and blow off steam, she was able to get them to accept the change. In other words, she changed their outlook from "would not stand for it" to acceptance by *working with them to accept the change*.

The fourth foundation, *make best use of each person's ability*, was another foundation that applies to this case. To begin with, the company wanted to upgrade the responsibilities of the team leaders and give them more management authority. Since the team leaders were already helping with a variety of tasks over and above what the other operators were doing, they had potential leadership skills that were *not now being used*. Giving them management responsibilities would help them to develop and grow, and would also free up the supervisors to take on additional duties. Instead of being a threat to the supervisors, this change gave the supervisors a chance to make the best use of their own abilities, and take away the perceived need to *stand in the way* of the team leaders' growth. Smart companies are always looking for ways to expand the capabilities of all of their people at all levels. Mary understood this principle, and it helped her to implement her action with poise and confidence.

Before implementing the change, Mary met with the team leaders who were being asked to take on these new responsibilities to ask for their cooperation and discuss possible difficulties. She explained that it was important for them to not only accept the challenge, but also perform well, because their success or failure would affect all future team leaders. By telling them not to be offended by remarks from other supervisors or operators, and by providing training to meet their new responsibilities, Mary was *letting them know what she expected of them* and *how they could improve*. As their new roles unfolded, she would be in a position to apply the first foundation, *let each worker know how he or she is getting along*.

Mary also used the second foundation, *give credit when due*. She thanked the supervisors and natural leaders, *right on the first day*, for their help in getting the change started. Given what we know about how meticulous she was on follow-up processes for checking results, it seems reasonable to assume that she will also give credit on a timely basis to all those who do well implementing the new team leader responsibilities. In particular, she will be looking to give credit to those in the group who work *diligently and reliably*, quietly going the extra mile to help bring good results from the new arrangement.

Conclusion: The Effect of Change and Problem Prevention

The best thing you can do in good job relations is to prevent problems from occurring in the first place. This is never truer than when you look at the effect change has on people. In the section on Job Methods improvement, you learned that people resist most changes that affect their workplace: the placement of tools or equipment, the procedures they use to get the work done, change in payment plans, new responsibilities, and even the people they work with or sit next to. It is important to prepare individuals and groups before introducing and implementing changes.

When you prepare for change, you can prevent problems from arising later, and this saves you time and helps to improve and maintain relationships with your people. Once you are sure people have fully accepted the change, you can move on to other important matters and allow the changes to reap the benefits they were designed to bring.

In the daily execution of the work, we have also seen how the foundations for good relations can serve as the preventive medicine that helps us avoid problems. A JR trainer from India told us, in the unique perspective of people from that country, that the foundations are like "TPM* for people." In other words, to keep a machine in top running condition, you must perform daily preventive maintenance like cleaning, oiling, adjustment, and calibration. The same can be said for people. If we do not perform these foundations on a daily basis, relations with people break down, and before long we are running into problems. By regularly applying the foundations, we keep our people in top form, motivated, and working well together with others and prevent those problems from happening.

Supervisor Team Exercise: Have each team member track down and compile a new list of potential people problems, in other words, problems they can size up before they happen or problems they are tipped off about by changes they notice in the work environment. For each potential problem, apply the foundations for good relations to see if you can prevent these problems or address them early. Discuss with the group specifically what you will do in each foundation and how it will help to prevent or resolve the problem.

---

* Total productive maintenance.

JOB SAFETY

V

Chapter 12

Four Steps of Job Safety: Preventing Accidents before They Happen

---

The original Training Within Industry (TWI) program consisted of three modules—Job Instruction (JI), Job Methods (JM), and Job Relations (JR)—as we have presented in this book. When TWI went to Japan in the early 1950s, Japanese industry embraced all three of these methods but eventually felt that an important subject, safety, was missing. In 1967, a group of safety experts organized by the Japan Ministry of Labor created a fourth TWI module called Job Safety (JS)* exactly following all of the standard conventions of TWI: a four-step method, a 10-hour delivery schedule, a learn-by-doing approach, and so forth. Since then, TWI has always been promoted in Japan consisting of these four modules.

This chapter brings out the need for accident prevention and introduces the JS four-step method for preventing them. In Chapter 13, you will use the JS pocket card to go through two examples that focus on both the things and the people aspects of preventing safety incidents and injuries. Then, in Chapter 14, we will present a problem for you to work through to hone your ability in Job Safety.

Supervisors' Roles and Responsibilities in Safety

In Chapter 2 we presented the five needs model and explained how a good supervisor has five needs that are indispensable in fulfilling his or her responsibilities: knowledge of the work, knowledge of responsibilities, skill in instructing,

---

* This is different from the Job Safety program promoted by the Canadian Vocational Training, Department of Labor after WWII. That version promotes safety as a development of the JI method of instruction, adding another dimension to the job breakdown covering safety instructions.

skill in improving methods, and skill in leading. The two kinds of knowledge must be acquired locally, but the three kinds of skills are universal and can be learned through practice of the three TWI methods: Job Instruction, Job Methods improvement, and Job Relations. But regardless of the work or industry, when we instruct people how to do their jobs, when we improve their operations, and when we deal with people under our supervision, we must always consider *safety* a foundation in everything we do.

Safety is an integral part of each of these five needs. When consolidating our *knowledge of work*, we must know the safety factors related to the machines, materials, and methods we use to get out production. For example, do we use materials that are dangerous or harmful to the people who come into close contact with them? We must understand the characteristics of these materials so we know how to handle and store them safely. Our *knowledge of responsibilities* would include safety rules and procedures that must be enforced to protect the safety of the people who come to work under our charge. In Job Instruction, when we teach people how to do their jobs, we always include the safety key points so that they perform the jobs in a safe way every time they do them. When we exercise Job Methods improvement, we are looking for an easier and safer way to do the job. For example, when we simplify a job, we are looking for ways to reduce strain, focusing on ergonomics and preventing long-term injuries. Finally, when developing and maintaining good job relations, the example set by a leader can help create or damage a safe working environment. Figure 12.1 shows the five needs model, including safety as an integral part of each of the five needs.

We can make good quality products and services inexpensively and quickly only when we use these five needs *in a safe environment*. In that sense, safety is the foundation to any of the supervisor's responsibilities concerning production, quality, cost, and everything else. When it comes to regulations and plans

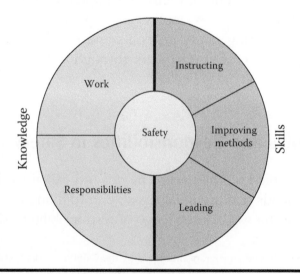

Figure 12.1 The five needs for good supervisors model.

regarding the safety of the workplace, the supervisor's role is to maintain a safe working environment. The supervisor is the key person at the front line of work regarding

- Work problems, difficulties, and dangers
- Correct work methods
- Past accident cases and injuries
- Operator abilities, attitudes, skills (good and bad), desires, and requests
- Close relationships with operators based on a mutual understanding of past work and experience

Therefore, supervisors are in the best position to

- Find possibilities for accidents and take preventive measures.
- Promote safety activities at the workplace.
- Raise safety awareness and promote workplace teamwork.
- Educate workers and promote safety regulations.

Supervisors directly educate and lead workers on safety. They are the *last line of defense* in regard to this responsibility. Supervisors' roles and responsibilities include planning the work and giving employees direction and training so that that work is done safely. It also includes setting work standards and giving proper work assignments so that the right people are doing jobs in the right way. Moreover, they are in charge of both the equipment and the working environment and can create good awareness of safety while listening to people's ideas on how to maintain a safe working environment. Finally, supervisors are responsible for taking action on abnormalities or injuries if they occur. Table 12.1 sums up these duties.

Table 12.1 Supervisor Duties in Regard to Safety

Supervision/leadership	Pretask planning and hazard analysis Giving direction while work is being carried out Training and guidance of workers
Jobs	Setting work standards Improving work methods Proper assignment of workers
Things	Equipment safety Maintenance and improvement of work environment Safety inspection
People	Raising safety awareness of workers Bringing out people's ideas
People–things–jobs	Taking action on abnormalities Taking action when injuries occur

Need for Accident Prevention

When we look at the relationship between safety and production, we can immediately see the need for accident prevention. For instance, consider the harm that is done when someone is hurt at work. Of course, the person who got hurt will suffer from the injuries. He or she will also face other difficulties, such as lost earnings or extra expenses. The injuries may also lead to additional physical problems, such as decreased physical strength or a loss of other capabilities. How about the person's family or dependents? They certainly will not be happy with the situation, and this will cause them a lot of anxiety as well.

Some of these costs can be measured in money, but we know from experience that money received from insurance benefits or other compensation or relief can never fully cover a loss from an accident. Therefore, *for humanitarian reasons*, accident prevention is extremely important.

Next, consider the cost to the workplace and the victim's coworkers. The injured person must be rescued and treated, and much time will be lost due to the distraction. Other workers will naturally be both sympathetic to the injured person and curious about what happened and why. Machines may also be damaged or left idle due to the accident and its aftermath. If the injured person cannot return to work, there could be overtime costs as the work plan is rearranged or other people are trained as substitutes. Depending on the severity of the accident, there may also be an investigation or even legal actions that must be addressed. What about the morale and productivity of the workforce? They will most certainly go down as employees lose confidence in their supervisors and the management of the worksite.

Supervisor Team Exercise: Have someone who has access to the company's accident record bring that data and statistics to the group and have a general discussion around the total cost of these accidents to the company. Be sure to first define the period and content of the analysis. Consider both direct and indirect costs. Direct costs would be things like

- Medical care compensation fees (workers' compensation insurance, examination and treatment, medicines, materials for treatment, hospital fees, etc.)
- Sick leave compensation
- Compensation for additional days off

Indirect costs would include

- Pay for time not worked (by the victim while getting medical relief or aid, by coworkers while the operation is held up, by coworkers while adjustments and restorations are being made, by those handling investigations, etc.)

- Material losses (machines and equipment, tools, instruments, raw materials, etc.)
- Production losses
- Other losses, like transportation (ambulance) costs or other outlays

Calculate and discuss the total cost incurred by the company in both money and time. How much does it cost to produce the product your company makes? How many products could you buy with the amount of money lost because of accidents? How many products could have been made during the time lost due to the accidents?

As you can see from the above exercise, accidents create a huge loss. Losses that are easy to overlook or difficult to calculate must be taken into consideration and added in to get a full view of the situation. Taken one by one, these amounts of money and time may not seem like much, but from a company-wide basis, they constitute a significant figure. Thus, *for economic reasons*, accident prevention is extremely important.

Next, let's consider things from the public point of view. If the accident affects ordinary members of the public, what might happen? Here is a story about an accident that actually took place at a research center of a major electronics manufacturer:

There was a fire at the center, and naturally the fire department showed up in force. However, they could do absolutely nothing. Why? Lithium was being processed there and they could not use water to put out the fire. If water is applied to lithium, it explodes. All they could do was evacuate the neighbors and wait until the fire burned itself out. This accident was broadcast nationwide, and it became very controversial. In fact, as all the lithium in the research center was sealed, they could have used water to extinguish the fire. Unfortunately, though, the person in charge of the lithium processing was not there due to some other business.

So, an accident can sometimes cause direct harm to the community. In that case, we will, of course, have to compensate for damages, and it will lead to the loss of the company's reputation or, even worse, a threat to the company's survival. Public facilities like parks, roads, water pipes, and so on, may also be damaged. As we have seen here, the accident may not be confined only to the person and company involved, but may create a lot of public damage as well. Thus, also *for community reasons*, accident prevention is extremely important.

If we are to raise production at our own workplaces, we must always be aware of and practice safety in the workplace. For the reasons we have mentioned, it is clear that *the meaning of safety is to consider measures and take action before an accident occurs rather than to handle the aftermath.*

But, while everyone knows that safety is necessary and important, accidents still occur and cause losses. When we haven't had an accident for a while, we forget the importance of safety. Then when an accident does happen, we are rudely reminded of it and we sadly wonder why we didn't think of taking precautions before it occured. So, *disaster occurs when we forget.* According to the Occupational Safety and Health Administration, 4585 workers were killed on the job in the United States in 2013. This means that while we have come a long way in terms of economic growth and progress, we can't say that we have been thorough enough about reducing accidents.

New work and technology means a new need for safety. We must always maintain vigilance when it comes to understanding the safety challenges we will meet with new methods and advanced equipment and materials. In any case, the majority of the accidents we experience are ones that supervisors can and must prevent.

Factors Common to Most Accidents: The Packing Section Example

In order to strive for accident prevention, we must first know what things and what conditions lead up to the accident itself. If we know what to look for, we can take precautions. As we have done throughout this book, let's look at an actual case, something that happened in the packing section of a factory, in order to understand how the method works. With Job Safety, first we'll look at the factors that led up to the accident in order to understand how most accidents develop. Then we'll introduce the JS four-step method, which would have enabled us to prevent this problem from happening in the first place.

This is a very busy workplace that packs and ships products. In addition to Foreman Anderson, 10 people work here. Nelson transfers packed products and brings in packing materials. King sweeps up the trash, which he does fairly frequently. His method is to sweep it into small piles in the aisle near the dumpsters, load it into a wheelbarrow, open the sliding door, and take it to a dumpster. This sliding door is not used by the other workers.

Figure 12.2 shows the layout of the packing section. On the top right, you can see a separate workplace, but in this particular workplace where the accident occurred, there are eight workbenches, four each on both sides of the central aisle, two sliding doors, and a scale. There are some dumpsters outside of the building near sliding door 1. An accident occurred in this workplace, and Nelson suffered lacerations and bruises that took a week to recover from.

Door 1 had been working poorly for about 2 weeks. King, who used the door, had reported this to Foreman Anderson, but nothing had been done about it.

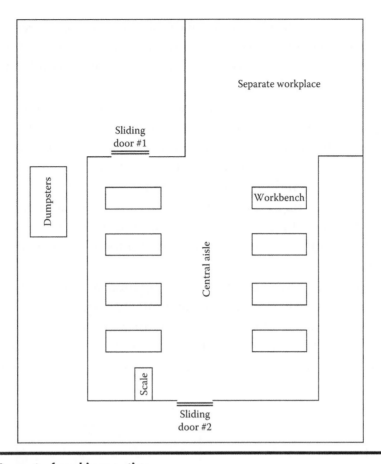

Figure 12.2   Layout of packing section.

On the day Nelson was hurt, Foreman Anderson had been told by his boss that the plant manager would be showing some visitors around their workplace. Around 10:30, when Foreman Anderson finished his morning's work and came to look around the work area, he noticed a pile of trash and told King, "The plant manager may be here any minute, so get rid of this right away." As Foreman Anderson watched, King, working like a beaver trying to get rid of the trash in one load, began to pile the trash high in the wheelbarrow.

Meanwhile, Foreman Anderson, satisfied that King had begun the job, looked elsewhere, and found an empty box left in the central aisle. The box had been left there momentarily by Nelson. Since the foreman was always telling his people not to leave anything in the aisles, he immediately looked for Nelson, but couldn't find him. Assuming that he was probably moving some packed products or packing materials and would be back soon, the foreman decided to wait for him to come back.

While he was waiting, he saw King, who had finished loading the wheelbarrow, coming along the central aisle headed for the dumpsters through sliding door 2, not his usual route, and that reminded him of the poorly working door. As soon as the empty box was removed, he decided, he would have to do something about the door.

Then Nelson came walking back to talk to a fellow worker. Seeing Foreman Anderson, he got quickly back to work with an embarrassed smile. Foreman Anderson, pointing to the empty box, said to him, "Haven't you been told not to leave anything in the aisles? Get it out of here before some idiot trips over it!" A flustered Nelson said, "I'm sorry," and started to remove the box.

Look at Figure 12.3 showing the circumstances up to this point. You'll notice that the trash piles that were near sliding door 1 have been moved by King to the dumpsters. King used the central aisle to remove the trash because sliding door 1 was not working and he had to go around the box that was left in the aisle in order to pass through sliding door 2. Here is what happened next. After carrying the box two or three steps, Nelson slipped. In trying to catch himself, he caught his left hand between a workbench and the box, lacerating and bruising it. The box was also broken.

The details became clear later, but what happened was that Nelson, being rushed by the foreman, had no time to watch his step and slipped on a small paste brush. The brush was old and had been thrown away by a worker and swept into the pile of trash. But it had fallen off of the overloaded wheelbarrow when it bounced over a repaired spot in the floor while passing along the central aisle.

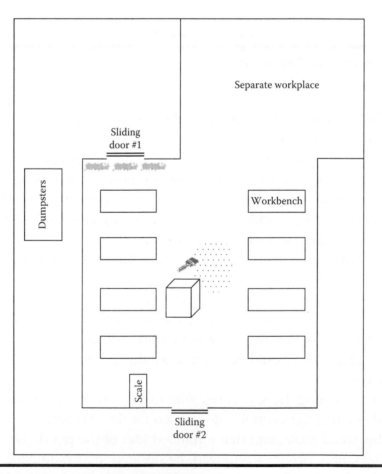

Figure 12.3 Circumstances at time of accident.

Let's think about this accident. Do you think it was unavoidable? If not, then what do you think caused the accident? The bad door? The rushed atmosphere because of the visitors coming to the area? King overloading the wheelbarrow? The imperfect floor repair? Nelson leaving the box in the aisle? In our TWI classes, we ask this question and most of the trainees respond enthusiastically, "All of them!" But when we ask them to choose just one, the one item that was most influential in causing the accident, everyone has a different idea and viewpoint, and we can never get complete agreement on a conclusion.

When looking at the situation, it is certainly important and appropriate to do an analysis of the causes. But when studying the problem, it will be very helpful to know the *chain of events common to many accidents*. Let's look at what forms this chain. First, there are what we can call *indirect causes*. Next, there are what we may call *direct causes*, in other words, the unsafe acts and conditions that led to the accident. These things cause a chain reaction, and what happens is commonly called an accident. But, for our purposes, we'll call this result an incident (see the "Accidents or Incidents?" section). We say that an *incident* is an abnormal occurrence that has the potential to lead to injury or losses. An incident may not necessarily lead to injury. Because the majority of incidents do not result in injury, we use this term instead of the more common word *accident*, which implies a resulting injury. Table 12.2 gives examples of each of these elements.

Accidents or Incidents?

The word *accident* usually implies that an injury or fatality has already occurred—"He was in a car accident." But as can be seen by the model in Figure 12.4, for every fatality there are more than 100 more serious injuries, and for each one of these, there are yet 10 times more who suffer only minor injuries and 100 times more who are fortunate enough to escape injury in near-miss situations.

So we will use the word *incident* to represent *all* of these situations, even those hazardous situations that may not necessarily lead to injury but have the potential to do so. What is more, the word *accident* implies the notion that it couldn't be helped, as in "it was just an accident." Incidents have causes that can and must be prevented.

If a fatality represented, say, a major defect in your company's product, you might think the above ratio was not so terribly bad. But when it comes to safety and human life, this one case alone presents a very serious problem and is totally unacceptable. Let's say there were 100 cream puffs. If only one were found to have some toxic substance in it, of course we would destroy all of them so that there was no chance for anyone to get sick or critically ill. Would you dare to eat one of those cream puffs?

Table 12.2   Examples of the Four Elements of the Incident Chain

1. Indirect causes

   a. Poor physical or emotional conditions: These are conditions that make it easier for unsafe acts to be performed or unsafe physical conditions to exist, for example, horseplay, despair, anxiety, dissatisfaction, fatigue, lack of sleep, childishness, inadequate knowledge or skills, inadequate strength, or indifference to regulations and instructions.

   b. Individual inadequacies: These are things caused by poor work environment or social conditions, for example, inappropriate supervision from above, unsuitable or excessive work, inadequate education and training, work methods that are not standardized, poor discipline at the workplace, poor habits or arrangements at the workplace, or an unhappy home life.

2. Direct causes (unsafe acts and conditions)

This means human acts or physical conditions that are unsafe, that is, dangerous. These differ from the points above in that many of them can be concretely and clearly recognized. They are things that cause accidents, for example, poor location, poor position, poor footing, excessive speed, errors in operation, throwing of tools, use of makeshift ladders, lack of safety devices and personal protective equipment or failure to use them even though they are available, performance of acts that ignore regulations, and poor arrangements.

3. Incidents

We call it an incident when there is an abnormal occurrence that has the potential to lead to injury or losses, for example, falling over, colliding, falling from a height, suffering an electric shock, touching something hot, getting something in your eye, coming in contact with dangerous or harmful objects, things exploding or catching fire, and inhalation of toxic gas.

4. Injuries

This includes both injuries to people and damage to things, for example, injuries that don't require time off from work, those that do, damage to bodily functions, death, and losses to equipment, machines, materials, and production.

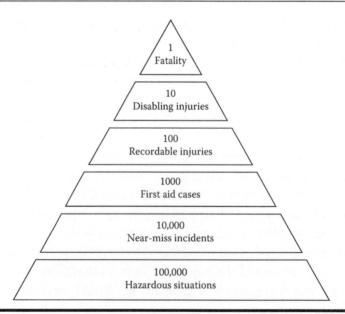

Figure 12.4   The incident pyramid.

Incidents may be considered occurrences that cause *personal injury*: injuries to people that may or may not require time off from work, injuries to limbs or bodily functions, fatal injuries, and so on. We may also consider *property damage* incidents: losses to facilities, machines, materials, production, and so on. These can be called injuries as well. *Injuries* then mean losses such as these to both people and property.

Figure 12.5 is a representation of the *incident chain*. The events leading up to a safety incident are interlocked just like the links of a chain.

Now, let's consider how we can apply this incident chain to the packing section example we are looking at. First, what kind of injury was there? Nelson received lacerations and bruises. This was a personal injury from the aspect of people. Was there any damage to property or things? Yes, the broken box.

Then, what kind of incident occurred to cause this injury to people and things? In other words, when who tried to do what and how, what happened, and what were the results? When Nelson tried to move the box in a rush, he slipped on the brush and fell.

Next, what direct causes—unsafe acts and conditions—led up to this incident? Here, recall the conditions right before the incident. We noted that Nelson slipped on a paste brush, but this was because the brush had fallen off of the wheelbarrow. The fallen paste brush is a direct cause of the incident. Also, we can say that a direct cause was Nelson not watching his step because he was in a rush. Finally, the reason he had to move the box was because he left it in the aisle. The box in the aisle is a direct cause of this incident.

What about the indirect causes? These would be the causes of the direct causes, these unsafe acts and conditions. We said a direct cause was the fallen paste brush, but why did it fall to the floor? Because King overloaded the wheelbarrow with trash due to the fact that he was forced to get rid of the trash quickly. What is more, because the floor was imperfectly repaired, the wheelbarrow bounced, causing the brush to fall off. These are also indirect causes. But that is not all. Why was King going down the central aisle in the first place? That was because sliding door 1 was not working and he had to go around to the other door to get to the dumpsters.

As is clear from this discussion, *incidents and injuries do not just happen; they are caused.* Incidents have causes, and *if only we eliminate the causes, we can prevent safety incidents before they happen.* Let's begin to think about what we have to do to prevent safety incidents before they happen.

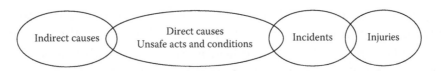

Figure 12.5   The incident chain.

Supervisor Team Exercise: Write four headings across the top of the board from left to right: "Indirect Causes," "Direct Causes (Unsafe Acts and Conditions)," "Incidents," and "Injuries." Then, working from right to left, have the group tell first what kind of injury there was in the packing section example. Discuss injury from both the people aspect and the things aspect. Write it down under the "Injuries" heading. Then have the group bring out what kind of incident occurred to cause this injury to people and things, in other words, when who tried to do what and how, what happened and what were the results? Write this down under the "Incidents" heading. Next, have the group recall the conditions right before the incident. What direct causes—unsafe acts and conditions—led up to this incident? Write these down under the "Direct Causes" heading. Finally, under the "Indirect Causes" heading, list the causes of the direct causes. Reviewing this incident chain, discuss what could have been done to prevent the incident before it happened.

Four Steps of Job Safety

If you had been Foreman Anderson of this workplace, what would you have done to prevent the incident before it happened? It's clear that the answer is to eliminate or prevent the indirect causes and the direct causes, that is, the unsafe acts and conditions. In this example, we used an incident that had already occurred, so it was easy to find the causes, but in order to prevent real incidents at our workplaces, we will have to think of these things before safety incidents happen. That is, we will have to detect various factors that we think might lead to a safety incident before the incident happens.

TWI note: Many safety programs deal directly with accident investigation in order to find the cause of an accident that has already happened and eliminate it so that it never happens again. This is very important work. The TWI Job Safety program, though, is designed to teach supervisors to recognize the *potential* causes, direct and indirect, of safety incidents that have not yet happened and eliminate them *before* an incident or injury ever occurs. In order to learn to recognize these causes, however, we have to look at safety incidents that have happened in order to understand better the things we missed and failed to prevent. This is just the learning process. The intent of the JS method is to recognize the causes of danger and eliminate them before they ever have a chance to do harm.

JOB SAFETY

The meaning of safety is to consider measures and take action *before* a safety incident. It is *NOT* to handle the aftermath.

Step 1: Spot the causes of danger

     Check the situation; check the record; talk to people
     Consider both things and people
     Check regulations and standards
     Always be aware
     Foresee risks of incidents and injuries
Dig down deep

Step 2: Decide on the countermeasures

     Fit the causes together; consider their bearings on each other
     Ask people who have detailed knowledge
     Think of several countermeasures
     Make sure of accordance with policies, regulations, standards
     Decide on back-up measures too
Are you yourself the cause?

Step 3: Enforce countermeasures

     Can you handle this yourself?
     Do you need support from your supervisor?
     Whose cooperation should you get?
Put into effect immediately

Step 4: Check results

     Check again and again
     Was it carried out for certain?
     Were the causes eliminated?
Have any new causes arisen?

**SAFETY INCIDENTS ARE CAUSED
BREAK THE CHAIN**

Figure 12.6   JS four-step method pocket card—front side.

*The meaning of safety is to consider measures and take action before a safety incident occurs. It is **not** to handle the aftermath.* The JS pocket card (Figure 12.6) outlines the method you need to follow in order to prevent safety incidents. Let's review the card and its contents by examining the packing section example.

Step 1: Spot the Causes of Danger

Did Foreman Anderson spot the causes of danger? If he had paid a little more attention, this sort of incident probably wouldn't have occurred. Now, let's use the card to see if we spot such causes of danger.

Item 1: Check the Situation, Check the Record, Talk to the People

If Foreman Anderson had paid attention to the poorly working sliding door and the condition of the floor, if he had checked past records of the workplace for similar incidents, and if he had talked to his people, would there have been this kind of incident?

Item 2: Consider Both Things and People

If things are in bad condition, safe operation may be impossible. Did the bad spot on the floor, the paste brush thrown into the trash, and the poorly working door interfere with safe operation? It is said that accidents are very often caused by people. People's feelings and emotions are especially important, and Foreman Anderson did not consider the feelings of King and Nelson. In particular, Foreman Anderson's own attitude toward the situation was directly related to this incident, as shown by his hastily having the trash removed, waiting for Nelson to come back, and thinking that he should do something about the door after the empty box was removed.

Item 3: Check Regulations and Standards

Safety regulations and other regulations and standards are all made for a reason. What does it show that Nelson left an empty box in the aisle, even for a moment? Foreman Anderson admonished Nelson for leaving the box in the aisle, but that was just before the visitor tour with the plant manager. His regular management of the regulations seems slack given Nelson's behavior.

Item 4: Always Be Aware

Awareness must first to be taken literally. Foreman Anderson took a look around the workplace before the plant manager's visit but nevertheless had forgotten about the bad door and hadn't noticed the fallen paste brush. Next, it means *systematic planning*. Foreman Anderson had done nothing about the bad door for 2 weeks and only remembered it as an afterthought when seeing King go down the central aisle to get to the dumpsters.

Item 5: Foresee Risks of Incidents and Injuries

It is hard to notice anything unusual with only a casual look around the workplace. Foreman Anderson spent some time in the workplace, but only to be sure that King and Nelson cleaned up for the visit. He did not foresee an accident.

Caution Point: Dig Down Deep

This is a caution for all of step 1. Step 1 shows us how to look for the potential causes of safety incidents, but you have to look for the *underlying causes*, without getting wrapped up only in what you can see.

Step 2: Decide on the Countermeasures

Once you have identified causes of danger, you must consider how they can be eliminated. Let's consider how to do this.

Item 1: Fit the Causes Together and Consider Their Bearings on Each Other

Foreman Anderson did not consider the bearing of the bad door on the use of the central aisle. Nor did he consider the relationship of the overloaded wheelbarrow on the falling of the brush, or of his own manner of giving orders to King and Nelson and their state of mind.

Item 2: Ask People Who Have Detailed Knowledge

Foreman Anderson did not show the bad door to a repairman, or ask Nelson why he left the box there.

Item 3: Think of Several Countermeasures

Don't think of only one countermeasure for each cause; think of several. Foreman Anderson only thought of one countermeasure: to wait for Nelson's return. If you had been him, what countermeasures would you have thought of?

Item 4: Make Sure of Accordance with Policies, Regulations, and Standards

Before you decide on countermeasures, you first have to make sure they comply with company policies, regulations, and standards.

Item 5: Decide on Backup Measures, Too

When you decide on countermeasures, also think of interim or contingency measures just in case. You have to *be doubly sure.*

Caution Point: Are You Yourself the Cause?

This is a caution for all of step 2. We should reflect again and again on whether the cause lies with us, the supervisor himself or herself. What sort of things should Foreman Anderson have considered in this vein?

Step 3: Enforce Countermeasures

Habitual enforcement of safety measures is important, and when we enforce them, there are several things we have to watch.

Item 1: Can You Handle This Yourself?

This is something that the supervisor must decide for himself or herself. In our example, the problem was one for Foreman Anderson himself to handle.

Item 2: Do You Need Support from Your Supervisor?

For problems not within your authority, you need to consult your own supervisor. But in this case, it probably wasn't necessary.

Item 3: Whose Cooperation Should You Get?

You should get help from as many people as possible.

Caution Point: Put into Effect Immediately

This is a caution for all of step 3. To decide on a countermeasure and then hesitate and shrink from putting it into effect is even worse than not to think of a countermeasure at all.

Step 4: Check Results

Foreman Anderson gave orders to King and Nelson, but did he check the results?

Item 1: Check Again and Again

There are times when just one check is not enough and you can't take your eye off something even for a moment. Foreman Anderson was keeping an eye on how King was doing his job, but only to the extent that King was going to get the job done. Once he felt King was underway, he didn't pay attention to the details of what King was doing and went on to check on Nelson.

Item 2: Was It Carried Out for Certain?

"For certain" doesn't only mean carried out according to plan; it also means carried out *so that the effects of the countermeasure are noticeable*. What does the imperfect repairing of the floor indicate?

Item 3: Were the Causes Eliminated?

You have to make sure that the causes of danger were eliminated by the countermeasures taken.

Caution Point: Have Any New Causes Arisen?

This is a caution for all of step 4. Sometimes measures taken lead to new causes. A good supervisor always *consciously searches* for new causes, in order to keep safety incidents out of his or her workplace.

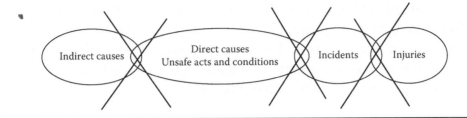

Figure 12.7 Break the chain.

Safety Incidents Are Caused; Break the Chain

Safety incidents always have causes. It is important to take measures not only against what you can see but also to eliminate the real underlying causes. That is, it is our job as supervisors to *break the links of the chain* so that indirect causes and direct causes—the unsafe acts and conditions—cannot combine to lead to an incident. In other words, *don't end up dealing with the aftermath of a safety incident; take countermeasures before it occurs* (Figure 12.7).

The four-step method on this card is a practical method that will help us in continuous maintenance of safety at our workplaces. The card shows us a method of looking at our workplaces and the workers under us from the point of view of safety. The card shows us first of all *what kinds of things may cause safety incidents* and *what we should do* to find those things; then it tells us *what we have to do next,* after we have put our finger on the real cause. Especially concerning safety, we must thoroughly learn how to spot potential causes of safety incidents in acts and conditions that look normal at first glance, to foresee incidents, and to take measures against them.

> **Supervisor Team Exercise:** Have the group discuss safety at their workplaces. What kinds of safety incidents and injuries have they had so far? Give concrete examples, no matter how minor, and list them for later reference. Discuss what they can do to prevent these kinds of incidents before they happen. Review the JS card and have members explain where the card can help them in preventing incidents and injuries.

Risky Supervisor Styles

Nobody wants to get hurt in the workplace. Moreover, nobody wants to cause injury to somebody else. Nonetheless, there are people among us who are indifferent to unsafe acts and conditions. Whatever the reason for their indifference, there is never any reason or cause important enough to barter for a human life. It is our duty as supervisors to make these people see the potential tragedy of such an attitude.

People are greatly influenced by their supervisor's way of thinking and supervision, and it is highly possible that the indifferent attitude on the part of the workers toward safety is created by their own supervisors. There are several types of supervisors. Let's review these different types to see how their attitude affects the environment for safety in the workplace.

- *"Production first" style.* This is a supervisor who concentrates all of his or her energies on the work, only emphasizing production and quality. This is a person who thinks, "Don't worry, nothing like that will ever happen," or "Some amount of danger can't be helped in getting the work done," and so on. He or she also thinks highly of selfless, loyal subordinates and regards the unsafe acts and conditions among them as evidence of their willingness and reliability.
- *"Let them learn" style.* This type of supervisor lets the workers find out for themselves about both safety and their work. They don't believe they should nag them. Their feeling about people who get hurt is that, rather than through teaching, they will only learn the hard way through experience, so they leave their people alone without guidance.
- *"Different every day" style.* This person's words and deeds depend on their daily moods, and they leave it up to their people to figure them out. They don't listen to their people's opinions, feel that those who offer opinions are insubordinate, and time and again make unfair work assignments and treat people unfairly.
- *"Safety before everything" style.* This is a supervisor who is constantly nervous about safety, preaches about it incessantly, and goes to extremes avoiding doing anything at all unless he or she is firmly convinced that it is safe. The people who work under this kind of supervisor do not have confidence in their work and become so used to hearing about safety all the time that they begin to pay only token attention to it. In the end, their safety winds up being threatened.

We have to always watch out for changes in ourselves depending on time, place, and circumstances. We must avoid developing any of these types of risky supervisory styles. There are certainly many other types of supervisors, but we won't try to cover all of them here. What we must remember is that *supervisors' ways of thinking and supervision are reflected in the people under us.* It is not too much to say that a supervisor's people are mirror images of himself or herself. That's why supervisors first of all must consider their own actions and attitudes. So as supervisors we must take a *firm stance* on safety. And in order to overcome obstacles to safety in the workplace, we must develop our knowledge and skills concerning safety.

Safe work methods and a safe workplace are indispensable for improving efficiency in quality and increasing production. So safety is an integral part of production, and it is unthinkable to separate the two. Safety means to *think of and take countermeasures before a safety incident happens.* In other problems, there may be a chance to take corrective action after something happens, and there are some problems we can never know about until after they occur. But in the case of safety, this is not permissible.

The key point of safety is to find abnormalities in workplaces that look normal at first glance, and to always stay a step ahead in thinking and acting. To do so, we must acquire a talent for spotting unusual behavior or unusual conditions at the workplace, for sensing the dangers of safety incidents occurring and eliminating them. Whenever you anticipate some change of circumstances—such as the introduction of new operations or techniques, the placement of new workers, the handling of new products and raw materials, the use of new machines, and so on—you must foresee new risks of incidents and take countermeasures.

That is the supervisor's job, and it has a company-wide effect on safety and production. Safety of the workplace is something that is preserved through human effort, not something that is best left to fate. *A perfect safety record is not a record of fate; it is a record of our efforts as supervisors.*

Supervisor Team Exercise: Have members discuss their own supervisory styles in regards to safety and if they recognize any of the risky supervisory styles in their own attitudes and behaviors. Discuss the ramifications of the different styles in their workplaces and how they would negatively affect safety. Then bring out ideas and suggestions on how they can reverse these patterns and what behaviors they could use to replace them.

Chapter 13

Two Key Aspects to Safety: Things and People

In Chapter 12, we defined an *incident* as an *abnormal occurrence that has the potential to lead to injury.* To prevent incidents, first we must dig down and find the direct causes, like unsafe acts and conditions, as well as the indirect causes that lead to these incidents. As you learned, these causes, both direct and indirect, do not exist independently, but form a chain. The next thing is to break the chain. We have to remove these direct and indirect causes to prevent incidents and injuries. This may be called preventive work or prediction of danger. For example, we tend to neglect our health and then have to go to the doctor and get a prescription only after we catch a cold.

As our Job Safety (JS) pocket card says, safety means to take action *before* a safety incident occurs, and it is *not* to handle the aftermath. This is the most important point, and the four steps for Job Safety on the card will assist you in achieving this. When using these four steps, merely following the card is not enough, we must also make correct judgments based on our safety consciousness.

Safety is an integral part of production, and safe work and a safe work environment help us to increase production. In this chapter we look at two examples that help bring out this point, the first focusing on the aspect of things and the second on the aspect of people. In doing so, we will get a chance to review and understand in more depth the JS four-step method.

A Problem with Things: The Miller Example

Let's look at a problem that occurred at a factory that manufactures parts for electrical appliances. Since we are going to be emphasizing the physical aspects of the workplace, what we have been calling things, pay special attention to how the supervisor in this story regarded the things aspect of the problem.

The Miller Example

A supervisor at the parts factory of a manufacturer of electrical appliances was going through the records of workers who would be coming to work under her in a personnel reshuffle and deciding who to put in charge of what. When she looked at one person's record, a woman named Miller, she thought to herself that they were sending her a problem person. Miller's record showed that she had been working for the company for 1 year and 6 months and during that time had suffered two injuries, one that didn't require any time off and another that required 2 days off. So the supervisor figured that since Miller was accident-prone, she would need special training and guidance.

The supervisor started Miller's training immediately the day she was transferred in. Her job was to strip vinyl insulation off electrical wire, install it in the product, cut it to the prescribed length, and attach a plug to it. She was to use a wire-stripper to peel the insulation. For about 2 days, the supervisor had Miller do the job while she kept a close watch on her. After that, since Miller seemed pretty much able to do it, she left her on her own.

After about a week on the job, Miller hurt herself by injuring the index finger of her left hand. Even though the wire-stripper is supposed to be used with the right hand only, Miller was performing the job by putting the vinyl wire into the tool, then stripping the insulation while holding the tip of the wire-stripper between the thumb and index finger of her left hand. At the time she hurt herself, Miller was just trying to squeeze the wire-stripper shut with both hands when a fellow worker tripped over the vinyl wire and jerked it, causing the index finger of Miller's left hand to slip and get pinched. The vinyl wire was being stored on a reel about 10 feet behind the workbench, and it had been casually pulled across the floor. In addition, the wire-stripper that Miller was using at the time was not the new one that had been given her when she was transferred in, but an old one that was hard to use because the stops were loose.

Let's examine this incident and lay out the incident chain that led to the injury. First, confirm what kind of *injury* was suffered. In this case her left index finger was hurt. From the aspect of things there was no damage done. Next, what kind of *incident* caused this injury? When who tried to do what, how, what happened, and what were the results? These are the conditions right before the injuries: as Miller was trying to squeeze the wire-stripper shut with both hands, the wire was jerked and her finger was pinched.

Then what *direct causes*, that is, unsafe acts and conditions, led up to this? The incident states, "She was trying to squeeze the wire-stripper shut with both hands." Why? It seems that the stops were loose on the wire-stripper and she could not hold firmly the vinyl wire to be stripped off. That is why she held the tip of the wire-stripper with her left hand even though the wire-stripper is to be used with the right hand only. The incident also states that the wire was jerked. That was because a fellow worker tripped over the vinyl wire behind her workstation. Where was the location of the wire reel that her fellow worker tripped over? The wire had been casually pulled from 10 feet behind where the vinyl wire was being stored on a reel. These were the direct causes of the incident and the injury.

What were the causes of these unsafe acts and conditions? This is the next link in the incident chain, the *indirect causes*. A direct cause was the stops were loose. Why? She was supposed to be using a new wire-stripper, but at the time of the incident, she wasn't using the new tool she received when she transferred in. That's why she was holding the tip. Another direct cause was a fellow worker tripping over the vinyl wire. Though it wasn't mentioned in the story, do you think the walkways and aisles were clearly marked in this work area? We can assume the aisle was not clearly marked. In addition to that, because the wire was pulled casually over the floor, we might also assume that there was poor housekeeping in the work area. These were the indirect causes of the incident and the injury.

We have mentioned over and over again that the meaning of safety is to consider measures and take action before a safety incident occurs. It is *not* to handle the aftermath. Now that we have practiced identifying and recognizing the direct and indirect causes that led to an incident that resulted in an injury, let's turn to the JS four-step method and practice it with an eye on learning how to prevent these incidents and injuries from occurring in the first place. In other words, let's study how the method can help us recognize these causes and deal with them *before* disaster strikes.

Supervisor Team Exercise: Review the list of safety incidents and injuries the team made in Chapter 12. Have each member bring in a safety incident (this includes what we call near misses) that was recently handled. It must be something that took place at his or her own work-site and upon which he or she has already taken action. Don't let members bring in problems that are too complicated, but it is best that their problems have a clear cause-and-effect relationship.

Have one person tell briefly what kind of injury was suffered in what kind of incident *without saying the action or countermeasures taken*. Did it require time off? How many days? What about damage to things? Write these details on the right side of the board under the heading "Injury." Next, have the person explain what kind of incident caused the injury. When who tried to do what, how, what happened, and what were the results? Write these down to the left of the injury statement under the heading "Incident." Then bring out the direct causes—the unsafe acts and conditions—that led up to this incident. This is what happened, but why? How did it happen? Write these to the left of the incident statement under the heading "Direct Causes." Now, what sort of indirect causes were behind these direct causes? In other words, what are the causes of these direct causes? Write them down to the left of the direct causes under the heading "Indirect Causes." If there are any other things that would make it easier to understand the circumstances, have the lead person tell them and list them to the far left under the heading "Items." For example, is there anything else about this person we should know? Where was the supervisor of the work at that time?

Have the group recognize and discuss the chain of events that culminated in the injury to the worker. Could it have been prevented? What do the team members think? The remaining team members will have a chance to practice the same process on their incidents in the last exercise in this chapter.

Step 1: Spot the Causes of Danger

When spotting the causes of danger, the first two items on the card instruct us to *check the situation, check the record, and talk to people* for *both things and people.* Let's look at the three elements of item 1 one at a time. The causes we have already pointed out in the previous discussion when *Checking the situation* for *Both things and people* would be

- The stops were loose on the wire-cutters.
- Miller held the tip of the wire-stripper with her left hand.
- The wire had been casually pulled from 10 feet behind.
- Miller wasn't using the new tool she received when she transferred in.
- The aisle was not clearly marked.
- Housekeeping was poor.

By checking the situation you can learn the true state of the workplace and spot any abnormalities. Are there any other causes besides these that could be discovered by checking the situation? It seems as though we have them all.

Next, which of the causes were discovered by *checking the record* for *both things and people?* By checking the record you can learn about the history of the person and the workplace, and by learning about the past, you can foresee what might happen in the future. When did she join the company? She has been with the company 1 year and 6 months. Did she have any record of incidents or injuries? Yes, two injuries: one injury requiring no time off and the second incident requiring 2 days off.

Finally, which of the causes identified so far were discovered by *talking to people* for *both things and people?* You cannot get a complete picture of a situation only by looking in from the outside. By talking to the person involved and his or her fellow workers and getting their opinions and feelings, you can better understand what is going on. It seems that the supervisor here did not talk to anyone about the conditions just before the incident occurred, so there are no causes or items here. Let's move on to the next item, then: *check regulations and standards.* These are the minimum requirements that must be met in order to ensure safe work. Miller was using the wire-stripper with both hands, but the standard is that the wire-stripper should be used with the right hand only. So this is another item to add to the list of causes that you picked up by using the card.

The next two items under step 1 are to *always be aware* and *foresee risks of incidents and injuries.* By being constantly aware of problems you can systematically think about possible causes of incidents. And if you hypothesize and foresee incidents that may arise from the causes you are searching for, you sometimes notice things you hadn't seen before. The caution point for step 1 is to *dig down deep,* and this is the point to watch for in all of step 1. In other words, don't get wrapped up only in what you can see. You must dig down deep for the true underlying causes. This attitude is critical to maintaining a safety consciousness.

Supervisor Team Exercise: Have the lead member review the causes listed on the board for the injury described in the last exercise. Which of these causes were discovered by *checking the situation for both things and people?* Are there any causes not written on that board that could be discovered by checking the situation for things and people both? Write any additions on the board. Ask the same two questions for *check the record* and *talk to people* while writing any additions on the board. Then identify which of the causes on the board were discovered by *checking regulations and standards.* Are there any causes not written that could be discovered by checking regulations and standards? Emphasize the importance of *always being aware* and *foreseeing risks of incidents and injuries.* Team members can then ask questions about the incident, which might bring out additional causes. When the team feels they have *dug down deep* to get to the underlying causes, then move on to step 2.

Step 2: Decide on Countermeasures

In step 2 you decide on countermeasures to take that will eliminate the causes of danger. In order to do this, the first item under this step is to *fit the causes together and consider their bearings on each other.* Fitting the causes together means to consider whether there are any omissions or inconsistencies in the causes you have found, and consider their bearings on each other means to consider the diverse relationships between the causes, in other words, the cause-and-effect relationships or interrelationships. The next two items are to *ask people who have detailed knowledge* and *think of several countermeasures*. When you are considering countermeasures, you should get good ideas and hints by talking to experienced people and specialists as much as possible. When thinking of countermeasures, consider if we can (1) engineer the hazard out, (2) add administrative controls, and (3) apply personal protective equipment (PPE). And don't settle with just one or two ideas for countermeasures. By thinking of several countermeasures you will be better able to ensure that the cause of danger will be eliminated.

In live Training Within Industry (TWI) classes participants consider the Miller example along with the causes that were available to Miller's supervisor at the time of the injury, and they can think of several countermeasures, such as the following:

- Have her do a different job.
- Change the wire-stripper for a new one.
- Move the vinyl wire closer.
- Get fellow workers' cooperation.
- Give her more training.
- Inspect the workplace.

All of these countermeasures are derived from the causes of danger spotted in step 1. Before giving consideration to each countermeasure, though, we must check them one by one against the fourth item under step 2, *make sure of accordance with policies, regulations, and standards*. In the list of countermeasures above, we can see that all of them comply with these criteria and can be enforced in the workplace. The last item under step 2 is to *decide on backup measures, too*, which means the supervisor should not be satisfied even if she has several countermeasures to consider. She must make doubly sure that she will be able to eliminate the causes of danger without fail and she can do this by coming up with secondary measures to use in case the first countermeasures cannot be implemented for any reason.

> **TWI note:** Once a countermeasure has been identified, it must be developed more concretely so that it can be carried out with assurance. If the countermeasure has to do with people, use the TWI Job Instruction (JI) and Job Relations (JR) methods to implement it. If the countermeasure has to do with things and procedures, use the Job Methods (JM) improvement plan to implement it. These methods, described in this book, will ensure that the countermeasure will be both effective and successful.

Unfortunately, Miller's supervisor did not have training in Job Safety and was not able to carry out the careful analysis of the problem you are doing here. The caution point for step 2 is, *Are you yourself the cause?* Do you think the supervisor's attitude and leadership style played a role in the outcome? Having decided that Miller was just an accident-prone person, she failed to see past her own preconceptions and did not try to get to the true causes of the accident. Below is what she did.

The Miller Example (continued)

After sending Miller to the nurse, where it turned out not to be a serious injury, the supervisor made out a safety report for her boss. Then, the supervisor immediately decided to assign Miller to an easy job. Her reasoning was that Miller was an accident-prone person who had already had two accidents at her former workplace. So she figured she would find some way or other as soon as possible to do something about Miller.

She gave Miller's job to a more experienced worker named Kelly, who had been working in the section for several months, and assigned Miller to sweeping the workplace, emptying the trash, and so on. Not 1 week after this change, though, Kelly had exactly the same kind of accident that Miller had experienced. After these repeated accidents, the supervisor warned everyone, beginning with Kelly.

Two or three days later, Miller came to ask the supervisor for a transfer. The supervisor went immediately to her boss, told him about Miller's accident, and recommended that she be transferred. But when Miller's coworkers heard about it, they complained that Miller had been treated unfairly. They felt she had not been given a chance to prove herself, and their complaints created a disruption in the department. Hence the supervisor sought help from her boss.

From her boss's investigation, the following points became clear. Miller's two earlier accidents had occurred during her 4-month training period. In the year and 2 months she had been at her former workplace, she had had no other accidents. Furthermore, although new workers entering the workplace were given new tools, the senior employees had been appropriating those new tools for their own use and making the new workers work with the old tools that were hard to use. When Kelly was hurt, he was using the old worn-out wire-stripper that Miller had been using.

Since the aisle at this workplace was not clearly defined, people often walked haphazardly across the work area, which was also poorly arranged. The supervisor had noticed these things, but it had not occurred to her that they presented a safety problem.

Some new items came out of the investigation by the supervisor's boss: Miller's two earlier accidents happened in the 4-month training period, and Miller had no accidents in 1 year and 2 months at her former workplace. Moreover, Kelly was hurt using the old tool that Miller had been using when she got hurt. We were also able to confirm two conjectures made earlier when looking at the incident chain, namely, that the aisle was not clearly marked and the poor housekeeping in the work area. A new indirect cause not known before also came out: senior employees were appropriating the new tools so that senior employees used new ones and new workers used old ones.

Supervisor Team Exercise: Have the group look at the lead member's incident chain, the indirect and direct causes, as well as other items that led to the incident and injury, and *fit the causes together* considering whether or not there are any omissions or inconsistencies. Then *consider their bearings on each other* considering the cause-and-effect relationships or interrelationships. Then have team members suggest *countermeasures* for eliminating the causes of danger. Each member who proposes a countermeasure should identify which causes and items he or she used to come up with that countermeasure. The lead member should state whether the countermeasure goes against any *policies, regulations, or standards* in his or her department. If so, it should be discarded. Have lead member consider if he/she may be the cause in anyway of the incident.

Step 3: Enforce Countermeasures

On the day Miller was transferred in, the supervisor gave her some training because she felt, from her review of Miller's record, that she was an accident-prone person. This was a countermeasure she took before the accident happened. Then, after she got injured, she assigned Miller to an easy job and assigned Kelly to Miller's job. She felt these countermeasures would solve the problem, though she was still left trying to figure out what to do with Miller besides just having her sweeping and emptying the trash. However, after a week, Kelly was also injured, so what did the supervisor do then? She warned everyone after Kelly's accident, beginning with Kelly. When Miller came to ask for a transfer, the supervisor jumped on the chance to rid herself of her problem employee and recommended Miller's transfer to her own boss. But the problem continued. Miller's coworkers complained about the treatment she was getting, and this disrupted the work in the department. Finally, the supervisor ran out of options and sought help from her boss.

In taking her countermeasures, the supervisor overlooked many of the causes she knew about, such as the wire pulled across the floor and the loose stops on the old wire-stripper Miller was using instead of the new one she had been given. Then there were the things she didn't know that were discovered from the boss's investigation. What do you think is shown by the fact that Miller applied for a transfer and her coworkers disrupted the workplace with their complaints? This supervisor couldn't see any of these other things because she had already made up her mind that Miller was just an accident-prone person. By giving consideration to the causes she overlooked we could think of different countermeasures, like the ones listed in step 2 above.

Did this supervisor's countermeasures work out well? The first item under step 3 is, *Can you handle this yourself?* She did enforce them herself, but they ended in failure. Item 2 is, *Do you need support from your supervisor?* Did she report to her own boss? What did she report? She recommended Miller's transfer. Item 3 is, *Whose cooperation should you get?* In the end, she had to ask for her boss's help. The caution point for this step is to *put into effect immediately*, and here we can say that the supervisor did take her countermeasures right away. But were they the correct countermeasures?

Supervisor Team Exercise: Have the lead member now tell what countermeasure he or she took and point out which causes were used to come to that decision.

Apply the three items of step 3 to the problem. Was the member the appropriate person to handle the problem? Did he or she seek help from his or her supervisor? Whose cooperation was received? Was the countermeasure put into effect immediately?

Step 4: Check Results

When you enforce countermeasures, you have to check the results. This supervisor didn't check the results, but let's think about how this should have been done. The first item is to *check again and again*. First, you need to check several times. Then the second item is, *Was it carried out for certain?* If the actual effect of the countermeasures is *not* noticeable, then they are useless. What does the occurrence of a second accident, when Kelly got hurt, signify? Obviously her initial countermeasures were not effective. The third item is, *Were the causes eliminated?* Were the causes eliminated by the supervisor's countermeasures? What about the fellow worker tripping over the wire? The caution point for this step is, *Have any new causes arisen?* Since countermeasures taken sometimes become the cause of the next safety incident, you have to be especially careful here.

The last line on the card, at the bottom, is "Safety incidents are caused; break the chain." Did the supervisor get to the root causes and break the incident chain? Obviously not. While she did consider some aspects of people in the problem, she overlooked many important points concerning the physical aspects, or things. If she had given a little more thought to causes from the aspect of things, she probably wouldn't have taken the countermeasures she did.

Supervisor Team Exercise: Discuss the lead member's safety incident, applying the three items in step 4. How often did he or she check? Just once, or again and again? Does the lead member think it was carried out for certain? Is he or she sure that all the causes were eliminated? Finally, have any new causes arisen? In the end, does the team think that the chain has been broken?

Rules for Things

Let's look in more detail about the aspect of things in the workplace. As we saw in the Miller case, if you get too absorbed in just the people aspect of the problem, you may fail to consider the things involved, like the tools, materials, and layout. No matter how conscientious people are about safety, if the workplace is poorly arranged, accidents will happen. Our responsibility as supervisors is to create and maintain a safe workplace that is easy to work in.

First, then, we must look at the work from the aspect of things. The back side of the JS card is shown in Figure 13.1 and lists the items we need to consider when looking at things. Let's look at these items one by one:

- *Parts and materials.* These must of course meet safety standards. Depending on shape, people might be hurt on corners or edges. Depending on type of material or weight, safety incidents might arise when things split or break.
- *Facilities, machines, and tools.* It must be possible to actually use these things. For example, it's useless to have an aisle that is an aisle in name only,

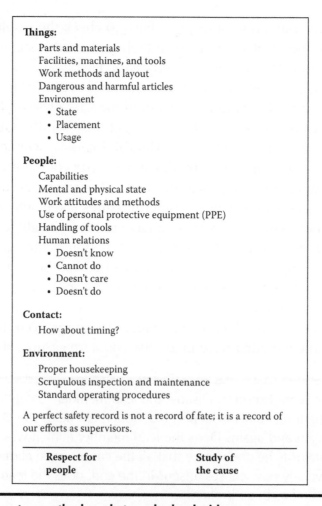

Things:

    Parts and materials
    Facilities, machines, and tools
    Work methods and layout
    Dangerous and harmful articles
    Environment
      • State
      • Placement
      • Usage

People:

    Capabilities
    Mental and physical state
    Work attitudes and methods
    Use of personal protective equipment (PPE)
    Handling of tools
    Human relations
      • Doesn't know
      • Cannot do
      • Doesn't care
      • Doesn't do

Contact:

    How about timing?

Environment:

    Proper housekeeping
    Scrupulous inspection and maintenance
    Standard operating procedures

A perfect safety record is not a record of fate; it is a record of our efforts as supervisors.

Respect for people	Study of the cause

Figure 13.1 JS four-step method pocket card—back side.

safety devices that don't work, or an emergency door that won't open. Sharp things that rotate; smooth, slippery, or inclined surfaces; and so on, may be terribly dangerous things depending on how they are secured and handled. Don't think we're covered just because we have the proper number of fire extinguishers and sufficient PPE in place.

■ *Work methods and layout.* Work methods must be decided on with respect to safety. You can't have set standards while actual working methods differ from these standards simply for convenience. Safe work is impossible if the work method itself or the layout is dangerous.

■ *Dangerous and harmful articles.* Dangerous articles mean explosive, flammable, or combustible articles, for instance, gunpowder, gasoline, and matches. Harmful articles mean things like gas, vapor, dust, and radioactive and carcinogenic substances that are harmful to the human body. Special attention must be paid to the daily handling and storage of these things.

■ *Environment.* Various factors such as temperature, humidity, ventilation, lighting, and noise often act to make dangerous and harmful articles even more dangerous. Moreover, they also act on people to cause unstable emotional states and behavior. If it's too bright, you get dizzy; if it's too dark, it's hard to see things; if it's too noisy, you don't know when something heavy is approaching.

 – *State, placement, and usage.* *State* means the nature and characteristics of a thing. Gasses that are heavier than air settle; lighter ones diffuse. *Placement* means the method of storing or securing things. Special methods may be necessary depending on the storage period or thing being stored, and things that move easily must be specially secured, by wheel blocks, for example. It's safer to store ladders and such things on their sides than to leave them standing. *Usage* means how things are handled, transported, and so on. Some things are absolutely forbidden; others must be done only in a certain way. That's the purpose of regulations, standards, and rules. Even a stick may become a dangerous weapon, depending on its use.

We have to understand these things and consider all of them together. We have been looking at the aspect of things here, but things, different from people, are pretty straightforward. Things in themselves don't cause incidents. Causes of incidents are created by people or by the interaction of things. By creating and maintaining correct conditions right from the start, you will be able to notice any deviations in things immediately and thus be able to cut off and prevent incidents and injuries from occurring.

A Problem with People: The Thomas Example

In the Miller example, a supervisor ended up creating another problem because she considered the situation only from the aspect of people. She failed to consider it from the aspect of things when thinking about the causes and missed the true source of the problem. In this example, a supervisor handles a problem by giving careful attention to the nature of the people under him as well as the conditions in the workplace. And by speaking thoroughly with the people concerned and checking the record, he was able to get good results. This is a case where a safety incident hasn't happened yet and will demonstrate the true nature of how the JS four-step method should work. So observe where this supervisor looks, what he considers, and how he talks with his people. Also, look at the way the supervisor treats his people, that is, how the workers feel and how they do their jobs.

The Thomas Example

A factory was expanding rapidly and decided to rationalize product inspection by placing the inspection staff, who were part of the test section, under the engineering section. Though by custom the change would not be announced until a week before it took effect, the supervisor in charge found out that workers had already found out and were gossiping about whether a group–leader system would be adopted to facilitate the change. They were also discussing who would become group leaders.

Thomas was an ambitious worker who had been in the section for 6 years. He was now one of the natural leaders, and his name was included in the candidates rumored to become group leader. It may have been the supervisor's imagination, but Thomas even seemed to be acting that way. The supervisor tried talking to Thomas casually at lunchtime. As usual, the good-natured Thomas had a lot to say without being asked. "I've been thinking about getting married. As soon as I'm promoted to a certain position, I'd like to start a family and I expect that time will come before long. When the time comes, I'm sure I'll be needing your advice," he said. With all that, the supervisor could hardly get a word in edgewise.

The supervisor checked Thomas's records, which were spotless. But when he looked into the records of some of Thomas's coworkers, those who looked to him as a leader, he found that two of them had cut themselves one after another just 8 months ago. The supervisor had been transferred to this section 6 months ago and was not in charge when these injuries occurred. The supervisor spoke to the two workers, and after some initial reluctance, they told him that at the time of the accidents another section had been added to the engineering section and Thomas had thought then, as now, that he would become a group leader.

As it turned out, a group–leader system was not implemented and a disappointed Thomas, as the only way to get himself recognized, pushed them to increase production. These two tried to help him out of sympathy, and as a result of pushing themselves to work so hard, they cut themselves.

Supervisor Team Exercise: Before reading the next part, review all the items of step 1 with the team and list all of the causes of danger present in the Thomas example. First, list the causes by checking the situation for both things and people, then the causes found by checking the record for both things and people, and then by talking to people for both things and people. Next, bring out details that apply to regulations and standards that are not being met. Throughout the discussion, emphasize the items always be aware and foresee risks of incidents and injuries so that the team learns to build a safety consciousness. Finish up by asking if anything was missed? The caution point here is to *dig down deep* so we get to the true causes of the potential incident.

As we pointed out, there have been no incidents or injuries in this situation. Therefore, we cannot outline the chain of events that ended up in an injury since none has occurred yet. But by practicing and understanding the incident chain common to most accidents, we have already seen how seemingly normal or inconsequential conditions can lead to other causes that ultimately end up in an incident and potentially an injury. These exercises were meant *only to help us learn to recognize these potential causes of danger,* so now, in the Thomas example, let's see how to do that for a situation where no incident has occurred yet.

Step 1 is to *spot the causes of danger,* so let's take a look at this situation and follow the items one by one on the card. First, we will *check the situation for both things and people.* What are the possible causes of an incident considering the current situation? We know that an organizational change is to be made due to rapid expansion and the subsequent need to rationalize product inspection. We have also found out that people already know about the change, and there are rumors about who would be a group leader in the new organization. According to the rumors, Thomas is a candidate, and it appears that Thomas thinks so, too. Thomas has been working 6 years with the company and is both an ambitious worker and a natural leader. These points are items and possible causes of danger in the current situation.

Next, we must *check the record for both things and people.* The supervisor found out that Thomas has a spotless record, but when he dug deeper into the records of those who looked to Thomas as a leader, he found that two of Thomas' coworkers were hurt 8 months ago. This supervisor had only been in charge of this section for 6 months and was unaware of the injuries until he found them in the record.

The next item on the card is to *talk to people,* and here is where the supervisor was able to learn a great deal about the true causes of potential danger. He spoke to Thomas and found out that Thomas wanted to get married and start a family. He had dreams for his future and was looking to the supervisor to help him get ahead in life. When he spoke to the two coworkers who had been hurt 8 months earlier, they reluctantly told him that there were rumors 8 months ago of a group–leader system to be started, but that the system was not implemented. At that time, Thomas had also been considered a candidate. The two workers told about how a disappointed Thomas pushed them to increase production to get himself recognized. The two coworkers said they cut themselves as a result.

The third item under step 1 is to *check regulations and standards*, and here the supervisor considered that the standard was for releasing organizational change notices 1 week before the change. That standard had obviously been broken. He also had to deal with the regulations around safe use of tools so that workers would not cut themselves. The last two items here are *always be aware* and *foresee risks of incidents and injuries*, and the supervisor had to keep an open mind and hypothesize about what potential risks there might be that he wasn't seeing. The caution is to *dig down deep* and notice things he hadn't noticed before.

Step 2 is to *decide on countermeasures*, and the first item here is to *fit the causes together, considering their bearings on each other*. Then the second and third items are to *ask people who have detailed knowledge* and *think of several countermeasures*. Here again, let's practice this in a supervisor team exercise using the information Thomas's supervisor gathered in step 1.

Supervisor Team Exercise: Reviewing the causes of danger found in step 1, have the team members consider countermeasures for eliminating those causes. Each member who suggests a countermeasure should identify which causes he or she used to come up with the idea. Try to bring out in the discussion how these causes might contribute to a chain of events that could potentially lead to an incident or injury. Then discuss with the group whether that countermeasure might go against any policies, regulations, or standards. If it does, take it down. Try to get as many countermeasures as possible and bring out any backup measures that could be taken as well.

Some possible countermeasures in this example might be to *explain the situation to Thomas, forbid gossip at the workplace*, or *recommend a change in the announcements policy*. Once you have come up with a countermeasure, it is important to follow the final two items of step 2. As we practiced in the supervisor team exercise, the second item is to make sure of accordance with policies, regulations, standards, and this is always critical so that you do not create additional problems with the countermeasures that you take. The last item is to *decide on backup measures, too*, so you can see how step 2 requires us to do a thorough job of coming up with enough measures to completely eliminate the causes of danger.

The Thomas Example (continued)

Here is how the supervisor handled the situation. The supervisor spoke to Thomas the next day. He told him what a good job he was doing, but that he needed his help maintaining safety in the rapidly changing workplace. He asked Thomas if he would be willing to learn about the safety program from Mr. Sanders, the safety supervisor, and come up with a plan to promote safety in their department.

Though at first he seemed unconcerned, Thomas enthusiastically accepted the assignment. After getting a safety overview from Sanders, Thomas returned to his work and, whenever he could get a break, went through the safety incident records and reports. In about a week, he prepared a detailed proposal on his findings and suggestions. Several times during the week he asked his supervisor for help, saying he had never done anything like this before.

Together with Thomas, the supervisor took the completed proposal to their section head, pointing out that it was Thomas's accomplishment. The section head gave the order to implement the proposal immediately as is and named Thomas to lead the effort.

The supervisor thanked Thomas for his effort and encouraged him in his new assignment. Thomas admitted that he had not always been conscious of safety, but he understood now how important it was not only to himself but also to everyone in the plant. Then, the supervisor assembled the entire team, explained the proposal and its necessity, and explicitly named Thomas to carry it out.

These were the countermeasures that the supervisor took:

- Requested Thomas' cooperation on safety
- Sent him to Sanders to get safety knowledge and skills
- Gave him supplementary guidance
- Made a recommendation to the section head
- Encouraged Thomas to learn and grow

The supervisor followed step 3 to *enforce countermeasures* by following the card item by item. Item 1 is "Can you handle this yourself?" The supervisor was fully capable of doing these things himself, such as assembling everyone when he was going to implement Thomas's proposal and letting them know its necessity and that Thomas would be the person to carry it out. Item 2 is "Do you need support from your supervisor?" He did consult his boss in order to get approval and support for Thomas's proposal. Item 3 is "Whose cooperation should you get?" Do you think it had a big effect on Thomas that the supervisor sent him to Sanders, the safety supervisor, to learn about safety instead of trying to teach Thomas himself? The caution point is to *put into effect immediately*, and the supervisor sent Thomas to Sanders right away with the order to draw up a proposal.

It is always important to *check results*, which is step 4. The first item here is to *check again and again*. Did you notice how the supervisor kept a constant eye on Thomas after he returned from Sanders to see how Thomas's attitude toward safety developed as he struggled to complete the proposal? Thomas was not impressed at first with the assignment, but with the supervisor's guidance and Sanders's instruction, he gradually came to understand the importance of safety in the workplace. Item 2 is "Was it carried out for certain?" We noted how Thomas's nonchalant attitude became serious. The supervisor wanted to see first how Thomas would change on his own. The supervisor will have to keep a constant eye on whether Thomas's proposal will work just as planned or not. Item 3 is "Were the causes eliminated?" We saw how Thomas's attitude changed for the better, and this will most likely improve his relationship with his coworkers.

As we stated at the beginning, the purpose of giving this example was to not only see the importance of thinking about causes, but also help understand how important your people's *feelings* are, and learn how the supervisor can *grasp those feelings* and use them to help people learn and grow. If this supervisor had not considered Thomas's feelings, could he have thought of the countermeasures he took? As you have probably noticed, when the supervisor checked the record and then talked to the people involved in the injuries that happened 8 months ago, which appeared to be caused by Thomas's attitude, he chose to appeal to Thomas's strengths rather than critique his errors. By assigning Thomas to the safety project, he let Thomas learn for himself the importance of his own attitude on the safety of others.

Whether we know it or not, all of us as people have desires and want our wishes to come true. A good supervisor understands and respects these feelings, giving his or her people appropriate guidance that leads them in a good direction.

Rules for People

As we did with *things*, let's look in more detail about the aspect of *people* in the workplace. In Chapter 12, we brought out how people's behavior and attitudes in the workplace are greatly influenced by the example set by their supervisors. So it is important, first of all, for us to consider the appropriateness of our own attitudes and actions. The very nature of the supervisor may bring about wastefulness, unsteadiness, unreasonableness, or recklessness in the workplace. The result of this will be inappropriate directions, layout, and work assignments; incomplete training and guidance on safety regulations; superficial enforcement of safety regulations; and so on. Nevertheless, we must still take into account the unique aspects of each and everyone of our people in relation to safety. Figure 13.1, (p. 234), the back of the JS pocket card, lists items to be considered under the aspect of people.

- *Capabilities.* You must have thorough knowledge of your people's capabilities. There is no reason why this shouldn't be possible. To force them beyond their capabilities is to invite an accident.
- *Mental and physical state.* We say, "Sound in body, sound in mind," and a healthy body is a prerequisite for safe work. It is important to take heed of your people's health. How your people feel is very important. Each one has different feelings, thoughts, and hopes. Moreover, their physical conditions, feelings, thoughts, hopes, and so on, change from day to day.
- *Work attitudes and methods.* Do they devote themselves to their work? Also, you have to see that their methods follow prescribed work standards.
- *Use of personal protective equipment (PPE).* Use of protective equipment must be a *habit.* Moreover, you have to make them understand clearly that the reason for its use is not just to follow regulations, but also to protect their own bodies.
- *Handling of tools.* To use a proper tool properly is to work safely.
- *Human relations.* The work environment is a product of people interacting together. For example, one person's personality can make everyone else unhappy. If people's relations with their supervisors and their fellow workers are not good, they will lose their motivation. A person may be distracted. And, if you invite emotional instability, this distraction may lead to a safety incident.
  - *Doesn't know, cannot do, doesn't care, won't do.* If you dig down deep into a person's problems, you find that sometimes a person's knowledge or skill creates a problem with the person's feelings. When a person doesn't know or cannot do something, teach him or her well. Here the Job Instruction (JI) method will help you. When a person doesn't care or won't do something, it is important to think carefully about the reason why before you try to do anything about it. Here the Job Relations (JR) method will help you.

However, there are also people who do know their jobs, can do them, and do care about them, but are nevertheless accident-prone. These may be divided into the following general kinds of behavior:

- *Overcautious.* A person lacking self-confidence or who has low self-esteem may act passively instead of actively. He or she causes accidents by being overcautious.
- *Timid.* A person acting this way doesn't see things as a whole and pays attention to one thing only, worrying about trivial things. They may cause accidents by being heedless of danger from other people.

■ *Short attention span.* People like this are cheerfully active, but you can see at a glance that they are inattentive. They easily get careless. They could easily cause a much bigger accident than you would expect. You must keep an eye on them, especially when they are working with others.

■ *Tense.* When people are behaving this way they are extremely particular. They even move stiffly. This behavior may get them involved in an accident because they won't be able to adapt to changing circumstances. This person presents a danger to the people with whom he or she is working.

■ *Nervous.* These people are always on edge and hypersensitive. They frequently cause accidents because they overreact or react too quickly and burn out easily.

■ *Rash.* A person acting this way constantly causes a commotion and upsets the people around him or her. He or she charges forward without thinking of the consequences of his or her actions.

People's behavior is complicated. People will differ according to the time, the place, and the circumstances. Supervisors must not think that our jobs are finished if we only know our workplace people, teach them, and train them. We must watch their personalities carefully and give appropriate individual assistance.

Supervisor Team Exercise: Now is the time for all of the other members of the team to review their safety incident examples with the team. Have each member present his or her example, covering all four steps and following the instructions from the previous team exercises at the end of each step. Have the member outline the incident chain, stating and recording the injury, the incident, the direct causes (unsafe acts and conditions), the indirect causes, and any other items related to the problem. In step 1, spot all the causes of danger following the card to be sure you haven't missed any. Let the group join in with questions so that additional causes may be brought out. In step 2, let members of the team offer countermeasures and state which causes were used to come up with them. The team member presenting the example should confirm if any policies, regulations, or standards would be violated. Then, in steps 3 and 4, let the presenter tell how he or she handled each item of each step and why.

Chapter 14

Practicing the JS Method

We have said from the very start that the meaning of safety is to consider measures and take action *before* a safety incident occurs. It is *not* to handle the aftermath. The Job Safety (JS) four-step method is a skill we can use for preventing incidents and injuries before they occur. In that sense, we are learning to foresee the causes of danger and eliminate them before they have the chance to start or contribute to a chain reaction of events that culminates in an incident or injury. If we can break the chain of these indirect or direct causes of incidents, we can prevent disaster from happening.

In order to be able to recognize these causes, though, we practiced by looking at incidents and injuries that had already happened in order to see what we missed that led to the unfortunate incident. But this was only a skills-building exercise. The correct usage of the method is for prevention and not for mere accident analysis. In this chapter, then, we create an exercise that simulates the correct and true use of the method. We also give suggestions for a workplace inspection exercise to get you started on using the JS method regularly and effectively.

The Foreman Morley Example

Let's consider a problem at the workplace from a different angle. This is the example of Foreman Morley of a press factory, and you, the reader, will only get details you want to know and hear about as if you were Foreman Morley. If you don't inquire, you won't get the information. It will be tricky simulating this process in book form, so no cheating! After going through this questioning process, you'll be asked to consider countermeasures, so be sure to make your questioning thorough.

First, a little background. Foreman Morley is the foreman of the press workshop. In this workshop there are 12 presses from 40 to 150 tons, and the personnel consist of 4 group leaders, 24 press operators, and 24 assistants.

They work in two shifts, and every other week the early shift moves over to the late shift, but the foreman's hours are fixed.

One day, as Foreman Morley was looking around the workshop, his attention was drawn to the work method of Osborne and his assistant, Ashford, who were working on the 120-ton press. In Figure 14.1 you can see there is an upper die and a lower die in the center of the press. When the lever is pulled, the ram goes down and up. This is a hydraulic press and the lever is stopped by a stopper so it won't cycle again. In Figure 14.2 you can see the location of the two workers, Osborne and Ashford, who are working on this machine. Osborne's operation is

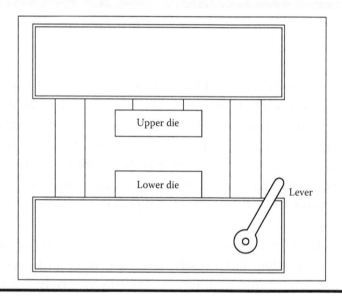

Figure 14.1   Press diagram.

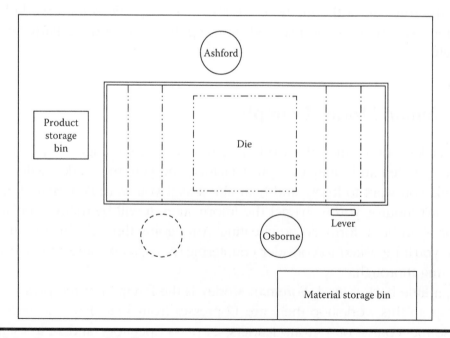

Figure 14.2   Press operation diagram.

to insert materials, operate the lever, and take out products. Ashford's operation is to take products from Osborne and put them in the storage area. The dotted circle shows Ashford's designated working position according to the regulations.

These are the circumstances that caught Foreman Morley's attention. Morley is 51 years old and has been working here since he was 20. He is confident in his knowledge of press operations and machines. In fact, he noticed a play in the lever of the machine Osborne was working. While he is a quiet person, he has a strong character and believes that experience is the best teacher. Maybe that is why the people working under him tend to avoid him.

Now put yourself in Morley's position and take 10 minutes (no more) to ask questions you want to know about this situation. On pages 253–259, *fold the pages over so you cannot see the answers to the questions on the right side of each page.* Peruse the questions and look *only* at the answers for which you have questions. Resist the temptation to read them all; real life does not automatically give you all the answers—you have to go and find them yourself.

Take a blank piece of paper and across the top of the long edge write the headings, from left to right: "Items," "Indirect Causes," "Direct Causes," "Incident," and "Injury." As you get answers to your questions, write them down under "Items," but if you recognize an unsafe act or an unsafe condition, write that down under "Direct Causes." If you feel it's a cause of a direct cause, then write that down under "Indirect Causes."

When your 10 minutes is up, go directly to the next section: "Step 1: Spot the Causes of Danger."

Step 1: Spot the Causes of Danger

The first thing to do in step 1 is to *check the situation for both things and people*. The back side of the JS card (Figure 13.1) gives us the items we need to consider for both things and people. Review these items as we go through step 1. Look at the incident chain you created while questioning the situation and identify which causes or items you found by checking the situation for both things and people. What are they? Is there anything else, like these points you already found, that you think you have missed concerning the situation? If so, go back to the questions and see if you can find the answer. Add these new facts to your table. Repeat the same procedure for *check the record* and *talk to people*.

Next, *check regulations and standards*. Can you find anything that applies here on your incident chain table? Are there any that you may have missed? In the role of Morley, you must *always be aware* and *foresee risks of incidents and injuries*. What do your senses and experiences tell you? Does this help you to think of anything else you may have missed? Continue to *dig down deep* until you truly understand the situation and have spotted the causes of danger.

Step 2: Decide on Countermeasures

In step 2 we *fit the causes together, consider their bearings on each other,* and *ask people who have detailed knowledge.* Looking at your answers, do you see any omissions or inconsistencies? Can you recognize the cause-and-effect relationships and interrelationships? These insights will help you with the next item, which is to *think of several countermeasures.* As Foreman Morley, what sort of countermeasures would you consider based on what you have learned about the situation and how you have analyzed it? If you are not considering the importance of *stopping work immediately,* you should go back and restudy the problem. When considering countermeasures, it is extremely important to think about **what you have to do right now** and **what you can leave until later**.

Write down on your table what countermeasures you think need enforcing. Some examples of countermeasures in this case might be:

- Stop work immediately.
- Replace lever.
- Make Ashford work in regulation position.
- Instruct Osborne on safe working.
- Have group leader watch them carefully.

For each of your countermeasures, make *sure of accordance with policies, regulations, and standards.* While we do not know the specifics of Morley's company, we can judge that any of the countermeasures listed above would certainly not be in violation. Then, *decide on backup measures, too.* Can you think of any backup measures you could put into place in case your countermeasures fail? Any stopgap measures or contingency plans? Finally, the caution point for step 2 is, *Are you yourself the cause?* As Foreman Morley, can you see any aspects of this situation where you yourself are culpable? What changes can you make in your own behavior that would enhance safety in the worksite?

Steps 3 and 4: Enforce Countermeasures *and* Check Results

Review the countermeasures you have listed and answer the questions for yourself in steps 3 and 4. In step 3, would you handle this yourself? Would you need your supervisor? Whose cooperation would you get? Would you put them into effect immediately? In step 4, would you have to check again and again? And make sure if the countermeasures were carried out, and all the causes were eliminated? How would you be sure? Also, you must check if any new causes have arisen.

Conclusion to Foreman Morley Example

We have two purposes in discussing this problem. First, there is the importance of considering *emergency countermeasures*. Here, it is important to consider the significance of what you notice. From things such as the play in the lever and Ashford's position, you considered the necessity of stopping the work immediately. The second point is the importance of spotting precisely *those causes that may lead to a safety incident.* Whenever you spot something, you always have to think, *What must you do right now? What can you do later?*

This is a true story that actually happened in a factory. As Ashford put his hands in to try to take out a product, the upper die suddenly fell, and he lost all of the fingers of both hands. Osborne had no idea how the upper die could have fallen. He had been handling the lever exactly as he always did. Only, just as the upper plate fell, he noticed a strange shock in the lever.

If this foreman had thought a little more about the importance of what he noticed, as you have done, and if he had thought of emergency countermeasures, this accident would probably not have happened. Later investigation revealed that the upper plate had fallen because the lever key fell out.

Action to Take on Abnormalities

We cannot emphasize enough times that safety means considering and taking countermeasures *before* an incident occurs, *not* handling the aftermath. Yet, as the incident record and case studies of incidents at any company show, safety incidents still do occur. When incidents or abnormalities associated with incidents occur, appropriate actions must be taken. In the example of Foreman Morley that we just studied, things like the key, which looked like it might fall out at any moment, or Ashford's not working in the correct position may be called dangerous, abnormal situations.

An abnormality means a condition that differs from the normal correct situation, a condition that forewarns of an incident, or a condition that exists while an incident is occurring. This includes unsafe acts and conditions. In effect, an abnormality indicates a serious situation that requires immediate emergency countermeasures. Because Foreman Morley failed to take proper action on the abnormalities he noticed, Ashford suffered the major injury of losing the fingers of both his hands.

A variety of abnormalities occur at workplaces every day. The following are some examples:

■ Abnormal noise, vibration, speed
■ Abnormal odors, emission of smoke

- Electrical power failure
- Defects in safety devices or protective gear
- Misuse of protective gear
- Misuse of machines, facilities, tools
- Use of defective machines or tools
- Repair or cleaning of machines while in operation
- Unauthorized entrance to dangerous places
- Unsafe working positions or postures
- Imprudent work above aisles

When such abnormalities occur, what sort of actions should you take? The following are some examples of actions that can be taken on abnormalities:

- Correctly size up the abnormal situation.
- Take emergency action.
- Report to your supervisor.
- Contact people concerned.
- Investigate causes.

First, it is important to correctly size up the abnormal situation. To learn where the abnormal situation occurred, and how serious it is, is the first step toward taking the correct action. After that you can proceed to eliminating the abnormality. As you did in the case of Foreman Morley, you have to judge what must be done right now and what can be left until later. When you suddenly encounter an emergency, it's easy to get flustered, and you may be unable to take proper action.

Sometimes, emergency countermeasures will cause trouble by interfering with normal operations. So we hesitate. We can prepare ourselves to handle emergency situations without getting flustered or without hesitating by deciding on standard procedures for emergency actions and repeatedly **conducting drills** according to prescribed procedures. We saw in the Morley example how important it is to prepare to take proper action quickly in emergencies. Preparing is preventing.

Along with taking such action on abnormalities, we must consult our own superiors and experts and get their instructions. Depending on the situation, we must also contact the people concerned or the associated workplaces and seek their support. Once we have eliminated an abnormal situation, we must swiftly dig down for the cause to ensure that the same situation does not repeat itself. To do so, it will probably be necessary to seek the cooperation of technical and safety staff. But in any event, *consider an abnormality as a symptom that may forewarn of some serious injury or even death.* To prevent serious incidents and injuries, we cannot afford to overlook even the most trifling abnormality. Moreover, it is important to conduct drills repeatedly according to standard emergency procedures.

What to Do When Injuries Occur

When an injury does occur, emergency measures need to be taken. What would you do if someone at your workplace suffered a serious injury such as Ashford did? The following are some things you can do when injuries occur:

- Stop the equipment or operation involved in the accident.
- Rescue the victim.
- Take emergency measures.
- Secure the scene.
- Write up communications and reports.
- Prevent secondary accidents.
- Investigate, get to the root cause, and enforce lessons learned.

When an injury occurs, both the supervisor and the other people at the workplace are apt to be frightened and flustered. We cannot afford to get flustered. The more flustered we get, the less we know what we are doing. To be able to take action without getting flustered when an accident occurs, you must prepare for such an eventuality in advance. Since emergency measures of first aid for the victim are only stopgap measures until you can get him or her to a doctor, you must also take care not to do too much, so that you don't further injure the victim.

Combination of Causes Involving People and Things

When considering emergency countermeasures, we have to dig a little deeper into *what sort of circumstances* result in the incident itself. A safety incident is caused by *contact*, in other words, by *collision*. There are various combinations of ways that objects come into contact, but all of them depend for occurrence on some kind of motion. That is because unintended contact is impossible when things are standing still.

The most frequent kind of contact that leads to incidents and injuries would be times when two moving objects come into contact, for instance, when you run into a moving vehicle. Next is where contact is made when only one of the objects is moving, for instance, when a person jumps onto or off of a stopped vehicle, or when a moving vehicle runs into a standing person. Why is this significant? We find that the *majority* of causes of incidents occur when *people are moving*. Thus, the greatest attention must be given when people are active.

Next is the movement of things, and this too is a major cause of safety incidents. But safety incidents occur even while we are paying attention and being careful. As we just stated, incidents are caused by contact, and such contact occurs precisely when two or more bodies or forces, like electricity or dangerous chemicals, *come together at the same time at the same place*. In other words, *timing* is a major cause of such contacts. As supervisors we must always consider timing when watching our workplaces, and it is a vital part of preventive safety. In other words, it is important to avoid bad timing by using emergency countermeasures and taking *permanent* measures to ensure that no unnecessary contact takes place.

On the back of the Job Instruction (JI) card (Figure 13.1), just below "Things" and "People," you will see a line reminding you to pay attention to this important point of contact, paying special attention to timing. There are limits to a human being's powers of attention, though. So we also have personal protective equipment and safety devices to avoid incidents when something unexpected happens. Here what we want is for the protective gear and safety devices to take the contact instead of ourselves. That is the purpose of using safety gear and protective devices, and we must ensure our people understand this.

Workplace Inspection

As a final **Supervisor Team Exercise**, have the team do a workplace inspection. This takes a considerable amount of preparation and planning, so we will lay out this exercise in a bit more detail. Select two members who work in the same area to take the team to their workplace for an on-site inspection. It is important that their superiors be notified ahead of time when the inspection will take place and why—as a practice of the Job Safety method. Instruct them to make diagrams on poster paper of the layout of the workplaces to be inspected so they can explain them before starting the inspection. Then arrange the place and time to meet and confirm that any safety equipment, like hard hats, clothing, gloves, and shoes, necessary for the inspection will be available.

For the safety inspection, make concrete use of both sides of the card that the team has been practicing up to now. In particular, you will make thorough use of step 1. When you *check a situation*, you must make sure not to overlook even the most trivial matter, which may involve a risk of injury. It will also be important to *check the records* of the workplace. Make note of any unsafe acts or conditions that you notice when checking a situation. These are things that you will want to question and investigate until we find any potential causes of danger.

A safety inspection tends to be an inspection of things, such as equipment and machines. But we must give our attention not only to the aspect of things but also to that of people. For example, we need to pay attention to the workers'

- Capabilities
- Mental and physical state
- Attitudes toward work
- Way of doing their jobs
- Use of personal protective equipment (PPE)
- Handling of tools
- Human relations

The best people to do this are supervisors who know the workers well. From the aspect of machines also, we need to pay attention to

- Their proper state
- Their placement
- Their usage

Supervisors are the ones who know these best.

We cannot think of workplace safety without considering provisions for controlling the environment of the workplace. On the back of the JS cards (Figure 13.1), under the heading of "Environment," there are three points we must always keep in mind. Safety incidents can only be eliminated through

1. Proper housekeeping
2. Scrupulous inspection and maintenance
3. Standard operating procedures

When the date and time for the safety inspection arrives, assemble at the site to be inspected. Divide the group into two, and have one of the persons who is offering his or her workplace for inspection stand at the front and give a safety orientation explaining the circumstances of the workplace: work content, layout, machines, staff, associated workplaces, and so forth. Have them pay special attention to dangerous places, dangerous areas, and dangerous and harmful objects.

Be sure to thank the people at the workplace for their cooperation in the group's study and explain that the members are not inspectors or evaluators. Remind the team members not to interfere with the work and not to get hurt. Take a note again of the dangerous places, dangerous areas, and dangerous or harmful objects.

Have each person inspect freely on his or her own. Then have each group sum up the results on poster paper identifying hazards found and recommended countermeasures. If possible, invite members of management as well as key operators from the area to a presentation of the results and comments. The leader of each of the two groups can come to the front and present the results of the inspection. By comparing what the two groups came up with and inviting questions from the area, the team will deepen their understanding of the JS method. Finally, have the manager of the area make some final comments on the presentation.

Questions and Answers for Foreman Morley Example

Questions Pertaining to Machines and Operation Methods	Answers
When was this machine installed?	The machine was installed 45 years ago. While old, it is still used to make standard parts and, with maintenance, has run well with few problems.
Are there any regulations for inspection of equipment?	Yes, there are regulations for the regular inspection of equipment.
What safety equipment is installed on the machine?	The arm is locked with a key as a safety device. There is a safety light curtain on the front of the machine.
Has anything happened recently with the lever?	Two weeks ago, the base of the lever broke during the night shift. The group leader on duty talked to the group leader in the welding shop and it was fixed.
Was the repair reported?	Neither Foreman Morley nor the maintenance staff knew about the lever repair that happened on the night shift.
What is the cause of the play in the lever?	The key looks like it may fall out at any time.
Did Osborne feel the play in the lever?	Osborne felt play in the lever when using it, but he was not too concerned.
Why was Ashford on the opposite side of the machine?	Ashford was on the opposite side of the machine because it was easier to take out the products from there.
Did Osborne seem concerned about Ashford's position?	Osborne wasn't concerned about Ashford's position.
Did the group leader check on their work?	The group leader looked around about 30 minutes ago, but at that time they had been working in regulation positions.
Where is the group leader now?	The group leader was temporarily filling in for an absent press operator.

Questions Pertaining to Organization and Job Responsibilities	*Answers*
What is the chain of command in Morley's section?	The setup of the manufacturing section consists of the section head, the foreman, group leaders, and the workers.
What other work is being done in this section?	The workshops of the manufacturing section consist of a press shop, an assembly shop, and a welding shop.
What are the rules and practices for communication between the different shops in the section?	Group leaders and foremen within the section may make lateral contact at any time to keep the work going smoothly.
Does the section head control this communication?	The section head neither encourages nor interferes with this contact.
What are the foreman's responsibilities?	The foreman checks the morale of the workers and watches the condition of the machines and how they are used. He makes work arrangements and assignments through the group leaders. With checking the progress of the work, encouraging the workers, inspecting the products, negotiating with other shops, and promoting safety, he works under a lot of pressure.
What are the group leaders' responsibilities?	The group leaders instruct the workers, arrange the materials, and fill in for absent workers.
How is the relationship between the foreman and the group leaders?	The division of work between the group leaders and that of the foreman is vague. The workers are sometimes troubled by conflicting instructions from the two.

Questions Pertaining to Individuals	Answers
Who is the section head and what is his leadership style?	The section head was transferred in from the technical department a year ago. He hasn't thoroughly grasped the work of the section, and he feels a little uneasy and impatient about the fact that the work goes on without his being consulted.
Who is Osborne and Ashford's group leader, and what kind of leader is he?	Age 31, graduate of technical school, sharp, highly skilled, workers respect him. Since he has a good head himself, he thinks his people will remember their jobs just as he does. He is meticulous in the arrangement of materials. He is sometimes doubtful of or dissatisfied with the foreman's instructions. He doesn't state his opinion much because he thinks the foreman would consider it impertinent. He is interested in machines and thinks he would like to manage them.
What kind of worker is Osborne?	Age 28, 7 years press work, skilled workman, married, no children. He was assigned to this machine about 2 months ago and has no recorded accidents.
What kind of worker is Ashford?	Age 24, transferred 1 month ago from another workshop where he was a temp and went to full-time status as an apprentice in this shop. He is serious, enterprising, single, and has no recorded accidents.

Questions Pertaining to Accident Record of Press Shop	Answers
What was the record on injuries requiring time off?	2 years ago, contusions, injury class 14, that is, 50 days.
What was the record on injuries not requiring time off?	In the past year, cuts, sprains, contusions, 1 each, total 3.

PROBLEM SOLVING

Chapter 15

TWI's Problem Solving Training

In the spring of 1951, Lowell Mellen and his associates from TWI, Inc. began teaching Training Within Industry (TWI) classes in Japan under contract with the U.S. military occupation. Mellen had been a district representative of the TWI Service during the war in Cleveland, and he formed TWI, Inc. in order to continue implementing the program when the service disbanded in September 1945 at the end of WWII. After successfully planting the three original J programs in Japan, TWI, Inc. was asked by the Japanese government in 1955 if they could teach supervisors how to solve workplace problems, and building on the success TWI was enjoying in Japan to that point, they then developed a new TWI program called Problem Solving training.

It seems strange today to think that the Japanese, with their manufacturing prowess in resolving production problems that results in the exceptional quality and durability of the goods they produce, would need lessons in problem solving. But things were different during these early years when TWI was still a new program. In a 1956 report, TWI, Inc. described how Japanese industry was controlled by "old hands" who didn't want to give up their "feudal prerogatives" and managed not by "definite policies, principles or fundamentals but by whim and caprice":

> This means that at all Supervisory levels below the very Top there is a reluctance to accept Responsibility for anything … so there is a constant crisis in waiting for someone to make a decision or come up with the answer to anything. The final result is that the average Japanese Supervisor is a very, very frustrated individual who hardly knows which way to turn.*

The "average Japanese supervisor" has certainly come a long way since then. By the time Patrick arrived in Japan in late 1980, frontline supervisors at Sanyo Electric Co., Ltd., where he worked, knew exactly which turns to take and were

---

* TWI, Inc., Final report, 1956, TWI, Cleveland, OH, 32.

active in confronting and solving the difficulties they faced each day. And the TWI Problem Solving training was a key piece of their training regimen.

To keep things in perspective, compare the situation in Japan in 1956 to the situation found at GM in 2009 after the company went into bankruptcy and was forced to open itself up to outside review and evaluation:

> When G.M. collapsed last year and turned to the government for an emergency bailout, its century-old way of conducting business was laid bare, with all its flaws in plain sight. Decisions were made, *if at all* [emphasis ours], at a glacial pace, bogged down by endless committees, reports and reviews that astonished members of President Obama's auto task force.*

While GM certainly learned a great deal about Lean and other quality techniques from its 25-year relationship working directly with Toyota in their joint venture plant in Fremont, California, they never updated their command-and-control corporate culture to a more humanistic approach, which is the essential change that needs to take place for the Lean tools to work. As we pointed out in the introduction of this book, the lessons learned in the United States during World War II developing and using TWI were lost after all the GIs came home and took their old jobs back, doing them the same way they did before they left for the war. In Japan, though, as we will now see, they not only fully embraced the TWI methods, but also expanded on them and pushed problem solving and decision making down to the factory floor.

Comparing TWI and Toyota Problem Solving Methods

As we reviewed in Chapter 1, Toyota, among many other things, experience tremendous success in its effective approach to problem solving with a focus on finding the root cause. So let's start by comparing the Toyota Problem Solving steps to the TWI method to show the direct correlation between the two. Knowing the strong influence TWI had on the early development, and current foundation, of the Toyota Production System, it will not be surprising to see how the two problem-solving approaches neatly align.

At the 2009 TWI Summit held in Cincinnati, David Meier, coauthor of *Toyota Talent* (McGraw-Hill, 2007), outlined the eight steps to problem solving currently being taught at Toyota. Table 15.1 shows the Toyota Problem Solving steps side by side with the four-step method of TWI Problem Solving developed in 1956 by TWI, Inc.

Both of these approaches spend a lot of effort at the beginning of the process seeking to correctly define the problem before beginning to solve it. As the saying goes, "a problem well stated is a problem half solved." Meier stressed in his

---

* "After Bankruptcy, G.M. Struggles to Shed a Legendary Bureaucracy," *New York Times*, November, 12, 2009.

Table 15.1   Comparison of Toyota and TWI Problem Solving Steps

Toyota Problem Solving Steps	TWI Problem Solving Steps

1. Clarify the problem	1. Isolate the problem
	  a. State the problem
	  b. Give proof or evidence
	  c. Explore the cause
	  d. Draw conclusions

2. Break down the problem	
3. Set targets	
4. Conduct root cause analysis	
5. Develop countermeasures	2. Prepare for solution a. Use JM, JI, and JR steps 1 and 2
6. See countermeasures through	3. Correct the problem a. Use JM, JI, and JR steps 3 and 4
7. Monitor both results and process	
8. Standardize successful processes	4. Check and evaluate results

presentation that, when dealing with a problem, where most people go wrong is that they immediately go out and try to fix it before they know what it is that is really broken. In other words, they want to go straight to the answer without taking the time to be sure they are dealing with the right question. The result of this haste and lack of clarity is to take shots at fixing symptoms, or perhaps even the wrong problem itself, while the true causes go on and continue to generate headaches.

Step 1 of TWI Problem Solving in effect covers the first four steps of the Toyota method. In both cases, the key is to get into the details of the problem, found at the gemba, so that we can understand clearly what we are actually dealing with. When we break down the problem, we are looking for the underlying components that are generating the visible problem, the thing that is causing the pain, and we can best do that by finding the proof or evidence of the various factors feeding the problem. In this way, we'll know that the problem exists as stated and have some idea of where it is coming from and on what scale. In other words, we should not "jump to solutions" after a cursory review of what we see happening on the surface of a problem.

Once we understand the details of the problem, then we can proceed to the ultimate goal, which is to determine the root cause of the problem. In TWI, when we say, "Explore the cause," we mean just that, finding the core or root cause that the TWI developers called the *problem point*. As we shall see, the TWI program devised a method of digging down deep to find the root cause of the problem, and this tool looks identical in practice to the famous Toyota method of "asking five whys." It is only when we get to the true cause of the problem that we can successfully correct it.

Where the two methods diverge is in how they prescribe resolving the problem at hand. The Toyota plan is much more open-ended, using tools such as brainstorming and consensus building in order to develop and enforce countermeasures. It stresses the vital need of taking time to work with other people related to the process in order to get their buy-in to the correction process. The key here, as John Shook explains in *Managing to Learn*, is to develop "a set of potential countermeasures rather than just one approach."* This allows for risk to be minimized by reviewing a variety of scenarios, and it also, more importantly, allows other stakeholders to take a more active role in evaluating and fine-tuning the correct solution. With various possible solutions on the table, the supervisor can entertain the needs and concerns of others while creating consensus and support around attaining the desired outcomes.

While the Toyota methodology takes this high-level approach to finding solutions, the TWI method gives specific prescriptions for solving the problem—namely, the use of the TWI methods of Job Methods (JM) improvement, Job Instruction (JI), and Job Relations (JR). It analyzes the core cause to determine if the problem is mechanical or people, or both, and then applies the proper TWI tool to bring that problem to a solution. Though this approach is narrower in scope than at Toyota, it allows frontline supervisors to use the TWI skills they possess, which are easy to learn and apply, quickly and effectively, to deal with the problems they face on a regular basis.

Finally, both the TWI and Toyota methods finish by thoroughly monitoring and evaluating the results of the problem-solving effort in a way that sustains the corrected processes. The Toyota method focuses a bit more on standardizing and sharing successful processes that have been found, an aspect covered in the Job Instruction portion of TWI, while the TWI Problem Solving method puts more emphasis on monitoring the people's reaction to the change—people resist change and see it as a threat to their basic needs—and looking for signs of new problems being created by the correction. But these aspects are well covered in both the Toyota and TWI methodologies.

It appears evident that the straightforward and commonsense approaches to supervisory management techniques originally proposed by the TWI programs in the 1950s are clearly reflected in the successful Toyota approaches to everything from standardized work to problem solving. The main differences in these two approaches, we feel, are the addition to the Toyota method of key aspects of Japanese culture and practice, such as consensus building, called *nemawashi* in Japanese, a focus on human development and mentoring, and the use of concise, easy-to-read-and-understand tools like A3 reports to support effective communication. These techniques are extremely powerful in bringing about lasting improvements, but they nonetheless do not take away the need for strong skills, as represented in the three basic TWI methods, in taking effective countermeasures to the problems themselves.

---

* John Shook, *Managing to Learn: Using the A3 Management Process to Solve Problems, Gain Agreement, Mentor and Lead* (Cambridge, MA: Lean Enterprise Institute, 2008), 75.

Therefore, the two approaches are quite complementary and can, and should, be used interactively. The A3 management process is, in many ways, a philosophical approach to dealing with the people who will be handling the problem. The TWI method is more of an on-the-ground tactical manual for frontline supervisors in solving problems. There are many good works describing the Toyota methodology, so here let's take a more in-depth view of the TWI Problem Solving method.

What Is a Problem?

A supervisor has a problem when the work assigned fails to produce the expected results. This straightforward definition of a problem is as true today as it was when it was written more than 50 years ago in the original TWI Problem Solving manual. In that manual, they created a simple graphic to display this gap between the current situation and the needed standard (Figure 15.1). Today, this model has been modified to reflect what is called the gap analysis, but, as can be seen in Figure 15.1, the idea is the same.

Some of the problems supervisors face are small and fairly simple and can be solved quickly by relying on the supervisor's experience and good judgment. But most of the problems we face will ultimately turn out to be much more complex and important than we at first anticipate, and we need to have an organized method of analyzing them before we rush to a decision on what to do. In order for supervisors to handle problems successfully, then, they need a clear sense of direction and specific steps that will lead them to a successful solution.

The TWI Problem Solving manual specified four facts that supervisors must understand if they are to resolve production problems successfully:

1. Their problems are seriously interfering with their ability to get out production.
2. Their problems have a direct effect upon cost and quality.
3. Their problems are not necessarily inevitable.
4. Their problems can be solved easily by following a definite pattern.

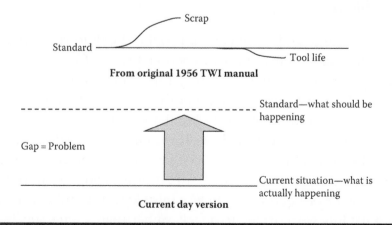

Figure 15.1 "Gap analysis" old and new.

The first two points have to do with an awareness of one's own responsibility toward resolving problems. Even as supervisors struggle daily to get out quality production while keeping costs under control, it's easy to be in denial about the problems surrounding them. They may consider these problems to be mere nuisances that get in their way and they don't realize that their struggles emanate from the very conditions they are trying to ignore. The second two points indicate that once they realize that they have problems that need to be addressed, there is a way to handle these problems.

Without a good method to handle problems, supervisors may have difficulty determining just what the problem is and confuse evidence of the problem with the problem itself. For example, if a machine is running poorly because it is low on oil, once the supervisor finds this out, he refills the oil and believes he has solved the problem. But the low oil level is just a symptom of a leaky valve, and so the supervisor's action is not conclusive and the problem continues, perhaps with even more serious consequences. Unless we are able to find the true cause of the poorly running machine, we will not be able to take the action that brings it back to normal performance.

Before we take action on any problem then, the first and most important step is to find, or isolate, the true problem.

Step 1: Isolate the Problem

As we pointed out earlier when comparing the TWI and Toyota methods, this first step of TWI Problem Solving consists of four distinct activities: (1) state the problem, (2) give proof or evidence, (3) explore the cause, and (4) draw conclusions. In this step, we want to clearly define the parameters of the problem so that we can search for the root cause. Once we find the root cause, we can decide on a solution course based on the makeup of the problem. Let's take a look at each one of these points.

State the Problem

When a problem is large and significant, it is not difficult to state what it is. But typically, problems are ongoing and in a continual state of flux. So they might be difficult to pin down. For example, you might find that you're having difficulties keeping up with the production schedule or that the morale of the workforce is not what it should be. How would you state these so that you knew more specifically the problem being addressed? We'll get into the actual figures, the data, of the problem in the next part, "Give Proof or Evidence of the Problem." But for now, to be more clear, you could state, "Parts delayed coming out of final inspection," or "Many minor errors due to careless mistakes." Careful consideration in defining just what it is we're trying to attack, rather than vague generalities or mere complaints, is the way to get off to a good start.

This does not mean, though, that we have to restrain our efforts to problems that are happening right now. We can also look for new problems just breaking out or ones that we see approaching so that we can get into them early while they're still small and easy to handle. We can also seek out and find problems by talking with other people and getting their perspectives and opinions, by reviewing reports and records to discover trends or hidden issues, or by simply anticipating problems and using our intuition. Having a "problem consciousness," or *mondai-ishiki* as the Japanese call it, means to always we aware and sensitive to where problems might be lurking so that we can take problem-solving actions to neutralize them before they interfere with our work.

Once we have identified the variety of current and potential problems we are facing, we should then prioritize them so they can be tackled one by one in order of importance. We can prioritize them by the level of impact they will have—some problems may be deemed emergencies that need immediate attention, while others might be considered threats that should be taken care of just as soon as reasonably possible. We could look at them by their level of importance or necessity—in other words, by the amount of benefits we receive if they are solved. Or we could look at them by the level of difficulty it would take to investigate and resolve them to see what amount of investment is necessary and available to resolve them. Based on this assessment, we can allocate our resources in the most effective way.

Give Proof or Evidence of the Problem

By proof or evidence of the problem we mean the actual facts, circumstances, figures, and so forth, that directly show the extent of the problem and prove that it is, in fact, something that needs to be dealt with. It is important at this early stage to look at data, wherever appropriate, that is concrete, well confirmed, and to the point. When faced with a problem, it is easy to get flustered and chase after something we think is causing trouble before we have confirmed its true validity. As we stated earlier in this chapter, we should resist the temptation to jump to solutions. On the contrary, once we have gotten specific data around a clearly identified problem, we are in a much better position to begin searching for the causes of that problem because we have taken the first step to locating just where those causes may be lurking and to what degree they are afflicting us. We are not on a wild goose chase—we have the proof and evidence.

What kind of evidence should we be looking for? This may at first appear self-evident—get data that are directly affecting the problem. But the TWI method makes a breakthrough here by beginning an analysis technique that continues throughout the entire problem-solving process: looking at the situation from two angles—the *mechanical* and the *people*. Especially in manufacturing settings, we commonly look at most everything from the aspect of physical things, like machines, parts and materials, tools and equipment, handling and storage, designs, processes, and facilities. But in doing effective problem solving, what we find, more often than not, is that what begins as a straightforward mechanical problem turns into, after careful analysis, a fundamental problem concerning people. As we point out in Job Relations, people are at the center of everything we do in fulfilling our responsibilities. So we must look equally at both aspects, the mechanical and the people.

From the mechanical angle, we look at things like

- Schedules
- Rework and scrap
- Tool wear and breakage
- Equipment breakdown
- Accidents
- Setup times
- Records and paperwork

From the people angle, we look at things like

- Productivity
- Work habits
- Knowledge and skill
- Safety
- Responsibilities
- Attitude and interest
- Job satisfaction
- Personality
- Physical condition and health

We have to take a fresh and honest approach when looking for this proof and evidence. In other words, we have to address the problem with an open mind and let go of our preconceived notions around the situation. We can do this by talking with people related to the problem to get new insights or contrasting points of view. In particular, if there are people who are directly involved in the problem, we need to find out who they are so that we can get a firsthand account of the facts. The purpose here, of course, is not to lay blame but to be sure we understand the true details of the situation. We should also review any available records to see if there is a history of similar or related issues.

Once we get these data, we should record them as concretely as possible. The TWI Problem Solving program created an easy-to-use problem analysis sheet to facilitate this (Figure 15.2). The facts from this part of the process are recorded under the section for proof or evidence, right under the statement of the problem.

Problem		Name:_____
		Date: _____

Proof or Evidence

Mechanical Angle			People Angle		
Behind schedule by			Productivity is		
Rework is up by			Work habits are		
Scrap is up by			Job interest is		
Tool breakage is up by			General attitude is		
Machine time is down by			Work quality is		
Accident rate is up by			Complaints are		
Setup time is			Attendance is		
Paperwork increased by			Job satisfaction is		

— Why?   Where?   When?   Who is responsible? —

Causes

The above problems are caused by…			The above problems are caused by…		
Job method			Incorrect job assignment		
Layout			Insufficient skill and experience		
Tools, fixtures, gages, etc.			Faulty instruction and follow-up		
Machines and equipment			Poor human relations		
Materials and parts			Personality situation		
Product design			Basic wants threatened		
Housekeeping and working conditions			Health and physical fitness		
Unsafe conditions			Unsafe acts		

This problem concerns: QUALITY? ○ COST? ○ QUANTITY? ○ SAFETY? ○ PEOPLE? ○

Conclusion

Problem Points (Core/Root Causes)	Mechanical	People	
	Things/Places	Don't know Can't do	Don't care Won't do

Figure 15.2 Problem analysis sheet.

Explore the Cause

Once we have identified visible evidence of the problem, the next thing to do is to find the causes, both direct and indirect, of each and every piece of evidence. When we search for these causes, we have to throw away our subjectivity and prejudice and think broadly. As the TWI method teaches, we have to dig down deep in order to get to the source of the problem, looking at each piece of evidence and asking "Why?" "Where?" "When?" and "Whose responsibility?" In doing so, we seek to get to the problem point, or root cause.

Here again, the method looks at the two aspects of mechanical and people when exploring the cause of each piece of evidence. While the topics are the same, what we are looking at now are those specific aspects of the process that contain the reasons for the problem.

From the mechanical angle, we look for causes in

- Method
- Layout
- Tools and equipment
- Materials
- Design
- Environment
- Unsafe conditions
- Standards

From the people angle, we look for causes in

- Job assignment
- Insufficient knowledge/skill
- Faulty instruction
- Human relations
- Personality/character
- Unsafe acts

We record these causes in the appropriate section of the problem analysis sheet right under the proof or evidence (Figure 15.2). In looking over these characteristics, we must consider the facts and piece together the cause-and-effect relationships between the various causes. In other words, we have to understand how there are "causes of causes," so that if we keep drilling down, we ultimately find the problem point, or root cause. This analysis leads us directly into the last section of step 1, draw conclusions, where we select these core causes as targets for our countermeasures (Figure 15.2).

The original TWI Problem Solving plan outlined this part of the method as we have described here. However, the Japanese later felt that the analysis was

Problem	Evidence	Causes		
		Direct	Indirect	Core/root
Customers complaining about late deliveries.	On-time delivery stands at 87%.	Packaging delays creating a bottleneck of finished product.	Delivery of packaging product is frequently delayed from printer. Films from art department are being held up waiting for confirmations. Need corporate approvals for correct usage of all company logo marks.	Poor communication between corporate marketing and plants.

Figure 15.3 Chain of causation analysis sheet—example.

a bit lacking in that, while it sought the root cause, it did not lead us there in a direct path. So they created another analysis form to be used at this point that better captured the cause-and-effect relationships we are seeking. By listing the problem, evidence, and causes—direct, indirect, and core—in a chain of causation, we can immediately see how these factors are all related to each other. So we call it the chain of causation analysis sheet, and we can see an example of its use in Figure 15.3.

Now that we have lined up this chain of causes to the stated problem, it's not hard to see that what we are doing here is continually asking "Why?" at each stage of discovery until we get to the bottom of the problem, or the root cause. This is exactly what Toyota does in their root cause analysis, what has been called the "five whys," or asking "Why?" five times until we get to the root cause. Looking at Figure 15.4, we can see that that is exactly what we're doing with the chain of causation analysis noting that, under indirect causes, there continue to be causes of causes until we finally find the core cause.

Draw Conclusions

The root cause analysis we have just completed does a good job of helping us identify the problem points. However, before we move on to try to solve them, the last thing to do in step 1 is to draw conclusions from our analysis and decide on a solution course. We need to ask ourselves, "If these causes were removed, would we still see evidence of the problem?" In other words, have we indeed found the true cause of the problem that is generating these difficulties? Is this a problem in my own area of responsibility? Should I handle it myself or report it to someone else? If it is my responsibility to handle, should I delegate it to someone below me or get help from other specialty staff functions like engineering, quality, and costing?

Problem	Evidence	Causes		
		Direct	Indirect	Core/root
Customers complaining about late deliveries.	On-time delivery stands at 87%. _Why #1_	Packaging delays creating a bottleneck of finished product. _Why #2_ _Why #3_ _Why #4_	Delivery of packaging product is frequently delayed from printer. Films from art department are being held up waiting for confirmations. Need corporate approvals for correct usage of all company logo marks. _Why #5_	Poor communication between corporate marketing and plants.

Figure 15.4   Chain of causation analysis sheet—example showing "5 whys."

Earlier in this step, we saw how we began to distinguish between the mechanical and the people aspects of the problem. Here, then, we have to determine if the problem points found are mechanical, people, or both. This determination will give us our solution course based on our TWI skills of Job Methods improvement, Job Instruction, and Job Relations. If the problem is mechanical in nature, if it concerns things, places, methods, designs, and so forth, then we will use our JM skill, along with other tools, to pursue a solution. If it is people in nature, then we have to think a little more deeply about the nature of the problem.

When problems are centered on people, we need to think about what is generating the problem behavior. Human motivation is complex, but we can do a simple analysis to help guide us to effective solutions. Since our focus is on resolving specific problems that have a bad effect on supervisors' duties to produce quality products or services at the proper cost, we can look at how people and the work they do are interfering with that goal. If the problem is because they *don't know* or *can't do* the tasks assigned to them, then the solution course is to use our Job Instruction skills. If the behavior is because they *don't care* or *won't do* those tasks, then the problem is a personal situation and we use our Job Relation skills to solve the problem (Table 15.2).

When deciding on any of these courses, we need to always keep in mind the company policies as well as the policies and direction of our own superiors. Even as we move forward toward solving problems in our own areas, we need to keep those actions in alignment with the overall goals and values of the organization. In describing how Toyota begins the process of problem solving, David Meier stressed the need for keeping in mind the long-term vision that will guide all of our decisions. This means adhering to our purpose, values, and philosophies (beliefs) to guide our strategic execution. This is especially true when it comes to taking actions to solve problems since these daily actions reflect the culture of the company we seek to build and support.

Table 15.2 Determine a Solution Course Using TWI Skills

Mechanical problems: • Use JM and other tools
People problems: • Don't know/can't do—use JI • Don't care/won't do—use JR

At this point we also need to consider how much of the problem we will take on at this time. Should we consider looking for a broad solution or stop at a partial solution? The important thing to consider here is which course will move us forward so that we can make progress on solving the problem. If we initially bite off too much, we quickly become bogged down and discouraged. The smarter course would be to address immediate concerns up front and then go on to address other problem areas later.

Summary of Step 1

Step 1 is the most important part of the TWI Problem Solving method because it systematically and precisely identifies the correct areas to address when going about solving a problem. By stating the problem clearly, giving proof or evidence of the problem from both the mechanical and people angles, then exploring the causes, both direct and indirect, of each and every piece of evidence, we can get down to the specific problem points that need to be addressed by our solution plan. Most significantly, because we have analyzed the problem from the mechanical and people angles, we can now determine the best course of action based on the nature of these root causes. Namely, we apply appropriately our TWI skills of Job Methods improvement, Job Instruction, and Job Relations to correct the problem.

Step 2: Prepare for Solution

Simply put, steps 2 and 3 of the TWI Problem Solving method are a recap of the four-step methods for each of the three original TWI programs: JM, JI, and JR. In other words, we implement these three TWI methods when we prepare for solution in step 2 and correct the problem in step 3. Step 2, *prepare for solution,* takes the preparatory phases of each of the TWI methods and applies them to the appropriate problem type (Table 15.2). Then, step 3, *correct the problem,* completes the remainder of each method so as to bring the problem to solution. Finally, step 4, *check and evaluate results,* is the follow-up step that ensures the problem is solved and does not reoccur.

Determine Objective		
Mechanical Problem	**People Problem**	
Job Method · Layout · Tools · Materials · Equipment · Design · Environment	Don't know or Can't do	Don't care or Won't do
Method Improvement	Knowledge and Skill Development	Attitude and Behavior Correction
Analyze	**Get ready to instruct**	**Get the facts**

1. Overall situation
   a. Flow chart
   b. Flow diagram
   c. Question overall job
2. Specific situation
   a. Work method—method breakdown
   b. Layout—discuss with operators
 	
Question every detail
 	
Why is it necessary?
What is its purpose?
Where should it be done?
When should it be done?
Who is best qualified to do it?
How is the "best way" to do it?
	1. Prepare yourself
	   a. Make a plan for training
	   b. Break down job for instruction
	      i. List important steps
	      ii. List key points
	
	2. Prepare the workplace
	   a. Correct equipment, tools, and materials
	   b. Have workplace set up properly
	
	3. Prepare the learner
	   a. Put the person at ease
	   b. State the job
	   c. Find out what the person already knows
	   d. Get the person interested in learning the job
	   e. Explain tools, equipment, and safety gear
	   f. Place the person in the correct position
		Review the record
		Find out what rules and customs apply
		Talk with individuals concerned
		Get opinions and feelings
		
		Be sure you have the whole story
		
		Weigh and decide
		
		Fit the facts together
		Consider their bearings on each other
		What possible actions are there?
		Check practices and policies
		Consider objective and effect on individual, group, and production
		
		Don't jump to conclusions

Figure 15.5   Step 2—prepare for solution.

Here, let's get a general overview of each problem-solving step, including a few additional tools and insights that were not part of the original TWI J methods. Figure 15.5 shows the details of step 2, prepare for solution, and readers of this book will recognize that the contents here, for the most part, come directly from the four-step methods of JM, JI, and JR.

Prepare for Solution of Mechanical Problems: Overall Situation Analysis

We said that mechanical problems are those involving things like methods, layout, tools, equipment, materials, and machines. While it is certainly true that all production problems will involve people in one way or another, either directly or indirectly, the fact that we are dealing with mechanical processes in producing a tangible product or service means that there will be many problems that are mechanical in nature. By mechanical we mean not only the use of industrial equipment, but any method or process of getting work done, including the handling of paper forms, the use of computers to process data, the creation and delivery of a service, medical procedures, and so on. These will affect the work in critical ways, such as the following:

- Quality: Scrap, rework, spoilage, etc.
- Quantity: Schedule bottlenecks, etc.
- Safety: Accidents, unsafe conditions and situations, etc.
- Cost: All of the above factors increase costs.

The first thing we want to do for mechanical problems is to question the job as a whole in order to bring to light troublesome or costly factors, such as transportation, inspections, delays, material handling, and safety hazards. Once we have found out in step 1 the problem points, or root causes, of the problem, the goal in step 2 is to search for the answers that eliminate the causes to these problems. This initial broad view of the work will oftentimes reveal the needed answers. For example, if our root cause analysis showed that the problem point was too much scrap caused by excessive handling of the raw materials, an analysis of the overall process would bring out where, when, and by whom the materials were over handled and suggest improvements on how this handling could be reduced to prevent the scrap.

When we question the work we have to keep an open mind. As the TWI developers pointed out, "The mind is like a parachute—it functions only when open." If we are going to find openings and opportunities for improvement and for solving problems, it is absolutely necessary to cultivate an open mind. To do this we must develop and maintain a questioning attitude. In other words, we need to question everything and never accept any method or procedure as being perfect. The greatest obstacle we have in problem solving is not created by technical difficulties but rather by the mental roadblocks we set up for ourselves when we cling to the attitude that we already are using the best methods available.

Here, there are three conditions that supervisors need to heed if they are to move on to effectively solving a problem with a specific job:

1. Just because a job is done in a certain way is no proof it is the best way.
2. Just because a job is done at all is no proof that it is necessary.
3. The fact that the method of doing the job has been in effect for years is no proof that it is the best way.

There are many tools available to us today to make this kind of a broad analysis. The original TWI Problem Solving manual taught the use of the flow-chart, which at a glance allows us to see the routing and production flow of the subject being analyzed (Figure 15.6). The subject of analysis, which we have identified in step 1 as a problem point, can be a part, assembly, material, paper-work, and so forth, but usually it is a part, so that we can use the flowchart

Flow chart (example)

Subject charted

Part: Angle plate	Date: _____
Material: _____	Department: _____
Person: _____	Charted by: _____
Paper form: _____	

	What and how current–proposed method	Oper. no.	Dept.	Distance	Time	Symbols
1	Materials warehouse					⇨ D O □ ▽
2	Move to press workshop			240 ft.		
3	Cut and stamp					
4	Move to boring section			90 ft.		
5	Cut hole					
6	Move to temporary storage			30 ft.		
7	Wait for inspection				25 min.	
8	Inspect					
9	Move to bolting area			60 ft.		
10	Bolt on					
11	Move to finished parts warehouse			180 ft.		
12	Finished parts warehouse					
13						
14						
15						
16						
17						
18						

Figure 15.6   Flow chart—example.

to resolve problems with work methods, layout, tools, materials, equipment, and so forth. The flowchart shows us the relationship between the subject and prior and subsequent operations, handlings, inspections, and storages. By clarifying the bigger picture of the problem area, we want to *cast a wide net* in our search for the correct solution so that we don't miss critical areas that have influence on the problem.

A second tool the TWI method introduced for this purpose was the flow diagram, which was none other than a graphic picture, or map, of the area to show the movement of the subject using lines and symbols (Figure 15.7). This is very similar in many ways to what we practice in Lean as a standard worksheet. It gives a more graphic view of the analysis area and makes it easy to see the layout of the process in order to make plans, reduce travel and movement, eliminate wasted space, and so forth.

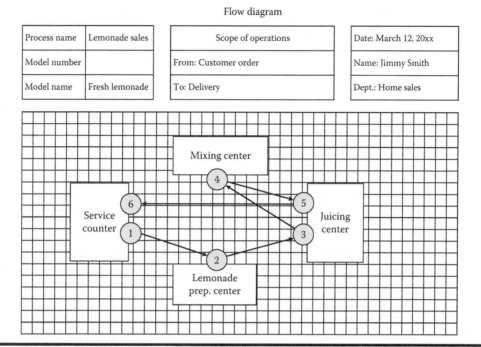

Figure 15.7   Flow diagram.

There are yet other, more contemporary, Lean tools, such as value stream maps and standard work combination sheets, which can be used here for the purpose of viewing the job as a whole in order to discover what needs to be done in order to correct the causes of our problem. The key is not which particular tool is used, but rather that we begin looking for answers from a wide perspective. More specifically, we need to grasp the actual conditions of the work we have identified as the problem point. If our analysis brings out the issues that need correction, we can move on to step 3, which would be to develop a new and improved method that corrects the problem. However, more often than not, what we learn from this overall analysis is not necessarily what specifically needs to be corrected, but only the location of a specific job or situation that is causing the trouble.

Prepare for Solution of Mechanical Problems: Specific Situation Analysis

Once we have located the specific job or situation causing the trouble, we then move on to analyze this using the Job Methods improvement plan. Here we take on the first two steps of the JM method, which are to break down the job and question every detail. As we learned in the JM section of this book, the breakdown is a complete and accurate record of the operation made right on the job as it is actually being done and just as you see it, not as you remember it or as you think it should be done. It lists all the details of the job, every single thing that happens, including all material handling, hand work, machine work, inspections, and delays.

Once we have listed all the details, we then move on to question each and every detail using the five W's and one H:

1. *Why* is it necessary? This is the most important question, and yet oftentimes the hardest to get answered. If the detail is not necessary, then it can be eliminated.
2. *What* is its purpose? If we're having difficulty answering the why, this is a check question to determine if the detail has a useful purpose or adds value. If the detail is found to be necessary, then we continue on with the other questions.
3. *Where* should it be done? Where is the best location to do the job? Why is it done there? Where else could it be done? Can it be combined with another detail?
4. *When* should it be done? When is the best time to do each detail? Must it follow or precede another detail? Are the details in proper sequence? Can it be done simultaneously with another detail?
5. *Who* is the best qualified to do it? Who is best qualified in terms of skill, experience, physical strength, and availability?
6. *How* is the best way to do it? Can it be done easier and safer? Can the layout of the workstation be improved? Are proper tools and equipment being used?

The key to this process is that the answers to these questions, asked energetically and thoughtfully, are the ideas that will lead to improvements and solutions to the problem at hand. At this stage, we only write down these ideas on our breakdown sheet and do not take any action yet; that will be taken up in the next step when we correct the problem. We are looking for new ideas on how to do the work that remove the problem points that are causing the problem. By questioning the details of the work method around that problem point, we can come up with answers to solve the problem.

The Problem Solving course added one more level of analysis here that is not part of the JM method: to look at the three parts of any job:

1. *Make ready.* This is the time and effort spent in getting things ready, such as materials, tools, equipment, and so forth. Also, the placing of materials or parts in the nearby work areas, from carts, containers, racks, and so on. It includes total productive maintenance (TPM) checks, 5S* activities, and safety precautions.

---

* The 5s's stand for 5 Japanese words that constitute good workplace housekeeping. Rughly translated they are: Sort (Seiri), Set in order (Seiton), S (Seiso), Standardize (Seiketsu), and Sustain (Shitsuke).

2. *Do.* This is the work that actually does accomplish the desired objective and adds value to the final product or service.
3. *Put away.* This includes all the details necessary to complete the job after the do operation is complete. It includes setting the part aside or placing it on carts, in containers, on racks, on conveyors, and so forth. It would also include paperwork and replacing tools.

When questioning the details of the job, we should first determine which of the three types of work each detail consists of and then *question the do details first.* If they are found to be unnecessary, then there is no need to question the rest of the operation around that unnecessary detail. If the do detail is necessary, then we continue to question the make ready and put away details. In fact, the greatest opportunity for improvement is in the make ready and put away details because they add to the time and cost, but not to the value of the product or service being created. In most jobs, less than 50% of the total time to get them done is taken up by the Do part of the job, and so these non-value-added details should be questioned with improvements in mind.

To sum up step 2 for solving mechanical problems, we should do the following:

1. Analyze the overall situation using tools such as the flowchart or flow diagram.
2. Make a job breakdown of the specific job where the trouble is located.
3. Question the details to find ideas upon which we can make the needed correction.

Prepare for Solution of People Problems: Don't Know or Can't Do

While not all problems are mechanical in nature, the truth of the matter is that almost all of them, in some way or another, are people problems. We said that we can break down these people problems into four distinct types: (1) people who *don't know* or don't understand the work assigned to them, (2) those who *can't do* the work due to lack of skill or practice, (3) people who *don't care* about the work and thus are not motivated to do the work properly, and (4) those who refuse to follow instructions and *won't do* the work as assigned.

We could think of many reasons for why these people problems occur. On careful consideration, though, we can boil them down to three main causes: faulty instruction, incorrect assignment, or personality situations that interfere with the harmony of a good work environment. Here, let's take up the first two categories of don't know and can't do, which are outcomes due to faulty instruction. What do we mean by *faulty instruction?* We can categorize faulty instruction into four categories:

1. Insufficient instruction
2. Incorrect instruction
3. Inefficient instruction
4. No instruction

The next question, then, is why do these faulty instruction situations occur? The major cause of these poor forms of instruction would be that little or no preparation has been done of the instructor, the workplace, or the learner. And these are just the points we looked at in the preparation portion of the Job Instruction method, which we call get ready to instruct. There are four things we do before we instruct:

1. Make a timetable for training.
2. Break down the job.
3. Get everything ready.
4. Arrange the worksite.

As we learned in Chapters 4 and 5, when making a training timetable, we determine *who* to train on *which job* and by *when*. The who and on which job factors are found in step 1, isolate the problem, where we identified the problem point causing the problem. What is left is to make a plan to determine when we will do the instruction. In addition, we also consider if it should be broken up into smaller instructional units for ease of training and effectiveness and, if so, look at the order in which we will instruct these smaller units.

Once we have made a plan for training, next we *break down the job* so that we have notes to clearly organize the job in our minds when teaching. The main reason for poor or incomplete instruction is that the person training the job did not take the time to identify the critical factors in the job, and the ensuing confusion leads to mistakes, rejects, accidents, delays, tool and equipment damage, material wastage, loss of productivity, reduction in morale, and so forth. The job breakdown allows you to put over the job to the learner quickly and completely because you know just what information you need, in the right amount, and in the correct order. The content of the breakdown includes *important steps* (what is done), *key points* (how it is done), and *reasons for key points* (why it is done that way).

Making breakdowns for Job Instruction is the most critical part of the method and takes great skill and practice. In particular, when we teach the key points we can be sure that operators know how to do the jobs correctly, safely, and easily. These key points are things that make or break the job (it has to be done just that way), things that injure the worker (safety), and things that make the work easier to do (a knack or feel for the job, a tip or a special piece of timing). These breakdowns don't try to cover every single thing that happens in a job, but are just simple, commonsense reminders of what is key to performing the job.

Now that the instructor is prepared to teach, the next thing is to prepare the workplace. We should *have everything ready*, like tools, materials, equipment, supplies, and anything else necessary to teaching the job. If we forget something and make excuses or use makeshift tools and parts, we set a low standard for the work and lose the respect of the worker. We also need to *have the workplace properly arranged*, just as we would want it maintained in actual working conditions. Otherwise, people will fall into bad habits and accidents are more likely to occur. In other words, we need to set the right example because these first impressions of the job they are learning will carry on into the future and affect the results we get moving forward.

The final thing we need to prepare for solution in these types of people problems is to *prepare the learner*. This is actually step 1 of the JI method as we saw in Chapter 3, and it gets the learner in the proper frame of mind to be ready to learn. Here we

- Put the person at ease.
- State the job.
- Find out what the person already knows.
- Get the person interested in learning the job.
- Explain tools, equipment, and safety gear (this is an additional item put into the JI method with the Problem Solving course).
- Place the person in the correct position.

To sum up, in order to prepare to instruct we should.

1. Prepare yourself (the instructor).
2. Prepare the workplace.
3. Prepare the learner.

Prepare for Solution of People Problems: Don't Care and Won't Do

Problems concerning people who don't care or won't do are situations concerning attitude and behavior that are unwieldy and difficult to handle. The Job Relations module of TWI was set up specifically to handle these kinds of problems and, more importantly, to show supervisors ways to prevent them from happening or, when they do occur, how to get into them early while they are still small and easy to resolve. In fact, the four-step method of JR is appropriately titled "How to Handle a Problem."

So it should not be surprising to see how the JR method, just as we learned it in this book, fits in perfectly with the Problem Solving program. In order to prepare for solution, first we *get the facts*, which means we have to be sure we have the whole story. Reviewing the record of the case is a way of being sure we know the full background of how the problem got to its present point. And since this is a problem with people, there are sure to be rules and customs that apply. Rules are conditions governing conduct and behavior and are written down in a policy manual, which supervisors need to know and abide by. Customs, on the other hand, are precedents or "unwritten rules," and many times these are even stronger than the written rules. Supervisors must take these into consideration as well.

Where supervisors usually fall down, though, in failing to prepare for a solution to a people problem, is that they don't talk with the individuals concerned in order to get their opinions and feelings. This is key to getting the facts because what a person thinks or feels, whether right or wrong, is a fact to that person and must be treated as such. If we fail to hear people out and learn where their bad behavior is coming from, then we'll never be able to take the correct action that solves the problem. We'll only be acting on assumptions, usually wrong ones, and attacking symptoms that do not get to the root cause of the problem.

After we get the facts, the next thing to do is to *weigh and decide*—in other words, to analyze the facts and evaluate options so that we can decide on a course of action. This analysis would include fitting the facts together while looking for gaps or contradictions in the facts. As we see the connections being made, we then consider their bearings on each other, looking for cause-and-effect relationships that help us understand the situation. Based on this understanding, we then consider what possible actions there are, being sure that these conform to practices and policies. We are now ready to evaluate these options considering whether each option meets our objective and what effect it will have on the individual, the group, and production. Through this careful consideration of the facts, we can be sure that we don't jump to conclusions and take a rash action, so common when it comes to dealing with people problems, which ultimately ends up not solving the problem.

The Problem Solving course added a few additional points to the JR method to consider that only further enhance the human aspect of the program. While evaluating the possible actions, it advised supervisors to

- Consider what the results of the action will be.
- Question the psychological effect.
- Not hurt the person's pride.
- Leave a way open for the individual to save face.

Step 3: Correct the Problem

Just as in step 2, the contents here again of step 3, *correct the problem*, come directly from the four-step methods of JM, JI, and JR. We'll briefly summarize the highlights of each method, but for a full description of how each is used, refer to the earlier parts of this book on each method. The contents of step 3 are seen in Figure 15.8.

Develop the New Method and Put Correction into Effect

For mechanical problems, we can make corrections when we improve the method in such a way that the causes of the problem are removed. We can make improvements when the details of the method are eliminated, combined, rearranged, or simplified. When we eliminate unnecessary details, we remove

Determine Objective		
Mechanical Problem	**People Problem**	
Develop the new method	**Present the operation**	**Take action**

1. Eliminate unnecessary details
2. Combine details when practical
3. Rearrange details for better sequence
4. Simplify all necessary details
5. Work out your ideas with others
6. Write up the proposed new method
   a. Flow chart
   b. Job breakdown sheet
	Tell, show, and illustrate one important step at a time
	Do it again stressing key points
	Do it again stating reasons for key points
	Instruct clearly, completely, and patiently but don't give them more information than they can master at one time
		Are you going to handle this yourself?
		
		Do you need help in handling?
		
		Should you refer this to your supervisor?
		
		Watch the timing of your action
		
		Explain and get agreement on action

Apply the new method	**Try out performance**	Take the action
1. Sell your proposal to the boss 2. Sell the new method to the operators 3. Get final approval of all concerned on safety, quality, quantity, cost, etc. 4. Put the new method to work; use it until a better way is developed 5. Give credit where credit is due	Have the person do the job—correct errors Have the person explain each Important Step to you as they do the job again Have the person explain each key point to you as they do the job again Have the person explain reasons for key points to you as they do the job again *Make sure the person understands*	Consider the person's feelings and attitude Inform everyone involved Don't pass the buck
	Follow up	
	Stress quality and safety Designate who the person goes to for help Encourage questions	

Figure 15.8 Step 3—correct the problem.

waste in our usage of manpower, machines, tools, materials, time, and so forth. We combine details when practical in order to improve problems with transportations, inspections, delays, and storages. We rearrange details for better sequence when the problem is one concerning location or excessive handlings, backtracking, delays, accident hazards, maintenance possibilities, or working conditions. And we simplify all necessary details when the resolution of the problem lies in reducing nonproductive work motions or making the work easier and safer to do. We are able to make these kinds of improvements based on the ideas we found in step 2, prepare for solution.

In developing the new method it is critical to write it down in the form of a proposal. This written proposal, which includes explanations of the current and the proposed methods as well as the expected results, will be indispensable when we apply the new method—in other words, when we sell the proposal to our boss and get final approvals of all concerned on safety, quality, quantity, cost, and so forth. It will be easy for these other parties to recognize and approve our changes when they know where our ideas came from and how they will go about solving the problem at hand. In addition, we must also make an effort to sell the new method to the operators because, without their cooperation, the changes will not be implemented and the problem will continue. The best way of getting this cooperation is to involve the operators right from the start of the improvement process using their ideas, along with any others, and giving credit when due. Finally, we must not let waiting kill our ideas and put the new method to work right away.

Instruct the Learner

For problems concerning people who don't know or can't do, in step 2 we prepared ourselves, the workplace, and the learner for instruction. It is our task in step 3 to deliver that instruction and teach them how to do the job correctly, safely, and conscientiously in order eliminate problems that result in scrap, rework, delays, accidents, damaged tools and equipment, spoilage of materials, low productivity, and so forth. We *present the operation* telling one important step at a time following the job breakdown sheet we made in step 2. Then we do the job again, this time stressing the key points for each step, again following the breakdown sheet. We do it yet one more time again, explaining the reasons for the key points. We can repeat this as often as necessary until they fully understand the job.

Once they understand how it is done, then have them do it in a *tryout performance*. The first time they perform the job, be sure to correct any errors so they don't develop bad habits—we do not want them to learn from their mistakes, but to repeat the correct performance that was presented to them by the instructor. Once you are sure they are able to do the job correctly, have them do it again telling you the important steps as they show you the job step by step. Have them do it again, this time stressing the key points. Have them state the reasons for each key point as they do it a fourth time. You can repeat this process until you are completely confident that they understand the job fully.

At this point, you can put them on their own, stressing the need to pay attention to their new work in terms of quality and safety. Be sure to encourage them to ask for help when needed. They are now able to do the job, but they are not yet experienced at it, and problems and questions will certainly come up. People are almost always hesitant to ask for help because they see it, mistakenly, as a sign of weakness and are afraid of negative consequences should they show their ignorance. Let them know that you are ready and willing to help when needed and assign a backup person in case you are not around.

Many decades of experience has shown that following this method of instruction produces good results and prevents many, if not most, of the common day-to-day problems supervisors have to deal with. In fact, a high percentage of production problems can be traced back to poor training, and the JI method is a powerful means of solving these problems.

Take Action on the Problem

For problems concerning people who don't care or won't do, these problems require quick and careful solution. In step 2, we collected the facts, weighed them carefully, and came to a decision on how to fix the problem. Now, in step 3, we have *to take action* on the problem and make the correction.

The important things to remember here are

■ *Are you going to handle this yourself?* Is it your responsibility to deal with this problem or should you pass it on to someone else?
■ *Do you need help in handling?* Do you have the ability to take this action, or do you need help from human resources, legal, professional counselors, and so forth?
■ *Should you refer this to your supervisor?* If you have the authority to take the action, don't bother your boss.
■ *Watch the timing of your action.* What is the best time and place to take the action?

The Problem Solving manual added a few more points to consider, above the basic method we learned in the JR section of this book. Here again, they were very concerned with the human approach to problem solving and stressed the overarching need, as dictated in the JR method, of maintaining strong relations with the people even as you go about taking action on problems that concern them:

■ Explain the action to the person—why it is best for him or her.
■ Give advantages and benefits; get acceptance.
■ Consider the person's feelings and attitudes when you take the action.
■ Secure clear understanding.
■ Inform everyone involved.

Because dealing with people problems is uncomfortable and unpleasant, it is very tempting to pass them on to others, like your boss or the HR department. When we do that, though, we lose the respect of our people, and that propels the downward spiral of deteriorating human relations. When taking action on problems, we must never pass the buck.

Step 4: Check and Evaluate Results

Once the correction of the problem has been made, it is vital to ensure that it takes hold and sticks and that the problem does not reoccur. The contents of this step are as follows:

■ Follow up to see that the change or correction has been made.
■ Look at what improvement the records show in quality, quantity, safety, and cost.

- Consider the human angle. Note changes in attitudes and relationships.
- Inform all those concerned of the progress and results of the action or correction.
- Look for ways to prevent a recurrence of the problem.

As one would expect, the key here is to find and evaluate data that show that the correction has worked, and to do this we can refer to records on production, quality, cost, safety, productivity, attendance, grievances, and so on. The method also stresses that once we have this information, we inform all those concerned on the progress being made and the results of the correction. This is particularly important when we consider the fact that sometimes our actions to correct problems may actually create new problems. By keeping a close check on this possibility and keeping everyone informed of the changes made and results obtained, we can be sure that the problem has been solved in a way that satisfies all parties.

As we have seen throughout this process, and in the overall TWI philosophy, the human angle is always given special attention, and even more so here because whenever changes are made, people will inevitably build up resistance or resentment to the change. These kinds of negative feelings will present themselves in the attitudes, behavior, and relationship situations of the people—not only the people directly involved with the problem, but also the overall group that will be affected by the change. It is simply a part of human nature that people react to change as a threat to their basic needs surrounding their jobs: stability, recognition, security, opportunity, participation, job satisfaction, and so forth.

When people resist change, it is an emotional reaction based on fear, not reason. They fear that their familiar routines will be upset, forcing a change in the work habits they have become accustomed to. They worry if they will be able to learn the new methods and what effect these new methods will have on their output and working conditions. When making changes to correct problems, then, telling people in advance about those changes will help pave the way for acceptance. In particular, telling them why it is necessary in a clear, simple, and concise manner while showing the benefits of the change to everyone involved helps to take down the resistance. If nothing else, just giving them a chance to blow off steam and have some say in the matter will help them to agree to the new standards.

Oftentimes people interpret our effort to solve problems as a personal criticism. In other words, they see the change as a way of blaming them for what has been done in the past and up to now. People do not like being told they are wrong, so in discussing the problem correction, we have to take special care to refrain from criticism and make it clear that we are looking for constructive actions on solving problems. Take special care, as well, when dealing with the people who originally proposed or installed the current methods so they do not feel the need to defend what they have done in the past.

Conclusion

Because the TWI Problem Solving method contains the full depth of all three of the other TWI methods, it is a much bigger and robust program. To properly use it, then, a supervisor must be well versed in Job Methods improvement, Job Instruction, and Job Relations skills. The practice of these three essential skills *is* the practice of problem solving, with the addition of the all-important step 1, isolating the problem—finding the true root cause first. Once we have identified these root causes, or problem points, we can quickly and effectively use our TWI skills to bring the problem to resolution.

In this way, the TWI approach to problem solving gives renewed meaning to the TWI skills we have been learning and practicing in this book and allows frontline supervisors to solve their everyday problems using these TWI skills. It also highlights the true leadership potential available to supervisors when they master these essential skills. A great leader is one who can guide the team to its objectives by overcoming the many obstacles that get in the way. These obstacles are problems, and problem solvers are the people we will follow because they have the skills to lead us to our goals.

Conclusion—TWI: Key to Changing the Way People Work in Lean

The two most compelling reasons why companies struggling with Lean implementation reach out to the TWI Institute for help are to learn how TWI's Job Instruction (JI) element provides a foundation for attaining and sustaining standardized work and to learn how the TWI program can provide shop floor supervisors and team leaders with the skills they need to engage people in Lean activities. Ironically, both of these basic needs are building blocks of the Toyota Production System (TPS) that were not carried over when companies learned about TPS and the tools that drive today's Lean system and culture. Toyota was delivering TWI hidden under the umbrella of TPS training when Lean was introduced but that changed with the publication of the *Toyota Way Fieldbook.**

The quickest way to understand the critical need for today's companies to allow TWI to revitalize their Lean initiative is to review what Toyota did differently in the 1950s with TWI to overcome their early struggles. As we saw in Chapter 1, by focusing on the basics to establish standardized work and improve shop floor management, they saved the company from going bankrupt. Solving these basic problems also launched Toyota on their never-ending Lean journey, and this is precisely what companies struggling with Lean need to do today. In fact, Toyota itself did corrective action to overcome problems with standardized work and shop floor management they were again struggling with in 2004.

Toyota Scrambles to Overhaul Itself 2004

After nearly doubling its revenue in the past decade and redefining competition in the key parts of the auto business, Toyota suddenly finds itself confronting mushrooming quality problems…. At Georgetown,

---

* Jeffrey K. Liker and David Meier, *Toyota Way Fieldbook*, The McGraw-Hill Company, Inc., 2006.

one glaring symptom of trouble, its top executives say, is that some hourly assemblers began ignoring standardized work processes—considered one of the biggest sins inside Toyota plants because of the impact on consistency and accuracy of manufacturing…. Among other things Mr. Oba [TPS guru] found many shop-floor leaders would spend too much time in their offices, instead of prowling the factory floor coaching and leading kaizen projects with assembly workers.*

Mr. Oba's report triggered a corporate review that resulted in Toyota introducing its Floor Management Development System (FMDS), which we learned about when visiting the Georgetown plant on October 21, 2004. FMDS was defined by Toyota at the time as a comprehensive system to align floor management and develop activities to achieve company targets by

1. Ensuring foundational skills are in place for people to perform work in accordance with the standard
2. Aligning hoshin† shop floor activities with hoshin goals and objectives
3. Visually demonstrating
   a. The management condition of the shop
   b. Alignment of daily activities to hoshin targets
4. Promoting two-way communication, creating the environment to
   a. Address abnormal conditions through targeted problem solving
   b. Determine needed support and resources
   c. Develop team members
5. Delivering and developing roles and responsibilities for all members

Gary Convis, president of the Georgetown plant, summed up having to overcome these struggles by saying, "We are getting back to basics." By returning to these fundamental elements, best represented by solid Job Instruction skill at the operator level, they were able to revive the very foundations that made the company great in the first place. Toyota has encountered many other challenges since 2004 that they have dealt with successfully and continues to be the most profitable manufacturer of automobiles in the world in 2014.

Focusing development efforts on the supervisor goes all the way back to Toyota's early days, when they introduced several management training programs in the company known collectively as Training Within Industry (TWI). These programs focused on the development of the production supervisor and his or her ability to instruct (JI),

* "As Toyota Closes in on GM, It Develops a Big Three Problem," *Wall Street Journal*, August 4, 2004, p. 1.
† Wikipedia: *Hoshin* is a strategic planning and management methodology based on a concept popularized in Japan in the late 1950s by Professor Yoji Akao. "Each person is the expert in his or her own job, and Japanese TQC [total quality control] is designed to use the collective thinking power of all employees to make their organization the best in its field."

improve (JM), and lead (JR) their work team…. To a very large degree, these programs are still the back bone of the supervisor development program in Toyota, and a big part of why the company is so successful.*

Implementing and sustaining Lean requires a specific set of skills and experiences for those responsible for leading employees, and this continuous effort directly and dramatically affects quality, cost, productivity, safety, and the morale of the team on a daily basis. Besides Toyota, companies from all industries in Japan used TWI to the same success in the postwar period, which led to a dramatic revival in Japan's manufacturing prominence. Today, with the reintroduction of the TWI methods across the globe, companies are making great strides using the TWI Institute standards to revitalize their Lean systems, creating and sustaining standardized work and developing shop floor management leaders in plants across diverse countries and cultures.

Implementing TWI

In our follow-up work to the first edition of this book, *Implementing TWI: Creating and Managing a Skills-Based Culture* (Productivity Press, 2010), we gave multiple case studies showing how companies are successfully introducing the TWI methods under current working environments. While the methods themselves, as taught in this book, are self-sustaining and can be learned and practiced individually, much more work is needed to create systems and structure so that organizations can successfully incorporate the TWI methods into the daily culture of how work gets done, as Toyota did in the 1950s and continues to do to this day. Without this effort at creating an environment for the methods to take hold and expand, the full benefits and rewards of TWI cannot be fully realized. Simply sending supervisors to a TWI training course and telling them to use the skills, while certainly giving better results than what we have now, will not create the overall foundation for Lean practice to take hold. A more structured approach is needed.

In *Implementing TWI* we cover the basic steps that are needed to accomplish a successful introduction and implementation of the TWI methods. When planning to use the TWI methods on a wider scale to reach larger organizational goals, we strongly recommend learning what other companies have done to successfully get the program to become a vital part of an organization's culture.

Using TWI to Create Corporate-Wide International Standards

Perhaps the ultimate expression of TWI practice is to use the methods as a "common language" across multiple production sites, even in different countries

---

* Art Smalley, "TPS versus Lean and the Law of Unintended Consequences," www.artoflean.com, 7.

with different languages, histories, and cultures. Because the four-step methods for each of the TWI modules are so foundational, they are understood in any country of the world, and today we are teaching the courses across every continent. No matter where we take the TWI programs, everyone understands and agrees with these principles of good leadership, which are basic to every human culture.

For example, a large tier 1 aerospace supplier consolidating smaller operations across the country and at several international sites wanted to create a unified approach to Lean thinking and standard work, not an easy challenge since each acquired company had its own unique history and work culture. They developed TWI trainers in each unit to promote a standard approach to training, and this enabled them to create a unified sense of what standard work should be. This, in turn, became the foundation for their larger efforts at developing a continuous improvement culture across the entire structure of companies.

At the LEGO Group, corporate HR was tasked with developing a training structure that would support the rapid expansion of their worldwide workforce. Their overriding goal was to create standard work practices across production sites in Denmark, the home country, Mexico, Hungary, the Czech Republic, and their newest plant, China. As one top executive put it early in the process, "any employee of the LEGO supply chain should be able to move from any factory to any other factory and notice nothing else but the language and the local temperature."[*] They selected TWI to be the tool they would use because it delivered a method that could be clearly translated into each language and practiced correctly and consistently. What is more, they developed an organizational structure that allowed key trainers in each plant to coordinate with each other on the development of the job standards (Job Instruction breakdowns) so that jobs at each site were taught in the local language following the same breakdowns and using the JI four-step method of instruction. These efforts were documented in the book *Building a Global Learning Organization: Using TWI to Succeed with Strategic Workforce Expansion in the LEGO Group* (CRC Press, 2014).

At one of the world's largest soft drink and beverage manufacturers, management at bottling plants struggled to get new equipment running at full capacity immediately after installation. Even though the equipment manufacturers were tasked with training the employees of the bottling facility, typically after the equipment was signed off and the manufacturers left the site, productivity of the line would drop from 100% to less than 30%–40% and would not recover to full capacity for up to 6 months. This was the time it took for local employees to actually learn how to use the equipment. In order to provide a better outcome,

---

[*] Graupp P., Jakobsen G., and Veltema J, *Building a Global Learning Organization* (CRC Press, Boca Raton, FL, 2014), 8.

the beverage group began insisting that equipment suppliers learn TWI and use the JI method to teach local employees how to use their equipment. In addition to that, they found that by developing their own internal JI trainers, they could use the JI breakdowns they learned from the equipment vendors to continue with the training even after the vendors left the facility.

In these ways, organizations are obtaining full value from their TWI skills, integrating and applying them across multiple sites throughout their organizations, including vendors, thus fully leveraging the effort of their work and multiplying the benefits.

The "Three-Legged Stool"

The three original skills taught in the TWI program—Job Instruction, Job Methods improvement, and Job Relations—work at a fundamental level to help get a Lean initiative off the ground, propel it forward, and sustain it as it develops to becoming truly continuous improvement. These three TWI programs are like the three legs of a three-legged stool: remove one and the stool does not stand. While each program can certainly be done on its own and give real value, the promotion of excellence in the work and the successful fulfillment of the varied responsibilities of a supervisor require all three used in conjunction with each other. We must always use our leadership skills to build solid relationships based on trust with our people (JR) so that they follow our instructions (JI). Even if we have a solid training method, people will not follow our instructions if we do not lead them well. When we determine standard work procedures and instruct our people in them properly (JI), we create a baseline of stable work performance. Work processes must be stabilized *before* they can be improved. We can then build on that standard performance by breaking down these jobs and questioning the details to come up with ideas for developing new and better ways of doing the work (JM). These improved methods must then be taught properly (JI) in order to have them stick. Otherwise, people fall back on their old habits. And by allowing people to participate with us enthusiastically in the search for the best ways to do the work (JM), we enhance strong relations and inspire a strong work ethic (JR), which multiplies exponentially the results of our kaizen effort. The three J programs, along with an understanding of your responsibilities and the company's objectives, will provide the essential tools and skills necessary to achieve good results on a regular basis.

We hope that you will practice these skills and reap the great benefits good supervisors have been enjoying for more than seven decades. As you gain control of your work, reduce problems, and improve output by using these tools regularly, your own value within your company will rise. So will the level of respect accorded to you by your superiors, your fellow supervisors, and especially your own people.

Training Trainers to Deliver TWI

Over the past 14 years, beginning with the initial pilot project in September 2001, the TWI Institute, in cooperation with Patrick Graupp, has recreated the pattern established by the original TWI Service to deliver TWI programs. Thanks to their efforts, large and small companies across the country and around the globe are benefiting from an ingenious training methodology that has stood the test of time. Fundamentals of the TWI program, explained in Chapter 2 of this workbook, are the key elements of this methodology and include a "learn by doing" format as well as a standardized template for delivering the training.

This workbook tries to recreate in written form the live version of the TWI classes, so that those who cannot attend a TWI class have the opportunity of learning and practicing TWI. No workbook, however, can replace the dynamic nature of a live classroom atmosphere. By the same token, a workbook can never fully provide the nuances that a skilled and practiced instructor can use to emphasize and clarify intangible concepts.

Having a specially trained facilitator to lead the team in doing the exercises outlined in this workbook ensures that the lessons are being properly learned and the methods correctly executed. For more information on how to train trainers using the TWI training delivery manuals as developed by the TWI Service, contact the TWI Institute at 315-412-0303 or visit its website at www.twi-institute.org.

We believe that this workbook, used in conjunction with a certified facilitator who has been trained to deliver the TWI programs, is the surest way to effectively implement TWI and reap the great rewards these skills bring to the work process.

Appendix: ESCO Turbine Technologies–Syracuse: Using Job Instruction as a Foundation for Standardized Work

The ability to train is one of the most important skills a supervisor must have to alleviate or eliminate common daily problems with production, quality, and cost and promote worker safety and job satisfaction. Trained workers can increase the profitability of a company and even help to create an environment that encourages people to improve the way they do their jobs. Nevertheless, many companies and supervisors continue to pass this responsibility on to support groups that are not accountable for the performance of employees after training is completed. Supervisors who do this mistakenly believe that it is the training department's responsibility to ensure that operators are trained to do their jobs. In practice, the training department can do little more than teach basic skills common to all areas of the company, not the specific procedures necessary to get a specific job done.

Since Training Within Industry (TWI) was originally developed many decades ago, one trend that has emerged in the workplace is the practice of placing many responsibilities that were once the domain of the supervisor into the hands of specific departments. One example of this is moving functions like hiring and firing, payroll, work procedures, training, disciplinary processes, and other duties, all previously handled by supervisors, to human resources. In today's complex business environment, this is not necessarily a bad thing. In many companies, however, this slow but inexorable trend has stripped important responsibilities (and the skills to handle them) from supervisors to such an extent that many have now become little more than "firefighters."

As a result, these supervisors spend their days chasing down problems and finding ways to make things work just to get the product out the door.

The TWI program reintroduces supervisors to and trains them in these lost skills—skills that are needed right at the worksite by the person responsible for the work there. The program operates from the premise that support functions, while they serve an important role, cannot provide the direction and leadership that employees need. Immediate supervisors can and should. Hence, TWI training's thrust is to return supervisors to a more active management role, reversing the way in which many companies operate today. Without the complete support of top management, however, the TWI Job Instruction (JI) program would not have had attained the desired impact on the performance of the ESCO Turbine Technologies–Syracuse plant that occurred during the period of this case study, from 2002 through 2007.

Job Instruction Training at ESCO Turbine Technologies–Syracuse

ESCO Turbine Technologies–Syracuse, formerly known as Gray–Syracuse and now part of Consolidated Precision Products Corp., is a world-class producer of precision investment casting parts that require exotic alloys and complex geometries for use by the aerospace and industrial gas turbine markets. Workforce competencies encompass computer modeling using complex dimensional integration software, metallurgical specialties, and foundry operations. Additional components in the value proposition include the production of high-quality precision products, timely delivery, and competitive pricing.

Located just east of Syracuse in Chittenango, New York, ESCO Turbine Technologies–Syracuse was then part of the ESCO Corporation family of companies; therefore, we will refer to this plant simply as ESCO in this case study. Our close relationship with ESCO began when Bob Wrona solicited Paul H. Smith, director of human resources, to have production and management people participate in the initial TWI pilot projects in September 2001 and March 2002. The timing could not have been better for CNYTDO and ESCO, which employed around 400 people, to reintroduce TWI, and for ESCO to become the first U.S.-owned operation to implement the TWI program as a strategy since the end of World War II.

Management introduced cellular manufacturing in 1995 to remove department silos and followed up with kaizen, synchronous manufacturing, and then Six Sigma to organize the casting and finishing areas into flow lines based on Lean and synchronous management principles. While running at full capacity, plant management focused on kaizen events to remove bottlenecks to maximize flow line production. The global investment casting business climate dramatically changed in 2001 when their very large customers began looking to offshore products to lower cost suppliers. Some of these ESCO customers were demanding immediate reduction in the price they paid for their products, by 6%–12%, and another 3% per year for the next 3 years.

Pressure from corporate to either reduce costs or run the risk of closing the plant motivated management to decide to replace existing products, items that would most likely move to low-cost poles, with technically challenging products that would not be affected. To make this move, the plant had to reduce inventory, increase speed to flow, and decrease lead time to improve the ability to make components for aftermarket suppliers of gas turbine parts, component parts that when they fail, must be designed, cast, and shipped as soon as possible for the customer to get the generator back into service. Needless to say, these were parts that could not be done offshore and would command higher prices. Strategic planning and execution was needed to focus on targeted market segments and for employees to see and believe that management had an aligned and integrated strategy. The future of the plant at this time depended on the innovative application of technology, Lean production, speed, 100% on-time delivery, and development of human capital. Smith, a strong advocate of the balanced scorecard,* influenced the ESCO management team to develop a measure of human capital readiness† that represents the availability of employee skills, talent, and know-how required to improve the performance of the internal processes critical to the strategy's success.

Developing the ESCO–Syracuse Human Capital Readiness Program‡

> All jobs are important to the organization: otherwise it wouldn't hire and pay people to perform them. Many jobs, however, provide basic capabilities and requirements, but not distinctive ones that create differentiation. Organizations may require truck drivers, computer operators, custodians, receptionists, and call center operators, and make it clear that contributions from all these employees will improve organizational performance. But while managers must develop the potential of everyone in the organization, they must also recognize that some jobs have a much greater impact on the strategy than others. The strategic human capital management process must identify and focus on the critical few jobs [strategic job families] that have the greatest impact on the strategy.§

TWI was introduced at a time when senior management developed a strategy map that identified the wax area as the strategic job family to improve quality

---

* Robert S. Kaplan and David P. Norton, *Strategy Maps: Converting Intangible Assets into Tangible Assets* (Boston: Harvard Business School Publishing Corporation, 2004), 225–239.

† Note: Readiness in this context is defined as being the "state of preparedness of persons, systems, or organizations to meet a situation and carry out a planned sequence of actions. Readiness is based on thoroughness of the planning, adequacy and training of personnel, and supply and reserve of support services or systems" (www.businessdictionary.com).

‡ Kaplan and Norton, *Strategy Maps*, 225–239.

§ Ibid., 228.

and reduce rework by 50%. Although kaizen events were completed on almost all of the processes, there was still significant variation at the operator level in the wax department, where as many as 4000 defects were detected in any given month in the assembly of initial molds. Since wax is the front end of the manufacturing processes, having to rework the molds increased touch time and adversely impacted on-time release and cost, affecting both manufacturing cycle times and customer delivery.

Management recognized that the need to train 30 people hired for their manual dexterity in a new set of competencies would require having a repeatable and verifiable training method to replace the current training for the entry-level position of mold assembly that was not effective. According to Smith, "employees were being trained utilizing the buddy technique or by assigning one of the best assemblers to train new employees. What we need is a repeatable and verifiable training method for employees." They found that method when his people participated in the CNYTDO, Inc. Job Instruction pilot project in March 2002, at which time JI became part of their human capital readiness framework (Figure A.1).

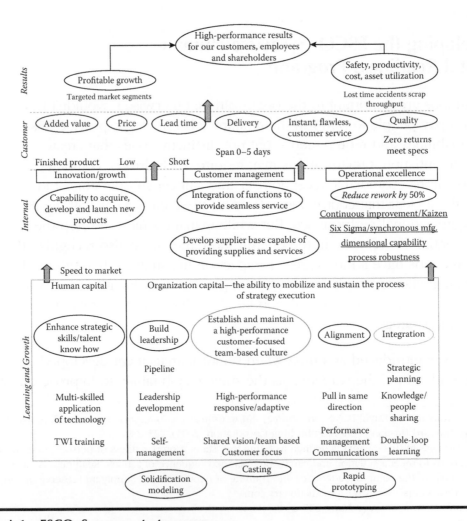

Figure A.1   ESCO–Syracuse strategy map.

Converting to Flexible Manufacturing

The plant had success using flexible manufacturing in the back end of the production process; however, it was now clear to management that to reduce rework and improve quality, they would first have to introduce flexible manufacturing to the wax area, where wax patterns are assembled into molds to be converted into castings. Since the new process required eight distinct configurations of activities known as cells that produce different types of products, the strategy of bringing flexible manufacturing to the front-end mold assembly process required a broad new set of competencies. According to Smith, "even though we manage everyone's competencies, we had been biased toward the high-skill jobs. The identification of strategic job families [Figure A.2] brought something to the forefront that we wouldn't have seen otherwise.... It showed us an entry-level job that was just as important. The benefits of focusing on these strategic job families will be huge."

Building the Competency Profile

HR leaders worked with key production personnel to develop competency profiles (Figure A.3) for mold assembly that defined the requirements of each job in considerable detail: knowledge, skills, and values required for each position to execute the new strategy.

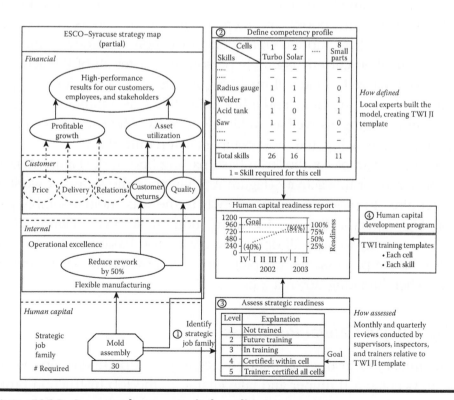

Figure A.2   ESCO–Syracuse human capital readiness program.

②	Competency profile			
Cells / Skills	1 Turbo	2 Solar	.....	8 Small parts
. . . .	–	–		–
Radius gauge	1	1		0
Welder	0	1		1
Acid tank	1	0		1
Saw	1	1		0
. . . .	–	–		–
. . . .	–	–		–
Total skills	26	16		11

1 = Skill required for this cell

Figure A.3 Competency profile: wax mold assembly jobs.

Implementing TWI Job Instruction Training

ESCO decided to focus on JI because the methodology requires breaking down each job into important steps, key points, and reasons for key points that document best practices on paper and then become the standard for training and performing each job. By requiring each worker to demonstrate competence in the job, it provides verification to the trainer that the employee has in fact learned to do the job correctly, safely, and conscientiously.

Patrick Graupp trained the entire wax area staff in the JI 10-hour training (outlined in Part II of this book), and then coached team leaders and operators on how use the JI method to create Job Instruction breakdowns that could be used to train all 30 current assembly persons to master all of the activities within each of their cells. One cell might require the use of welding equipment, an acid tank, an x-ray machine, and a hot knife, whereas another cell required shellacking and gauging, as well as welding and x-ray. The simplest cell required 11 different activities, while the most complex cell required 27.

The following example of the "trim flash parting line" task (Figure A.4) and the tools provided for this activity (Figure A.5) illustrate the scope of work and the skills required to properly use these tools in the wax mold assembly process. From a Six Sigma perspective, the Job Instruction breakdowns (Figure A.6) identified the current way to train all operators to establish basic stability by minimizing variation in the process. See Chapter 4 to learn how operators are engaged in their work when breaking down a job.

Assessing Human Capital Readiness

During the initial Job Instruction pilot project, a wax department supervisor, who was to become a JI trainer and take charge of the Job Instruction project, became extremely excited about the JI training timetable. She was charged to

Wax parting line—A positive, seam like in appearance.
Cause—Separation of the pattern die.

Figure A.4   Wax mold parting line defect.

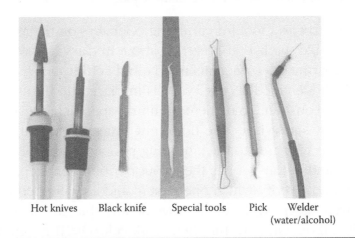

Hot knives   Black knife   Special tools   Pick   Welder
(water/alcohol)

Figure A.5   Wax mold finishing tools.

No. ASSM-15 Rev.1			
Job Instruction Breakdown			
Title: Trim flash parting line			
Part: All			
Tools: Wax mold finishing tools			
Step NO	**IMPORTANT STEPS**	**KEY POINTS**	**REASONS**
1	Remove flash parting line	1. Lightly with flat of pick 2. One direction and stopping in same spot 3. Away from your body 4. Over paper towel	1. Prevent gouging pattern 2. Prevent over trimming 3. Safety 4. Keep flash off piece
2	Blow off pattern	1. Air hose 2. One piece at a time	1. Free of debris 2. Prevent damage of pattern
3	Inspect	1. Visually inspect	1. Scratching 2. Negatives
4	Place pattern back on tray	1. Same way you took it off	1. Dimensional

Figure A.6   JI Breakdown (JIB), wax mold assembly.

③	Assess strategic readiness	

Level	Explanation
1	Not trained
2	Future training
3	In training
4	Qualified: within cell	←— Goal
5	Trainer: qualified in all cells

Figure A.7   Levels of readiness: wax mold assembly job.

develop a skills matrix as a tool for certifying operators on their jobs, and the JI TWI training timetable she had just learned about in class was what she needed to develop the department's own skills matrix and certification program. With the skills matrix, which identified necessary skills in place, the JI four-step method could be used as a consistent, multitiered training approach. Once it was learned and implemented by supervisors, the JI training timetable format was prominently posted in the wax area to track training people on the job. Since JI training is repeatable, and because it has the tryout performance step, trainers and supervisors could now verify which operators could actually perform the work.

Assemblers were assessed (Figure A.7) to identify the gaps that had to be closed to qualify all operators within their work cell. The JI program, then, became ESCO's tool for maintaining a job certification program that enforces standardized work. This new system was well received by all of the operators in the area, who took pride in attaining JI certification within their cell because this opened the door for them to be trained for jobs between cells (there were seven in the department at the time). This, in turn, provided operators with recognition and the opportunity for advancement while giving the company flexibility in scheduling work within the department. Figure A.7 shows the levels of training that ESCO developed to measure human capital readiness. By using this evaluation, management was able to mark progress accurately, the goal being to have everyone at level 4 after implementing the JI program.

Limited Training Dollars Invested in TWI JI to Train Mold Assembly Strategic Job Family

All 30 current assembly persons were then trained using the TWI JI method to master the activities required by each cell. Then the supervisor, the quality inspector, and the trainer used the JI job breakdown to evaluate monthly and quarterly whether the assembly persons continued to perform each task as trained, in order to bring all assembly persons to level 3 (in training) as soon as possible, and then quickly to level 4 (qualified: within cell). Once employees were certified within a line, their training continued to certify them in all lines, giving the company maximum flexibility to minimize cost by being able to move employees to where customers demanded at the front end of the production process.

Training all operators in the wax department required the need for hundreds of Job Instruction breakdowns that were controlled via a company database. The people at ESCO took the JI method one step further by using the job breakdown as a standard for auditing operators to ensure that each person was continuing to use the established best method. In other words, even after JI training, operators were observed at random intervals; if they passed six successful audits, they became JI certified operators. No additional audits were performed for 60 days, at which time operators were observed for recertification.

Employees observed not following the procedure exactly as described in the job breakdown were not recertified until retrained in the job. A star was placed after the name of a person on the JI training timetable to signify the level of proficiency of each individual as a certified operator, which provided a reference for cell leaders in need of an operator to fill a gap. Once employees were certified within a cell, their training continued to certify them in other cells, to give the wax area maximum flexibility to minimize cost by being able to move employees within the department based on customer demand.

In a book on strategy maps that came out in 2004, Kaplan and Norton reported on the work ESCO was doing with TWI:

> The readiness level was 400, an average level of 1.6 per person per cell, when the program was introduced in 2001. This level was only 40 percent of the phase 2 objective. One year later, the readiness level had risen to 810, an average level of 3.3 and 84 percent of the phase 2 objective. Paul Smith, the director of human resources at Gray–Syracuse, attributed the speed with which the competency levels rose to the TWI program.… He estimated that the TWI program cut the time to achieve strategic readiness in half (Figure A.8). Rework dropped by 76 percent during this period, creating dramatic economic benefits.[*]

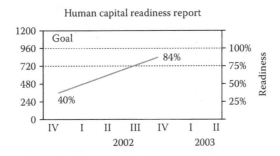

Figure A.8   **Human capital readiness: wax mold assembly.**

* Robert S. Kaplan and David P. Norton, *Strategy Maps: Converting Intangible Assets into Tangible Assets* (Boston: Harvard Business School Publishing Corporation, 2004), 239.

Impact of Job Instruction on the Wax Department (2002–2004)

■ Reduction in wax department assembly of molds and defects (Figure A.9)

2002 Up to 4000 defects in any given month

2003 vs. 2002 75% reduction

2004 vs. 2003 83% reduction

2004 vs. 2001 96% reduction

■ Improvement in the average monthly on-time release of wax molds

2002 average per month 73.2%

2003 average per month 89.5%

2004 average per month 98.6%

■ Significant leveling of month-to-month variability of on-time release of molds

2002 variability 38.0%–96.1%

2003 variability 67.3%–100%

2004 variability 98.3%– 99.9%

■ Improved mold release times contributed to increased productivity in other areas

Training time reduced 2 months to 2 weeks

Cycle time reduced 64%

Inventory reduced 50%

On-time delivery improved 80%

Impact of TWI on the ESCO Plant (2004–2007)

■ ESCO management credited the Job Instruction training at an award luncheon at the plant on June 21, 2005, for becoming the first and only recipient of the prestigious Platinum Supplier Award from the Dallas, Texas–based Lockheed Martin Missiles and Fire Control Division.

■ JI was introduced in the coating and finishing areas in 2006 as the next step to establishing a mobile workforce within the plant, as outlined in this case study.

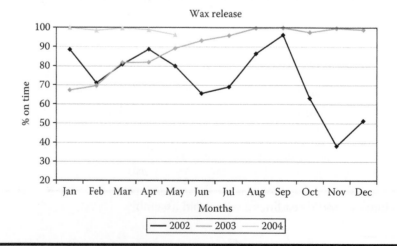

Figure A.9 Variability of on-time release of wax molds.

ESCO–Syracuse Human Capital Development Program

By following the Kaplan and Norton *Strategy Maps* model for capital invest-ments and development programs and focusing on the relatively small num-ber of employees in the wax mold assembly strategic jobs, ESCO achieved breakthrough performance faster and less expensively than by diffuse HR spending. Since this was our first project with TWI, we were especially pleased to hear Paul Smith attribute the speed with which the competency levels rose to the JI program because it "required breaking each job down into its important steps and key points, and then implementing training for each of these parts that includes having the trainee demonstrate performance to con-firm the worker has in fact learned the job." It is no surprise, then, that ESCO built its human capital development program (Figure A.10) around the TWI JI program.

JI Moves beyond Wax to Finishing to Create a Flexible Workforce (2006)

When Job Instruction was fully implemented in the wax department, two experienced operators with a proven competency in TWI were pulled from pro-duction to manage the daily TWI activities that would now be expanded to other parts of the plant that worked with metal instead of wax (Figures A.11 and A.12). In addition to training, the two were made responsible for maintaining and sustaining the TWI program with the following duties:

- Create and maintain files of Job Instruction breakdowns (JIBs) as they are created for all jobs in the plant.
- Monitor improvements to update JIBs as jobs are improved.
- Coordinate the training of new hires.
- Cross-train employees to create a mobile workforce.
- Use JIBs to conduct random audits of operators.
- Retrain operators when job methods change.
- Establish off-line training of skills operators need before being assigned to a job (Figures A.13 and A.14).

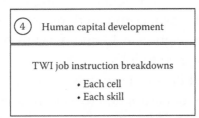

Figure A.10 JI breakdown method driven human capital development.

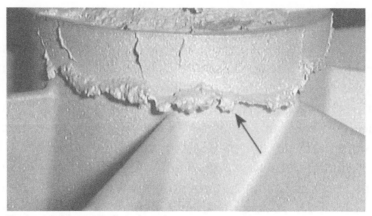

Finning—A thin positive line of metal.
Cause—Formed as a result of shell splitting.

Figure A.11 Finning defect.

Examples of die grinders

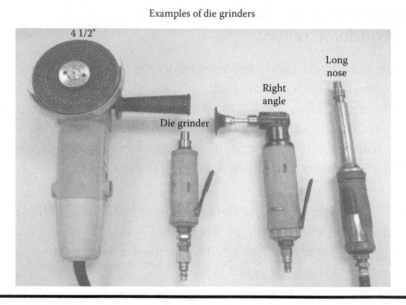

Figure A.12 Metal finishing power tools.

Competency profiles were maintained for all employees within flow lines, and cross-functional training was conducted between lines and departments. A plant-wide training matrix was maintained to audit, train, and retrain on a continuing basis through the team leaders. Looking for ways to improve the training process when TWI was incorporated into new employee training, the TWI team negotiated space (Figures A.13 and A.14) to provide off-line training to new hires before being assigned to jobs.

Although the tools and skills for these new areas were dramatically different from those used in the wax department, cross-trained employees were assigned based on daily production schedules. Employees voluntarily moved between

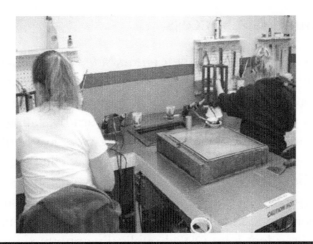

Figure A.13   Off-line wax department training.

Figure A.14   Off-line metal-line training area.

departments just for a change and to maintain both sets of skills. The initial results of the JI training in the metal end of the production were encouraging:

Category Tested	Improvement
Casting configuration	44%
Defect identification	67%
Quick check basics	79%
Quick check advanced	25%

   With the JI method steadily taking hold, Job Relations was added in 2007 as part of supervisor and team leader training. Job Methods was introduced at the same time for supervisors to help them introduce kaizen at the operator level.

ESCO Turnaround Is a Success

According to an article published in the *Central New York Business Journal* on July 8, 2005, "about three years ago, sales at ESCO Turbine Technologies–Syracuse dropped $20 million in one year. The company went from 400 employees to 297." John O'Neill, ESCO president, explained the downturn by stating, "Both our key markets had simultaneously tanked on us [and] we were just hunkering down and trying to weather the storm at that point. It's been slow climbing our way out."

In 2003, ESCO began aggressively recruiting new customers by entering the demanding sector of making components for aftermarket suppliers of gas turbine parts. Orders came in faster than expected, pushing employment back to pre-9/11 levels. President John O'Neil publically announced that the plant would spend $1.4 million on equipment and facility upgrades and hire 80 people to meet a projected sales increase from $30 million to $50 million over the next 3 years.* This is what Paul Smith meant when he initially stated that TWI was just what ESCO needed—the Job Instruction program not only helped the company resolve its current problems, it also empowered growth and expansion into more value-added product lines that would ultimately make it globally competitive.

---

* Kevin Tampone, ESCO turns around after challenging period. *Central New York Business Journal*, July 8, 2005, 3.

Index